IN OUR OUR OWN WORDS

IN OUR OWN WORDS

A TREASURY OF QUOTATIONS FROM THE AFRICAN-AMERICAN COMMUNITY

compiled by

ELZA DINWIDDIE-BOYD

AVON BOOKS ◆ NEW YORK

IN OUR OWN WORDS is an original publication of Avon Books. This work has never before appeared in book form.

AVON BOOKS
A division of
The Hearst Corporation
1350 Avenue of the Americas
New York, New York 10019

Copyright © 1996 by Elza Dinwiddie-Boyd
Published by arrangement with the author
Library of Congress Catalog Card Number: 95-38692
ISBN: 0-380-77910-2

Library of Congress Cataloging in Publication Data:
In our own words : quotes for the African-American community / [collected by] Elza Dinwiddie-Boyd.
    p.   cm.
1. Afro-Americans—Quotations.   I. Dinwiddie-Boyd, Elza.
PN6081.3.I5 1996   95-38692
081'.08996—dc20   CIP

First Avon Books Trade Printing: February 1996

AVON TRADEMARK REG. U.S. PAT. OFF. AND IN OTHER COUNTRIES, MARCA REGISTRADA, HECHO EN U.S.A.

Printed in the U.S.A.

OPM   10 9 8 7 6 5 4 3 2 1

*To Arlene Clark and Herb Boyd
for love, sustenance, and righteous thinking*

ACKNOWLEDGMENTS

Let me first acknowledge the people of my all-black hometown, Taft, Oklahoma, for their lessons in strength, courage, perseverance, friendship, and community. I offer thanks to my childhood friends who chewed on the red clay with me. And I am eternally grateful to my loving family who watched over me as I ran wild in the tall grass.

Thank you to Howard Campbell for so many trips to the research library, and always to Sharon Howard of the Schomburg Center for Research in Black Culture and History.

To my colleagues at the College of New Rochelle, School of New Resources at the New York Theological Seminary: Sharwyn, Sam, Charlene, Vanessa, David, Faye, Alan, Zina, Rosetta, Cade, Lucinda and Desmond, thank you for your friendship and many kindnesses. I am especially grateful to Dean Bessie Blake and Dr. Louis de Salle for their continued support of my work.

I owe a special word of gratitude to all of my students for love, faith, and belief in my leadership. I have drawn so much energy and inspiration from you. Thanks, Butch!

Appreciation's bright light goes out to Thelma Dinwiddie for coming through yet one more time and providing so many African proverbs and to Laverne "Safiyyah" Marks for sharing her research.

Friend Tonya, what would I do without your quick and "good moral mind"?

There is reserved a very special sense of appreciation for my editor, Tom Colgan. For without his friendly support this collection of black wisdom and wit would not be.

Thank you rings hollow when extended to the great long

distance runner, Marie Dutton Brown, my dear friend and literary agent, for her tireless work on behalf of all of us who would be black and in publishing.

Asante sana H.B.

The words I speak unto you, they are power. They are life.

—Jesus Christ

CONTENTS

Contents

IN OUR OWN WORDS

Introduction:
Life-Affirming Ideas

Herein lies a great celebration. It is a celebration of a people's ability to survive and thrive under awesome pressure. It is a celebration of our wit, clarity, creativity. It is a celebration of our intelligence. The provocative, incisive, searing, and life-affirming ideas collected here are a brilliant refutation of the claims made in that infamous book *The Bell Curve*.

* * * *

Whenever I think of this book and the philosophy behind my collecting of the voices assembled here I think: *Quotations: A Practical Guide to Life in Africa America.* You see, we have spoken so much wisdom in so many ways about our existence in a white-dominated society freighted with obstacles deliberately designed to thwart us. When I think of this book I think of the profound wisdom that so often has comprised black intellectual activity. Truly, I have found the process of this work to be a celebration of black intelligence, under pressure.

In Our Own Words: Quotations for the African-American Community is soul food for the mind, inspiration for the spirit, and an affirmation of our persistent humanity, our enduring struggle, and our continuing triumphs.

What sets *In Our Own Words* apart from other quotation books? For one thing, its focus on contemporary, young voices. Traditionally quotation books have focused on the historical wisdom of the elders. The overall emphasis of this quotation book is on those who live and work among us today. Although I have collected the pearls of wisdom that so many of our con-

1

temporaries have uttered, I am a staunch believer that we are a result of our history, and like Nikki Giovanni, I believe we "divine the future from the past," as the Sankofa legend implies, so that we cannot truly go forward without looking back. Therefore, today's voices are anchored in the historical. Another feature that sets *In Our Own Words* apart is the fact that the quotes are often arranged so that the reader feels that she or he is participating in a debate among opposing voices or a symposium designed to fully explicate such issues as welfare reform, Afrocentricity, or integration. Furthermore, the quotes contained here are often long so that the reader achieves a greater sense of the context from which the quotation was drawn.

Black folks have something to say about everything, and we are putting mouth to mikes, pen to paper, fingers to keyboard, and getting published in unprecedented numbers. Don't ever let anyone tell you that we black people do not possess a literary tradition, a canon. We are speaking out and up. Just check out the pages that follow.

You will find many heroic voices of triumph and victory in tune with the sagacious wisdom of a Derrick Bell when he alerts us that racism is "intractable" and that our very fight against it is that which personifies our humanity. Here are collected beacons of courage that urge us to our highest possibilities.

And sometimes the quotes represent our tradition of spreading the word, letting one another know about something worthwhile that is happening out there such as the Birthing Project USA, which pairs at-risk pregnant women with volunteer "sisters" and is lowering infant mortality rates.

Between these pages you will discover big thoughts in small doses, points of insight from which to draw empowerment. You will find sister talk, girlfriend speak, brothers rapping, mothers struggling, fathers standing tall, and a people under siege ever hopeful, faithful and triumphant. You will find the ideas and ways of thinking that produce positive outcomes. Contained here are enduring truths.

There are quotes on healing and affirming ourselves, on developing and maintaining fortitude, responsibility, parents, children, success, the merits of tenacity, and seeing the connections between me and thee. There are great quotes from the famous, great quotes from those who are not so recognizable, and some everyday people like you and me speaking on achieving excellence, surviving against the odds, and the art of living your life well.

I am a teacher and I don't apologize for it, for as my father always said it "is an honorable pursuit." So to that extent I have been overwhelmingly concerned with providing as much information as possible, on as many levels as space and time will allow, hoping that each reader upon putting this book down will be all the more enthralled with the great dignity of black people, our consistent achievement in the face of those who would obliterate us.

I so love the African contribution to our society. I am ceaselessly astounded by its vastness at the very same time that I am stunned by our humility. A humility so great that it too often permits us to believe others when they tell us we are inferior, that we have less of a right to the good life, to the world's resources. What a lie! Don't believe it, brothers and sisters; look around, choose any field, and look down deep and you will find African creativity at a critical juncture.

I am presenting here to you, my dear readers, chunks of logic from people whose eloquence and wisdom help me along my way on this sometimes perilous journey. It is among these writers, speakers, painters, sculptors, teachers, doctors, lawyers, diplomats, preachers, students, mothers, fathers, sisters, singers, brothers, coworkers, neighbors, musicians, poets, carpenters, accountants, friends, folks, that I gain my exuberance for life, see once again what right thinking can do for me, and am reinforced in seeking joy in the Divine One–Timeless One.

Much of what is collected here is good advice we have always heard but is so easily forgotten in day-to-day living. Cultivating these habits will help us to reach our goals, to accomplish life's many satisfactions, and to smell the roses along the way. They are affirmations for building and maintaining strong, positive characteristics. They are ideas that teach history, predict the future, mold morals and manners, and ultimately civilize humanity.

Before a good habit can occur a good thought must be

formed. The point that I am trying to convey is that our actions are all too often the results of our thinking patterns and that there are ways of thinking that will get you the actions and thus results that you want. I submit that there is an inevitable cause-and-effect relationship that exists between what we think, what we do, and what we get. Here collected are ways of thinking that have produced positive ways of doing and getting. Moreover, in most instances, the results of this wholesome intellectual activity has had positive intergenerational impact.

Many of the narratives ring poignantly with our genius for introspection. Reclamation is also a recurring theme. A large part of our time is spent in reclaiming our allegiance to the birthplace of our ancestors, so naturally a significant portion of our experience is given over to this need. To establish firmly our identity in our roots provides an energy source for our strivings to achieve balance, to refute the notion that others can remake and rename us.

There are no promises here, however, that you will be raised to transcendental spiritual heights, for I am not capable of that—in that realm I defer to the Lord. But what I do claim is to have collected here some valuable insights into how to live life well, with integrity and wisdom spurred by the fear, and resulting love, of God.

It is principally a mind thing. I have relied upon the minds of the many great thinkers among us for the words and phrases by which to form a successful intellectual process and a mental perspective to live our lives with gusto, passion, and lasting fulfillment, fulfillment that prepares us to face death with courage and serenity. Such minds as John Oliver Killens, Mari Evans, Frances Ellen Watkins Harper, W. E. B. Du Bois, bell hooks, Cornel West, Halle Berry, Johnetta B. Cole, Ice T, and Spike Lee are represented here telling it like it is.

These pages will reveal to us once more the great beauty in the black world, the great dignity, and the heroic capacity to withstand the maafa—great suffering—of being black. We have had to build our lives from the wounding raw material America has given us. Oh, but how gloriously we've done it!

Perhaps there are those of you who wonder why we blacks have to put so much effort into praising our accomplishments.

Well, because the society puts so much effort into tarnishing and denying them. It is a defense mechanism that has taken the offensive. We know that we must constantly build ourselves up in a country that systematically bombards our image with negativity and cultural destruction. Emerging from the quotations contained within these binders is the marvelous Spirit of Triumph.

And it is my motivation, my sincere hope, my sense of project purpose that these stellar black voices in choir sing our glory song.

In these diamond mines of logic that define the spirit of wisdom and victory I have tried to capture our profound belief in the continuity of human experience and our indebtedness to the generations that preceded us—for it is the effort to practice such principles as these that builds moral character and personal strength, it is their fulfillment that brings peace of mind and self-confidence, and it is in moments of realizations like these that I am compelled to stop and thank God. Armed with these ideas we are better prepared to face life's inevitable ups and downs.

"This is so wonderful," is a recurring thought as I am flooded with the joy of investigating the vast expanse of black literature. Each quotation here represents a point on a wonderful trail of words, each a referent to a larger map. The great black chorus gathered here dwells not on our anguish; rather each voice reaching its own crescendo illuminates the qualities that have empowered us to outlast it all—and to keep on keeping on. The strain of optimism that permeates the literature is apparent in the work of Frances Ellen Watkins Harper. Harper's optimism, like that of poet Lucille Clifton, is fueled by her Christian faith.

Many times during the compiling of this book I have been stunned into stillness, perfectly captivated by the power of such voices as Haki Madhubuti and Gwendolyn Brooks. It is voices such as theirs who resonate with the affirmation that we do have choices that can be exercised; with the need to fight from generation to generation; who cry out with direction, hope and future; who emphasize that whatever we do has impact both materially and spiritually. They are burning with the energy of renewal.

We have survived by our faith—faith in God, faith in our humanity, faith in the humanity of others, faith in justice, faith in freedom, faith in faith . . .

So here, we let a thousand thoughts contend, but let the best ones win.

Sankofa:
The Value of History

The achievements of the Negro properly set forth will crown him as a factor in early human progress and a maker of modern civilization.

Carter G. Woodson,
Educator, Historian
founder of Negro History Week,
which became Black History Month

One need only gaze for a moment upon the majesty of the great pyramids or the sphinx at Giza to understand how Egyptian scholarship is at the base of Western culture.

Herb Boyd, *Historian*

There is an urgency for historians, like never before, to speak to the larger public. And if we don't we are going to leave the terrain to the Disney Corporation, and journalists, who when they are good, they are superb. But the historians have a training that is of value, and we have got to practice accessibility in our language and presentation. We must present history vividly, more concisely. There is nothing wrong with popularizing the material, if the research behind it is sound.

David Levering Lewis
Historian, Biographer

Unfortunately, no one has yet found a way to make most scholarly texts interesting enough to entice laymen to read them—unless they are assigned by teachers with the power to inflict punishment. So it is left to the historical novelist and other nonacademic writers to popularize the complex issues of academia.

PLAYTHELL BENJAMIN
Essayist, Novelist

We have no analysis of our history because we have no memory of our history.

DR. ASA HILLIARD
Professor of Urban Education, Georgia State University

If our study of black history is merely an exercise in feeling good about ourselves, then we will die feeling good. We must look at the lessons that history teaches us. We must understand the tremendous value of the study of history for the regaining of power. If our education is not about gaining real power, we are being miseducated and misled and we will die miseducated and misled.

AMOS WILSON
The Falsification of Afrikan Consciousness

African people can have a Golden Age or another Age of Continued Despair, depending on how they view themselves in relationship to the totality of history and its ironies. The cruelest thing slavery and colonialism did to the Africans was to destroy their memory of what they were before foreign contact.

JOHN HENRIK CLARK
Historian, Professor Emeritus, Hunter College

If the sculptors along the Gulf Coast were not African, to what then do we attribute the influence—*National Geographic*?

HERB BOYD
Historian, Down The Glory Road,
about the colossal Negroid heads standing
six to nine feet tall along Mexico's Gulf Coast

Affirming objectivity as equally necessary to any compassionate rendering of our flawed and splendid human striving, I have tried honestly to tell the story and to provide a rigorous analysis of the long black movement toward justice, equity, and truth. At the same time, identifying fully with the subjects of my study and the substance of their hope, I have freely allowed myself to celebrate. For I could not possibly remain silent and unmoved in the presence of the mysterious, transformative dance of the life that has produced the men and women, the ideas and institutions, the visions, betrayals, and heroic dreams renewed in blood that are at once the anguish and the glory of the river of our struggle in this land.

VINCENT HARDING
Author, Historian, There Is A River

It's up to the living to keep in touch with the ancestors.

JULIE DASH, Daughters of the Dust

I don't walk "correct" because I want to be super righteous. I simply want to say to the world—through my actions—that Black women, having endured, are certainly women who should be revered ... respected on the stage of history. And that is why I cannot produce a work or walk on a stage as if I am a whore, a harlot. I can't slide on a stage like "Here I am, baby." I must walk on stage saying, "Yes! This is me." I am coming with a whole host of women, unsung heroines, unsung women we will never know. I see them in my dreams. I hear them in my dreams. I walk with them every day ... that's why

I can answer your questions with names like Phillis Wheatley,
Frances Ellen Watkins Harper, Jessie Fauset, Nella Larsen, Zora
Hurston, Ann Petry, Margaret Walker, and Gwendolyn Brooks.
I can say them because I can truly *feel* history.

TONI CADE BAMBARA
Author, Activist

We might seek to turn to our advantage the interdependence
history has thrust upon us.

KWAME ANTHONY APPIAH

When my father taught me history, I began to understand. I
remember distinctly, for instance, how he taught us about the
nine Xhosa wars. Of course we had textbooks, naturally written
by white men, and they had *their* interpretation, why there were
nine "Kaffir" wars. Then he would put the textbook aside and
say: "Now, this is what the book says, but the truth is: these
white people invaded our country and stole the land from our
grandfathers. The clashes between white and black were originally the result of cattle thefts. The whites took the cattle and
the blacks would go and fetch them back." That's how he
taught us our history.

WINNIE MANDELA
Part of My Soul Went with Him

Then our people lived peacefully, under the democratic rule of
their kings ... Then the country was ours, in our own name
and right. The land belonged to the whole tribe. There were no
classes, no rich or poor and no exploitation of man by man.
All men were free and equal and this was the foundation of
government. The council was so completely democratic that all
members of the tribe could participate in its deliberations, Chief
and subject, warrior and medicine man, all took part and en-
deavoured to influence its decisions. There was much in such
a society that was primitive and insecure, and certainly could

never measure up to the demands of the present epoch. But in such a society are contained the seeds of revolutionary democracy, in which none will be held in slavery or servitude, and in which poverty, want and insecurity shall be no more. This is the inspiration which, even today, inspires me and my comrades in our political struggle.

NELSON MANDELA
Part of My Soul Went with Him

If a race has no history, if it has no worthwhile tradition, it becomes a negligible factor in the thought of the world, and it stands in danger of being exterminated.

CARTER G. WOODSON
Historian, Founder of Black History Week

Of all our studies, history is best qualified to reward our research.

MALCOLM X

We know from the historical record that under the barbaric system of slavery black women were afforded equal-opportunity employment, no less than black men; and black women bore the lash as well. Because they were the carriers of the next generation of the "master's" profit, to protect the unborn slave child, a pregnant black woman was made to put her extended belly into a deep hole so that the warm earth hugged her baby while her back received the cold cruelty of the whip. And, when the brutality of racism and capitalism had dealt its blow to black women by day, night brought the most bitter sting of sexism in the form of rape by "the master."

JOHNETTA B. COLE

The South didn't win the war, but it won the peace, and it's been going in that direction ever since. The critical period is the period following the war.... They were very firm on what they felt the position of the country should be in respect to race. And the North was interested primarily in the South's resources. It was the perfect trade-off—we'll let you take this race thing and run with it as long as you let us invest and exploit the South's resources.... Jim Crow came when the Northerners were coming down in large numbers and investing in the South.

JOHN HOPE FRANKLIN

If the Egyptians and the majority of the tribes of Northern Africa were not Negroes, then there are no Negroes in the United States.

CARTER G. WOODSON

If you know whence you came, there is really no limit to where you can go.

JAMES BALDWIN

Afrocentric:
To Be or Not to Be?

He who ask questions, cannot avoid the answers.

African proverb

What is the truth? Or, more precisely, whose truth shall we express, that of the oppressed or of the oppressors?

LARRY NEAL

Educated Negroes have the attitude of contempt toward their own people because in their own as well as in their mixed schools Negroes are taught to admire the Hebrews, the Greek, the Latin and the Teuton and to despise the African. We should not underrate the achievements of Mesopotamia, Greece, and Rome; but we should give equally as much attention to the internal African kingdoms, the Songhay empire, and Ethiopia, which through Egypt decidedly influenced the civilization of the Mediterranean world.

CARTER G. WOODSON
Educator, Historian

Multiculturalists require a common truth of history.

RALPH WILEY,
Author

13

I have avoided the discussion over the issue of Afrocentric versus Eurocentric thought because they don't seem to be genuine debates. They really seem to be opportunities for an exchange of insults. Issues are not as dichotomous to me as that; I don't see multiculturalism as a threat to the accepted canon. All this strikes me as rhetoric behind which people are protecting other things that have less to do with knowledge than who's running the department, or who's getting the grants. What disturbs me about the Afrocentric approach, is that too often it masks the absence of standards. A lot of the Afrocentrics don't know what they're talking about, because they have not read broadly. You saw a lot of this at the beginning of Black Studies, when people would go to conferences and declaim, but had not read anything. Well, that's very rare these days. But I can't see that there's a problem with Afrocentrism, in and of itself, after all Du Bois invented it; however, he didn't give up the standards.

DAVID LEVERING LEWIS
Professor of History

Those people who fill the curriculum with thousands of courses on Shakespeare would have denied Shakespeare a job because he lacked a degree.

ISHMAEL REED

Afrocentricity is a terribly maligned concept. Afrocentricity is the idea that African people and interests must be viewed as actors and agency in human history, rather than as marginal to the European historical experience—which has been institutionalized as universal.

MOLEFI KETE ASANTE

The Afrocentrists stand on solid ground when they charge that European and American academics still resist the inclusion of African contributions . . . But in their zeal to counter the heavy handed "Eurocentric" imbalance of history, some have crossed the thin line between historic fact and fantasy. They've constructed groundless theories in which Europeans are "Ice People," suffer "genetic defects," or are obsessed with "color phobias." They've replaced the shallow European "great man" theory of history with a feel good interpretation of history. Black scholar Molefi Asante sees the danger. He warns that Afrocentrism is not about "biological determinism" but showing that Africans are "subjects of history and human experience rather than objects."

EARL OFARI HUTCHINSON, *Author*

Reclaiming our history does not mean resorting to simplistic and symbolic maneuvers to identify with a mythic Africa.

SHEILA WALKER

As a beginning, Afrocentricity is good to strip away those layers of doubt and self-hate in Black people, the way old paint is scraped away for a new coat to adhere properly. But sooner or later we folks in America must admit to ourselves we are not pure African at all—we are out of Africa. Just as the origins of humanity are out of Africa.

RALPH WILEY
What Black People Should Do Now

The seed of African cosmology contains a view of the world that repeatedly attempts to prove that intelligence and reason must always overcome brute force. We have taken simple unassuming creatures, the Spider and the Rabbit, as our totem—no lions or tigers or dragons—a simple rabbit imbued with characteristics that we all can identify. Brer Rabbit is none other than the spider, Anansi, of African lore.

JOHNETTA B. COLE

Afrocentric scholarship requires understanding on a concrete level that "I am because We are; and because We are, therefore

I am." There can be no I unless there are We. And it requires more than Western thought and sensibility with its emphasis on the rational, objective, and logical. Afrocentric scholarship proceeds from a world view which incorporates both "rational" analysis and "intuitive, subjective, and communal" analysis.

ELSA BARKLEY BROWN, *Historian*

I'm not interested in a curriculum of inclusion. What we need is a curriculum of liberation.

JOHN HENRIK CLARK
Historian, Professor Emeritus, Hunter College

Our kids hear terrible things about themselves. They hear they are incapable of learning—or of learning certain things. Here, we show them that there is no work they cannot do. And the Afrocentricity of this school makes them much more receptive to learning.

DR. AYNIM PALMER
Founder, Marcus Garvey School in South Central Los Angeles

Children are begging to know who they are. Up until 14, a child needs to have a strong background in his or her heritage before he or she goes out into the world.

JACKIE TURNAGE, *Educator*

Eurocentric historiography is the most formidable ally of White racism and imperialism. Its treacherous role in this regard must be explored and reversed by an Afrikan-centered historiography written by Afrikan historians dedicated to historical accuracy and truth—historians who are unafraid to speak truth to power.

AMOS N. WILSON
The Falsification of Afrikan Consciousness

Afrocentrism is an idea whose time has come. You see a lot of resistance to it coming from people who think it's a movement to change history. It's a reexamination of stuff that we've been told. In almost all my writing there's a character who has to reexamine what he has been told about himself and his history. Kids come in here and ask why we want to just emphasize slavery or the hard times that we have had. They want a different sense of that past. The idea is not that we were slaves, but that we were *enslaved*. Even though the whole idea of rebellion was *there*, we haven't emphasized it.

BILL HARRIS
Playwright, Detroit Lives

It is the Eurocentrists who are panicking that the untrue among their myths are being exploded. It seems they're unwilling to stand on their own two feet with little help from the past, but they insist that we do it.

RALPH WILEY, *Author*

I mean, you couldn't say Ellison is prevailing when you've got all these people in colleges and so forth talking about being Afrocentric as if they never heard of Greenwich Mean Time.

ALBERT MURRAY, *Novelist*

Why are we tribes in Africa and ethnic groups in Europe?

A STUDENT

When I was in school, I had the feeling that African-American history didn't begin until slavery. We teach the children that these ethnic groups had a society, a culture, a value before they appeared in America.

EILEEN GRAY, *Principal*

Thus I follow a long tradition of African American scholars who understand the limitations of the paradigms and underlying assumptions that pervade Western educational institutions and bookshelves and who draw upon our communities—and for African American women especially, the women in our communities—to help us understand and depict the lives of African American people in a way that they/we would recognize as reality. I build upon the experience of my scholar/mothers in recognizing the difference between the two views and noting the important role that my community, especially the women in it, have played in my development.

ELSA BARKLEY BROWN
Doublestitch: Black Women Write
About Mothers and Daughters

. . . millions of Americans know now that the story of African-Americans is the story of one of the greatest flights of the human spirit in human history and that the history called American history cannot be understood or redeemed without a confrontation with the history called Black history.

Ebony *magazine*

I differ with the concept of Afrocentricity because it compromises the word Africa. The concept was old long before the current propagators began to promote it. This form of African awareness started early in the nineteenth century with Frederick Douglass, Prince Hall, Benjamin Banneker, Paul Cuffee and the African Colonization Society, Martin Delany and David Walker with his famous "Appeal," and the founding of the African Methodist Episcopal Church. So, Afrocentricity is a current development of this generation that is weakened by not having the background of this information. I think the concept is much too narrow; it's almost like popular music . . . next season you might not even remember today's hit songs . . . it just lacks depth.

JOHN HENRIK CLARK
Historian, Professor Emeritus, Hunter College

THE TRANSFORMING POWER OF EDUCATION

An educator in a system of oppression is either revolutionary or an oppressor.

LERONE BENNETT JR., *Historian*

Education is our passport to the future, for tomorrow belongs to the people who prepare for it today.

MALCOLM X

Education empowers you; it places you in a position to verbally challenge people who are giving you a whole lot of nonsense.

CAMILLE COSBY

There is no people that need all the benefits resulting from a well-directed education more than we do.

FRANCES ELLEN WATKINS HARPER
Abolitionist, Poet

Perhaps we should remind ourselves that the ultimate purpose of education is not to know but to act.

JOHNETTA B. COLE

Let there be light, two kinds of light: to light the outside world, to light the world within the soul. Each generation with its own lamp gave out the lamp of learning, education.

MARY McLEOD BETHUNE
Her Own Words of Inspiration

We have too long educated the mind and left the heart a moral waste.

ANONYMOUS

I'm also convinced that illiteracy is a factor contributing to suicide becoming one of the leading causes of death among white middle-class youngsters, who allow their souls to atrophy from the steady diet of spiritual Wonder Bread: bad music, and bad film, and the outrageous cheapness of superficial culture.

ISHMAEL REED

I feel that the problem that we have in the black community is education. The greatest impact on the community is education. Until we can educate our people to be healthy we are going to have problems; until we can improve the education in the schools in our community we are going to have problems; until we can start early with our bright young people, get them off to a good start so that they aren't already behind when they get to school we are going to have problems. So I feel that the problems are related to education.

DR. JOYCELYN ELDERS
First female black Surgeon General of the United States

I was very fortunate to have gone to one of the old-type segregated schools. My teachers saw me as an extension of themselves, and they probably would have committed mass suicide had I graduated from school not being able to read and write.

DR. AYNIM PALMER
Founder, Marcus Garvey School in South Central Los Angeles

He who learns, teaches.

Ethiopian proverb

In teaching me the alphabet, in the days of her simplicity and kindness, my mistress had given me the "inch," and now, no ordinary precaution could prevent me from taking the "ell."

FREDERICK DOUGLASS

The feeling that we had forgotten more than we had learned had shown us that school was no more than paying our dues for a place in life.

WILLIAM BANKS, *Novelist*

Good grades mean good dollars.

ANITA BAKER

Knowledge is gold.

Swahili proverb

When the studying gets hard, we should get hard too.

DR. BENJAMIN CARSON

The schoolteacher today has to be mother, father, counselor, everything. The majority of children have nobody to sit down with them and teach them the little things that are right from the things that are wrong. Sometimes I have to stop the class, close the book and say "let's talk." Because their parents just don't have the time.

RUBY MIDDLETON FORSYTHE, *Schoolteacher*

Surely we have wit enough to found a Negro college so manned and equipped as to steer successfully between the dilettante and the fool . . .

W. E. B. Du Bois

Going to school wasn't a requirement in our house, it was a sacrament.

Julia Boyd

Learn how to do or be a bum.

Tonya Bolden, Just Family

There are children of color in special education who have been taken off the express train and put on the local. The local never catches up with the express.

Anonymous

It is a significant and shameful fact, that I am constantly in receipt of letters from the still unprotected women in the South, begging to find employment for their daughters . . . to save them from going into the homes of the South as servants as there is nothing to save them from dishonor and degradation.

Fannie Barrier Williams
Turn-of-the Century Activist, Doublestitch: Black Women
Write About Mothers and Daughters

My whole family is really education based. Everybody says "You must go to school. You must be educated." It's been a strong push for me.

Geri Allen, *Jazz Pianist*

Because men are very dangerous to women's education. Why would I endanger my own child? I'm not crazy. A little eccentric, but not crazy.

> NTOZAKE SHANGE, *explaining why her daughter, Savannah,*
> *attends an all-girl school*

Again, an education (not a schooling, and not a *colleging* as Langston Hughes put it) about ourselves would empower black women because it would help us understand the source of our powerlessness. And, understanding is always the first step toward change.

> JOHNETTA B. COLE

Now that I'm out here teaching, the first thing I hear is, "We cannot afford that." And I say "Well, give up cigarettes for a month or those new tennis shoes that you don't have to have." You just no longer see that tradition about sacrificing.

> ANGELA FRANKLIN, *Artist-Teacher,*
> *about some parents' attitudes toward supporting*
> *a child's talents beyond the public school classroom*

The tendency is here, born of slavery and quickened to renewed life by the crazy imperialism of the day, to regard human beings as among the material resources of a land to be trained with an eye single to future dividends. Race-prejudices, which keep brown and black men in their "places," we are coming to regard as useful allies with such a theory, no matter how much they may dull the ambition and sicken the hearts of struggling human beings. And above all, we daily hear that an education that encourages aspiration that sets the loftiest of ideas and seeks as an end culture and character rather than bread-winning is the privilege of white men and the danger and delusion of black.

> W. E. B. DU BOIS
> "On the Training of Black Men"

ARCHITECTURAL DRAWING AND ELECTRICAL ENGINEERING

The Tuskegee Institute is now offering extended courses in both theory and practice to young men anxious to secure advanced instruction in Architectural Drawing Courses, to make plans for houses, and who can do the work required in Electrical Engineering. Every effort is being made to make these courses more helpful than ever before.

> BOOKER T. WASHINGTON, *Principal*
> *Tuskegee Institute, Ala.*
> (*Ad found in October 1907 issue of*
> The Colored American Magazine)

When we also learn that this country and the Western world have no monopoly of goodness and truth or of skills and scholarship, we begin to appreciate the ingredients that are indispensable to making a better world. In a life of learning that is, perhaps, the greatest lesson of all.

> JOHN HOPE FRANKLIN
> *Historian, Professor Emeritus*

It is not enough that the teachers of teachers should be trained in technical normal methods; they must also, as far as possible, be broad-minded, cultured men and women . . .

> W. E. B. DU BOIS

More and more African American parents have concluded that the nation's public schools are failing to meet their children's needs.

> CHARLENE MARMER SOLOMON, *Writer*

I got the feeling from people at the public school that if you have a nonwhite child who is doing O.K. you should be happy. In other words the attitude is "what more could you ask?"

> KIM BAKER, *Parent*

When a school child remains unchallenged he or she will shut down and lose interest in learning altogether.

BESSIE HOGAN
Retired School Principal

Generally, standardized tests don't serve African-American children well at all.

JUDITH BERRY GRIFFIN

Identify your child's needs, find a school that stresses diversity and get free professional help.

CHARLENE MARMER SOLOMON, *Writer*

The function of education in the United States is to develop citizens who are fully oriented to cultural diversity—and are not hung up on race.

ALBERT MURRAY, *Novelist*

It is very difficult for children to be the only child of color in a class.

JUDITH BERRY GRIFFIN

We have standards in our home that we want replicated in a school where you learn about choice and consequences.

ROYAL ALLEY-BARNES

Sometimes parents are thinking so much about saving for college that they believe they can't afford to pay for private school now. I tell them if they invest now, the child will have more options later.

MANASA HEKKYMARA, *Educator*

Knowledge is better than riches.

African proverb

We have got lots of folks who are colleged, but too few who are educated.

LANGSTON HUGHES

Not to know is bad; not to wish to know is worse.

Nigerian proverb

My classroom is the haven in a community that is sometimes chaotic. I serve as the teacher, preacher, counselor, tutor and giver of a needed hug. I use mathematics as the vehicle to build self-esteem, pride and racial understanding incorporating the contributions of various ethnic groups. My philosophy is simple, all can learn through listening, reading, touching, talking and writing—and holding fast to dreams.

KAY FRANCES TOLLIVER
Teacher of Mathematics

If you're illiterate, people can do anything they want to you . . .
   As you go through life X-ing documents, unable to defend yourself against forces hostile to you, people can deprive you of your voting rights through gerrymandering schemes, build a freeway next to your apartment building, or open a retail crack operation on your block, with people coming and going as though you lived next door to Burger King—because you're not articulate enough to fight back, because you don't have sense enough to know what is happening to you, and so you're shoveled under at each turn in your life; you might as well be dead.

ISHMAEL REED

To one who does not know, a small garden is a forest.

Ethiopian proverb

I was born knowing exactly nothing. I had no one, no one, to teach me the things of real value. The school systems are gauged to teach youth what to think, not how to think.

GEORGE JACKSON
Soledad Brother: The Prison Letters of George Jackson

Illiteracy not only affects members of the "underclass" but reaches into the centers of higher education.

ISHMAEL REED

I assume that if the students are in my class, they're here to learn. I emphasize hard work. It's hard work that separates so-called geniuses from the also-rans.

ABDULALIM SHABAZZ
Professor of Mathematics

Classroom motto: Let us think big, even though we may miss our aim.

RUBY MIDDLETON FORSYTHE, *Schoolteacher*

I'm not there to impress students with what I know. I'm there to impart to them what I know.

WENDY R. BROWN, *Law Professor*

It's painfully obvious that this nation and this world cannot allow white students to go through higher education without interacting with blacks in authoritative positions.

NIKKI GIOVANNI

After several years' work, suddenly, it was as if a door opened and I knew without a doubt that I was *inside*. I knew literature. And what was my joy!

JEAN TOOMER

One of the joys of reading is the ability to plug into the shared wisdom of mankind.

ISHMAEL REED

Most blacks emerging from the civil war, men and women, advocated the education of black women for two very practical reasons: One, better training and skills were rewarded with better wages and two, educated black women could escape domestic service in the homes of whites where they were too often economically exploited and sexually assaulted. The African American ex-slave community is one of the few [in world history] where the education of females was often placed ahead of males. Black men often sacrificed their formal training and undertook extra unskilled work, so that a wife, sister, or daughter could go to school.

JOHNETTA B. COLE

The influence that we have over the male sex demands, that our minds should be instructed and improved with the principles of education and religion, in order that this influence should be properly directed.

MATILDA *(surname unknown)*
in a letter to Freedom's Journal, *founded in 1827*
by Samuel Cornish and John Russwurm

Don't let your address be your destination.

CORLA WILSON-HAWKINS, PH.D.
Essence Awardee, Sixth-Grade Teacher

You cannot teach a child you fear.

JAWANZA KUNJUFU

It is better to be loved than feared.

Senegalese proverb

A law enforcement agenda, kicking kids out, is not an education agenda.

GEORGE MCKENNA III
High School Principal

Classroom cheer: One, two, three—HARD WORK.

CARTER BAYTON CLASSROOM

I had a strong and loving father. That's what I had to be for these boys.

CARTER BAYTON

I will not let you fail.

MARVA COLLINS
Founder, Collins Westside Preparatory School

Enter to learn; depart to serve.

MARY MCLEOD BETHUNE
Her Own Words of Inspiration

WISDOM WORDS

> *Right is of no sex*
> *Truth is of no color*
> *God is the Father of us all*
> *And all, we are brothers*

FREDERICK DOUGLASS

The beginning of wisdom is the fear of God.

Axiom

Do not live your life as if God does not exist.

ARLENE CLARK

A wise man who knows his proverbs can reconcile difficulties.

Nigerian proverb

There are moral laws of the universe just as abiding as the physical laws, and when we disobey these moral laws we suffer tragic consequences.

THE REVEREND MARTIN LUTHER KING JR.

Wisdom is not like money, to be tied up and hidden.

Proverb of the Akan people of Ghana

30

Life is a shadow and a mist; it passes quickly by, and is no more.

Madagascan proverb

Experiences teach the best lessons only when we reflect on them in the light of a Higher moral value.

MILDRED GREENE, *Armchair Philosopher*

The best way to live in this world is to live above it.

SONIA SANCHEZ
Poet, Lecturer, Teacher

Don't borrow trouble.

Traditional

There are rare instances when truth is best served by silence.

GORDON PARKS

When a man is coming toward you, you need not say: "Come here."

Ashanti proverb

One problem thoroughly understood is of more value than a score poorly mastered.

BOOKER T. WASHINGTON

Near the end of a long vacation, I was cleaning my tightly packed New York-sized closet getting it ready for back to work. As I repacked and expanded on the clothes, towels and bedding, I was saving to send to Haiti as soon as the embargo was lifted, I suddenly understood why it was so important to continue to grow in my ability to carry out the ritual of recycling items that I am not using. It came like a flash as I struggled to part with things I had been saving but had not used in over two years (my self-imposed cut-off period) that to hold on to things I accumulate in our consumer-driven society in a finite space is indeed the author of chaos and the enemy of order.

MONIFA HAKIM, *Writer*

The test of character is the amount of strain it can bear.

CHARLES HOUSTON

An idle mind is the devil's workshop.

African-American folk saying

Money talks. Bullshit walks.

African-American street folk saying

They say you should not suffer through the past. You should be able to wear it like a loose garment, take it off and let it drop.

EVA JESSYE

There is no need to have a meeting unless you can be productive. If you are not sure of what the meeting is expected to produce, don't have it.

MARIE DUTTON BROWN, *Literary Agent*

It works if you work it.

JOHNETTA B. COLE

In your lifetime if you can come up with one original idea you have accomplished a great deal.

MAX ROACH

A cutting word is worse than a cutting bowstring; a cut may heal, but the cut of the tongue does not.

Mauritanian proverb

Sophistication has to do with the way you think, the way you live.

CARMEN McRAE

New Yorkers need to learn more about the principle of arriving passengers. It is but common sense and indeed common courtesy to let the arriving passengers on a city bus or subway car disembark before ruthlessly pushing your way onto the car with no respect for those trying to exit. You see it works like this: the conductor sees you standing on the platform waiting to enter and will allow sufficient time for you to do so. "Let the passengers off before you enter" is a superb organizational principle for public transport. Imagine trying to board an aircraft or Greyhound bus or an Amtrak train before the arriving passengers discharge. The more impolite and disrespectful New Yorkers attempt to do so every day on their subway trains and motor coaches.

JOANN NICOL
Law student from Liverpool, England

It is in your self-interest to find a way to be very tender.

ANONYMOUS

Everything that IS was once IMAGINED!

TED JOANS

Distrust is motivated by fear, and fear is motivated by the unknown.

JULIA BOYD

As long as you keep a person down, some part of you has to be down there to hold him down, so it means you cannot soar as you otherwise might.

MARIAN ANDERSON

The seven wonders of the world I have seen, and many places I have been. Take my advice, folks, and see Beale Street first.

HENRY CHASE

I was having a good time visiting my friend, but I kept my stay short. She was lovingly and genuinely bending over backwards to show me a good time. I didn't want to keep her in that position too long.

A GIRLFRIEND

Leave everything a little better than you found it.

Axiom

Don't look back, something might be gaining on you!

SATCHEL PAIGE

He who digs too deep for a fish, may come out with a snake.

Ethiopian proverb

Confiding a secret to an unworthy person is like carrying grain in a bag with a hole.

Ethiopian proverb

A loose tooth will not rest until it's pulled out.

Ethiopian proverb

Reference determines value.

AMIRI BARAKA

When you make a mistake, correct it.

FRED HAMPTON, *Black Panther*

Men are condemned for what they do; men are even condemned for what they don't do. But the measure of a man isn't what he does or doesn't do. It is what he admits when caught.

EWIN JAMES, *Writer*

The measure of a man is in the lives he's touched.

ERNIE BANKS

Travellers with closed minds can tell us little except about themselves.

CHINUA ACHEBE
Hopes and Impediments: Selected Essays

The truth is never a finished product; it is a continuing process.

WILLIAM BANKS, *Author*

For generations, instead of seeking black independence, we have sought white acceptance.

GEORGE C. FRASER

We need a revolution inside of our own minds.

JOHN HENRIK CLARK

Folly is shortsighted.

Saying

But folly is shortsighted and for now [Benjamin Chavis] is out of the [NAACP] and will never make the contribution that he might have.

Ewin James, *Writer*

I realized that a hospital is not a place of gloom, but a place of last-minute hope.

A high school student
in an essay about his grandmother's terminal illness

Don't ever be jealous of anyone, because you never know how they got what they have.

West Indian proverb

You can't make chicken salad out of chicken shit.

Consuella Cunningham, *mother of Gene*

If you don't like something, change it. If you can't change it, change the way you think about it.

Traditional wisdom

Don't complain.

Traditional wisdom

Actions reproduce themselves.

Traditional wisdom

When deeds speak, words are nothing.

Traditional African wisdom

Actions are statements of character. It doesn't pay to ignore acts of malice, greed, backbiting in one situation, expecting it not to occur in another altogether different setting. If you do, you may find yourself saying in dismay, "I never thought she would do a thing like that," only to be reminded of the time past when she did a very similar thing to someone else in another venue. This is not to say that we break associations with people, but it is to suggest that we proceed thoughtfully with clarified expectations.

MILDRED GREENE, *Armchair Philosopher*

When you control a man's thinking you do not have to worry about his actions. You do not have to tell him not to stand here or go yonder. He will find his "proper place" and will stay in it. You do not need to send him to the back door. He will go without being told. In fact, if there is no back door, he will cut one for his special benefit. His education makes it necessary.

CARTER GOODWIN WOODSON

Actions do build attitudes, and attitudes, of course, build character. You have to watch what you are doing.

MARIE DUTTON BROWN, *Literary Agent*

To understand all is to forgive all.

Maxim

CREATIVITY

For four hundred years African creativity has been struggling to counter the narrow constraints of oppression, to circle it, turn it around, to seek order and meaning in the midst of chaos. My soul looks back in wonder at how African creativity has sustained us and how it still flows—seeking, searching for new ways to connect the ancient with the new, the young with the old, the unborn with the ancestors.

TOM FEELINGS, *Artist*
My Soul Looks Back in Wonder

I remember hearing Bird, Charlie Parker, play "Ain't She Sweet" three straight nights and he never played it the same way twice. I asked him why. He said the wind doesn't blow the same way every day, so why should I play the song the same way every time? I didn't gather the real import of what he said until years later when I was driving up in the country and I saw a dog on a leash. He was jumping to the right, jumping to the left, jumping up and down, but he could not jump beyond that leash. Now the dog had all kinds of liberty, but it could not go beyond the leash. Bird never stopped playing "Ain't She Sweet"; the parameters were the song, but his innovation was within the song.

JOHN HENRIK CLARK, *Historian*

The novel is fiction. History is fact. And the blending of fact and fiction has given writers no little trouble. Either fact or fiction must suffer; and in the successful historical novel, fact

38

usually suffers, for it has to be bent, that it may be made to blend.

WILLIAM H. DAWLEY
The Colored American Magazine, *October 1907*

... I do not deal in happiness, I deal in meaning.

RICHARD WRIGHT

Denied their original cultures, slaves created a new culture, one that embraced their African pasts and accommodated their new status as captives. Along with this new culture—African-American culture—came a new oral tradition, one that would give rise to rap.

K. MAURICE JONES, Say It Loud

And for everything they took away, we came up with something new ... We sang some new songs, and danced us some new dances ... See, you can put a hurting on the body, but you can't touch the soul.

AL YOUNG, *Novelist*

It's not that the cultural cutting edge has been influenced by black creativity; it's that black creativity, it so often seems today, is the cultural cutting edge.

HENRY LOUIS GATES JR.

Writing well is the same thing as thinking well.

CHARLES JOHNSON
about Ralph Ellison's Invisible Man

While some of the authors of the present day have been weaving their stories about white men marrying beautiful quadroon

girls, who in so doing were lost to us socially, I conceived of
one of that same class to whom I gave a higher, holier destiny;
a life of lofty self-sacrifice and beautiful self-consecration, finished at the post of duty, and rounded off with the fiery crown
of martyrdom, a circlet which ever changes into a diadem of
glory.

FRANCES ELLEN WATKINS HARPER,
Poet, Novelist, Abolitionist

Social function is the heart of literature.

*Credo of the Harlem Renaissance
and the Black Arts Movement*

I write the way I write because I am the kind of person that I
am. My styles and my content stem from my experience. I grew
up a well-loved child in a loving family and so I have always
known that being very poor, which we were, had nothing to
do with lovingness or familyness or character or any of that.
This doesn't mean that I or we were content with whatever we
had and never hoped or tried working at having more. It means
that we were quite clear that what we had didn't have anything
to do with what we were. We were/are quite sure that we
were/are among the best of people and not having any money
had nothing to do with that. Other people's opinions didn't
influence us about that. We were quite sure. When I write,
especially for children, I try to get that across, that being poor
or whatever your circumstance, you are capable of being the
best of people and that best, as a human, does not come from
the outside in, it comes from the inside out.

LUCILLE CLIFTON

The real hard terror of writing like this came when I found that
writing of one's life was vastly different from speaking of it. I
was rendering a close and emotionally connected account of my
experience, and the ease I had in speaking from notes at Fisk

[University] would not come again. I found that to tell the truth was the hardest thing on earth, harder than fighting in a war, harder than taking part in a revolution.

RICHARD WRIGHT

I continue to create because writing is a labor of love and also an act of defiance, a way to light a candle in a gale wind: "In the beginning was the Word, and the Word was with God, and the Word was God."

ALICE CHILDRESS,
Novelist, Playwright

At the same time when so many Black writers have decided that the thing to do is to "get over" with the great white racist publishing establishment, despite the price one may be forced to pay in terms of self-esteem, human dignity, and artistic integrity, Childress has made a deliberate choice of weapons; she has chosen the weapon of creative struggle. Black blessings on you, Alice Childress.

Love, struggle, humor. These are the hallmarks of her craft, of her artistry, these, like a trademark or a fingerprint.

JOHN OLIVER KILLENS, *Novelist*

If I could be cloned, I'd like to be three people. One would stay at the desk writing; one would be a public writer, the one who goes around making speeches and being personable; the third would be a normal human being. A writer cannot be all these things at one time.

ALEX HALEY

It is the dream of my life to be an author.

CHARLES CHESTNUTT

I have to figure out how to make these solos I'm hearing into people who are talking. If I wrote the music down, since I can't read music, it would be chaos.

NTOZAKE SHANGE

The irony of receiving flagrantly inequitable treatment in a society that boasts of its democratic heritage has been a main source of black humor ...

MEL WATKINS, On the Real Side

If you want to feel humor too exquisite and subtle for translation, sit invisibly among a gang of Negro workers.

W. E. B. DU BOIS

We raise de wheat,
Dey gib us de dorn;
We bake de bread,
Dey gib us de cruss;
We sif de meal,
Dey gib us de huss.

Antebellum African-American humor

One thing most Negroes learn early is how to laugh at their situation.

SADIE DELANY
Having Our Say: The Delany Sisters' First 100 Years

Humor is laughing at what you haven't got when you ought to have it. Of course, you laugh by proxy. You're really laughing at the other guy's lacks, not your own. That's what makes it funny—the fact that you don't know you are laughing at yourself. Humor is when the joke is on you but hits the other fellow first—because it boomerangs. Humor is what you wish in your secret heart were not funny, but it is, and you must laugh. Humor is your unconscious therapy.

LANGSTON HUGHES

The black comic tradition emerged as one of the major shaping forces on American humor in general.

MEL WATKINS, *Author*

How dare anyone, parent, schoolteacher, or literary critic, tell me not to act colored? White people have been enjoying the privilege of acting like Negroes for more than a hundred years.

ARNA BONTEMPS

Your talents are not yours to keep . . .

KALAMU CHACHE, *Poet*

Know your gifts and share them.

LES BROWN

My mother and grandmother were always ladies of style. They taught me that you didn't have to be rich to look good.

WILLI SMITH, *Fashion Designer*

All the pleasure I have had, I owe to my sewing.

ANN LOWE, *Fashion Designer*

White designers who have to run to Paris for color and fabric combinations should go to church on Sunday in Harlem. It's all right there.

WILLI SMITH, *Fashion Designer*

I design differently because I am Patrick Kelly, and Patrick Kelly is black, is from Mississippi.

PATRICK KELLY, *Fashion Designer*

If I can create the minimum of my plans and desires, there can be no regrets.

BESSIE COLEMAN, (1893–1926),
the first black woman—and possibly the first woman—to receive an international pilot's license

I have great belief in the fact that whenever there is chaos, it creates wonderful thinking. I consider chaos a gift.

SEPTIMA POINSETTE CLARK,
Founder, Freedom Schools, Charleston, South Carolina

I invented jazz and the stomps.

JELLY ROLL MORTON

The New African names have the cadence and structure of the old but they are created here ... The newly created names have music in them. They sing.

DR. IMANI HUMPHREY, *Educator*

One of the challenges in studios at that time was to paint a white egg, on a white tablecloth, on white marble ... although all white, you get the feeling of an egg, the feeling of the cloth, the feeling of a table. One of the fascinating things about two-dimensional art is that it has a magic.

JACOB LAWRENCE, *Painter*

Of course, the impact that black entertainers and athletes have had on American culture is nothing if not staggering.

CHARLES WHITAKER, *Actor*

Art and the Artist

It seems to me that the best art is political and you ought to be able to make it unquestionably political and irrevocably beautiful at the same time.

TONI MORRISON

The responsibility of an artist representing an oppressed people is to make revolution irresistible.

TONI CADE BAMBARA

I think every artist is obligated to dig deep within him- or herself if he or she intends on being true *and* real. . . . There is something grotesquely wrong with a society where millions of people face daily political, cultural, spiritual, psychological, and economic oppression by virtue of their skin complexion. That said, much of my work deals in some manner with the cancer we call racism as well as the all-important identity questions which accompany it.

KEVIN POWELL, Recognize

An artist is a sort of emotional or spiritual historian. His role is to make you realize the doom and glory of knowing who you are and what you are. He has to tell, because nobody else can tell, what it is like to be alive.

JAMES BALDWIN

The artist, always in an uphill battle, must engage truth.

SARAH WRIGHT, *Novelist*

It's a tremendous responsibility—responsibility and honor—to be a writer, an artist, a cultural worker . . . whatever you call this vocation. One's got to see what the factory worker sees, what the prisoner sees, got to see what the ruling-class myth maker sees as well, in order to tell the truth and not get trapped.

TONI CADE BAMBARA, *Author*

Art is confrontational in that it challenges someone's way of thinking.

DANNY GLOVER

Traditionally, African art objects did what art is meant to do: They were a part of society—they were teaching elements, instructive tools for reinforcing the community's morals and explaining the changes and challenges of life.

KAREN CARRILLO, *Writer*

I make the kinds of films I've always wanted to see.

JULIE DASH

Because a genuine artist, no matter what he says he believes, must feel in his blood the ultimate enmity between art and orthodoxy.

CHINUA ACHEBE
Anthills of the Savannah

I'm an African-American, and my role in the entertainment industry is to entertain—and to educate.

KADEEM HARDISON

When Ruby and I came into the professional theater in 1946 and 1947 ... [w]e in the theater had a sense of purpose. It wasn't about money. It wasn't about your name on the marquee.

OSSIE DAVIS

The ... debate over artistic integrity is as old as the prehistoric divorce between art and spiritual expression, and the subsequent marriage of the former to commerce.

MICHAEL ROBINSON

When you start making slight concessions, you find yourself making all of it ... There is always the danger to artistic integrity of conformity. That is not really what the artist is here to give. Even when the artist commits himself to work with other people to bring about a better society and really goes in, the artist must at the same time be aware that a time will come when he will ask himself if he did the right thing. Because somebody with political ambitions will have highjacked the movement and will be telling the artist that he must do this or that in the interest of the people. This is always dangerous.

CHINUA ACHEBE

Some entertainers have tried to make art of their coarseness, but in their public crudeness they have merely revealed their own vast senses of personal inferiority.

MAYA ANGELOU

When I was young I listened to music. I remember Marvin, Smokey and the Supremes singing about Black love and unity. As black women we respected ourselves and demanded respect from others. Nowadays, these children are calling each other "niggas," "skeezers," and "whores." As if that's not bad enough, they are getting paid millions of dollars to do it.

SISTA MONIFA

... I think a lot of women like our music because we're not calling them names. These guys who buy our records say they buy them for their girls, but I think a lot of them want to be able to say the things we say, they just can't. We know these young women will grow up to be somebody's mother, and the mother is the shaper of the family.

NATHAN MORRIS, *Boyz II Men*

I'm the son of a minister and I couldn't do it. Even if I could, I wouldn't. It really doesn't work. It's pandering. If you want to be funny, be funny. Look at Gleason, Berle, George Burns. They didn't go on television and do sex jokes. They were just funny.

SINBAD

Record companies have sacrificed artistic integrity. The bottom line is all that counts. This attitude is a big problem and has, unfortunately, been picked up by artists, especially the young ones. This is damaging to our art form and the recording industry as a whole.

QUEEN LATIFAH

I place no limits on what I can do as an actor or as a black man. It's time for more of us on the inside to speak up, and demand better roles and decisive control of the black images that people around the world and outside of our culture judge us by.

CHARLES S. DUTTON, *Actor*

I suppose you could say that I am basically kind of emotional, and there are some things, such as graduations and your husband being there when your baby is born, that are very important to me. I missed both of those. My husband wasn't there when my baby was born and I did miss my graduation. And I think the only constructive thing I have done about it is instead of crawling in a hole somewhere or dying on the vine, I use it in my acting, which comes out in an emotional way. If I have a scene to do that's emotional, it's easy for me to grab an emotion, because I already have them there—little hurts.

DOROTHY DANDRIDGE

I put on whatever face is required for whatever I'm doing. I try to realize who I'm reaching and what I want to say to those people, and I try to wear that face and put on that hat.

HALLE BERRY, *Actress*

This play is about the problem of minority groups. It concerns a blackamoor, who tried to find equality among the whites. It's right up my alley.

PAUL ROBESON, *on* Othello

Tell them I'll become a star when they start writing great roles for black women in films.

LONETTE MCKEE, *Actress*

The thing I love most about being in films is that they allow me to be other people.

JASMINE GUY, *Actress*

I love language and authors and music and how it can all interconnect. As an actor I want to explore life rhythms and the sounds in the silences.

RUBY DEE

We need to tell the full range of our stories, not just the ones about violence and poverty and pain. We need movies that show Black folks in all their dimensions, movies that portray us as the loving, complex, multifaceted people we are.

HALLE BERRY, *Actress*

So we've got to really expand the subject matter, because these films in the 'hood don't tell the total picture of our experience in this country. And I know that it's easier for young black filmmakers to get financed if the 'hood is the subject matter, the same way that if you're a rapper, if you go the hard-core gangster route, you'll probably get a quicker record deal that way too.

SPIKE LEE

It really doesn't make sense to rely upon another culture to describe you and define you . . . regardless of how well-meaning they may be.

MARY SMITH, *President,*
Black Filmmakers Hall of Fame

But I *would* like to see us—as Blacks in the industry—getting away from these stereotypical films. I'd like to see us change the picture of ourselves that we're presenting to the public. It's something that *we* have to do because the studios won't. They'll keep giving us money to make shoot-'em-up films.

HALLE BERRY, *Actress*

The great black performers did not simply play characters. Rather they played *against* their roles.

DONALD BOGLE

I am not hankering for an Oscar. That would be crazy. I'm hankering for the kind of work that makes you a contender for one.

JAMES EARL JONES, *Actor*

I consider myself an actress and have always worked hard to become a competent one. I interpret a role to the best of my ability, and more often than not—and more often than I would like—the role calls for a creature of abandon whose desires are stronger than her sense of morality.

DOROTHY DANDRIDGE

I don't want others outside of our community to define us, because they are doing a horrible job of it. And they are lying.

CAMILLE COSBY

Show business was class in the twenties and thirties.

MAUDE RUSSELL RUTHERFORD,
Former Broadway Showgirl, at age ninety-eight

Being an artist, I had an artist's instincts. Why, you have an advantage over the average photographer. You can see the picture before it's taken; then it's up to you to get the *camera* to see.

JAMES VAN DER ZEE, *Photographer*

He [Nat King Cole] had been all over the planet with roses to walk on, acknowledged as a goodwill ambassador, but in his own country, getting on television and into the homes of millions of Americans was a problem.

CAROLE COLE

The magic of artistry is found in the peace of knowing and accepting who you are.

AVERY BROOKS, *Actor*

Artists suffer so you don't have to.

MARVIN GAYE

A song has to become a part of you. It's something in you that you'll have for the rest of your life.

MARTHA REEVES,
Lead Singer, Martha and the Vandellas

My songs are not autobiographical. If I sang about everything I've experienced, I'd be in a straitjacket. But some of the songs I write and sing are reflective of my state of mind at that time. But this is true of all artists and composers. If you've been in a bad mood for a year, then you're going to write or sing the blues.

LUTHER VANDROSS

If I wrote autobiographically . . . I'd wind up getting into folks' business, plundering the lives of people around me, pulling the covers off of friends. I'd be an emotional gangster, a psychic thug, pimp and vampire.

TONI CADE BAMBARA

I used to say that I learned to write by listening to people talk. I still feel that the best of my writing comes from having *heard* rather than having read.

GAYLE JONES, *Author*

I kept quiet. . . . For the most part, I still do. I kept quiet and listened to all kinds of philosophy, ideas and attitudes.

AUGUST WILSON,
Playwright, speaking about teenage years spent in a cigar store with retired Pullman porters

She [the protagonist in *Liliane*] can figure out other things to do. She has lovers, she has friends, she has great intellectual adventures. And she never stops saying she doesn't like being oppressed. But she doesn't have to put Mary Dalton in that oven. That's something Richard Wright gave me.

NTOZAKE SHANGE

No single entity really influenced my life as did my father ... an oak of a man, his five-feet-eight frame loomed taller than Kilimanjaro. He lived as if he were poured from iron, and loved his family with a vulnerability that was touching. Indomitable, to the point that one could not have spent a lifetime in his presence without absorbing something beautiful and strong and special.

MARI EVANS, *Poet*

The Black writer at the present time must forgo the assimilationist tradition and redirect his (her) art to the striving within ... to do so, he (she) must write for and speak to the majority of Black people; not to a sophisticated elite fashioned out of the programmed computers of America's largest universities.

ADDISON GAYLE JR.,
Professor of English

What I do is write about what I see and what I feel and what I know in the hope that it will help the people who read it see more and feel more and know more.

PEARL CLEAGE
Deals with the Devil

... I cannot imagine a writer who is not continually reaching, who contains no discontent that what he or she is producing is not more than it is. So primarily, I suppose, discipline is the foundation of the profession, and that holds regardless of anything else.

MARI EVANS, *Poet*

Learning to sing one's own songs, to trust the particular cadences of one's own voice, is also the goal of any writer.

HENRY LOUIS GATES JR.

With a mass audience comes the peril of the gatekeepers to that audience, those whose task it is to turn art into a commodity.

MICHAEL ROBINSON

Most writers that "make it" in this country have to become literary and physical prostitutes in one form or another.

HAKI MADHUBUTI
Founder, Third World Press

Artists should follow their own visions and create whatever they want. That is because it is precisely the variety of those unique visions of the human condition that gives art its true value.

While the world knows and loves the dramas of Shakespeare and still recites his sonnets, only historians of the Elizabethan period can remember the names of the politicians who were his contemporaries. The moral of this story is clear. The value of great art will outlive the political controversies of the moment.

PLAYTHELL BENJAMIN,
Columnist, Daily News

Content is of great importance, but we must not underrate the value of style.

MAYA ANGELOU
Wouldn't Take Nothing for My Journey Now

In dance you have to be focused. And dance gives you the structure to help you use the focus.

ARTHUR MITCHELL,
Choreographer and Founder of Dance Theatre of Harlem

One endures and is fascinated by the amount, variety and ubiquity of urban debris. Its pervasive presence provides an endless source of form, texture and palette in my work.

LEROY JOHNSON, *Artist*

I wanted the face to have the appearance of being worn and stretched, but still holding up, which is the image of African and African-American women. We've weathered time and space and gone through many experiences, but we're still standing. We're still here.

ANGELA FRANKLIN, *Artist,*
about her 1993 copper and enamel work
"My Strength Flows Ever On"

No. I never had nothing like that. The only lesson I got, I got it from God, so that's the way I got it. I get it like that.

THORNTON DIAL,
Alabama-based Folk Artist, about art lessons

I've been treated like a dog [by the art world]. I wasn't paid fairly for [some pieces]. And some of them; I didn't get paid at all for them.

CHARLIE "TIN MAN" LUCAS,
Alabama-based Folk Artist

When you find someone who is very talented, very sensitive, and who works very hard, then you have a good artist.

ELIZABETH CATLETT

Why use three colors when you can use two? Why use five colors when you can use three? [This] idea ... forces you to work with less, to work with a degree of economy, and out of that you ... get a stronger work than you might get otherwise.

JACOB LAWRENCE, *Painter*

They say Negroes carry knives. That's a lie. My brother has been carrying an ice pick for years.

REDD FOXX

Human anguish is human anguish. Love is love. The difference between Shakespeare and lesser artists is eloquence.

RALPH ELLISON

Although I am an habitual pessimist, I believe that the future is bright for black literary artists and critics, if we do not destroy our art with our vanity.

DARWIN TURNER

True universality is seldom achieved through premeditation or compromise with superficiality.

GEORGE E. KENT

My grandmother made me feel safe. If I'm an artist today, it's because I was able to live within my childhood state for a long time. Because I rarely left that world until I was 13 or 14, I grew up with no concept of racial inferiority.

GEORGE C. WOLFE, *Producer*

All art makes us more powerfully whom we wish to become.

AUDRE LORDE

I do art like T. S. Eliot the bank teller, and William Carlos Williams the doctor—I am always doing something else for which society will grant me a living wage.

JUDY DOTHARD SIMMONS,
Journalist, Poet

When I discover who I am, I'll be free.

RALPH ELLISON

Seek to be an artist! Cease to be a drudge!

MARY MCLEOD BETHUNE
Her Own Words of Inspiration

Music

Music is the healing force of the universe.

SUN RA

Tuned to its grandest level, music, like light, reminds us that everything that matters, even in this world, is reducible to Spirit.

AL YOUNG, *Author*, Kinds of Blue

... music will be here when money is gone.

DUKE ELLINGTON

Way down yonder by myself and I couldn't hear nobody pray.

Spiritual

Since slavery times, black musical modes have evolved to create the phenomenon recognized and appreciated the world over as American music.

African American Voices of Triumph: Creative Fire

The spirituals teach us that the problem of the twentieth century is not the problem of the color line. The problem of the twentieth century is the problem of civilizing white people.

NIKKI GIOVANNI

Our house was always like a mecca for musicians. My mother had an excellent piano and a set of drums. Lester Young would come by with his mouthpiece and take mama's horn and play.

HAZEL SCOTT

In Europe and Japan I am an American idol. Here in the U.S., I am an idle American. You see, I'm kind of an Icon: I can't get a job, can't get a record date, and I can't get started.

WALTER BISHOP JR., *Jazz Pianist*

There should be a boycott by Negro musicians of all jazz clubs in the United States. I also propose that there should be a boycott by Negro jazz musicians of all record companies. I also propose that all Negro jazz musicians boycott all trade papers and journals dealing with music. And I also propose that all Negro musicians resign from every federated union in this country that has anything to do with music. We're no longer reflecting or vibrating to the white-energy principle. The point is: we know who we are. We have a whole history of music in this country.

CECIL TAYLOR, *Pianist*

In this business, an African American woman has to protect herself because precious few will.

ANITA BAKER

Music is my mistress, and she plays a second fiddle to no one.

DUKE ELLINGTON

Jazz is not just music, it's a way of life, it's a way of being, a way of thinking. I think that the Negro in America is jazz.

NINA SIMONE

Listen. The greatest feeling I ever had in my life—with my clothes on—was when I first heard Diz and Bird together.

MILES DAVIS

On this recording you can hear how the two friends talked to each other musically, and it bears all the similarities of timing and empathy of the conversation that afternoon in Englewood. They know intuitively where the other was heading and why.

HERB BOYD
about the historic album Max + Diz, in Paris, 1989

Diz [Dizzy Gillespie] was the catalyst. He brought us all together to create this most significant music of the twentieth century.

MAX ROACH
about the creation of bebop

It was a group thing. Everybody added a little bit to the concept. But most of the drummers followed [Max Roach].

DIZZY GILLESPIE

I was so nervous on that first real gig with Bird [Charlie Parker] that I used to ask if I could quit every night ... Man, I was scared to death that I was going to mess up.

MILES DAVIS

Miles and Monk weren't turning their backs to the audience, they were turning their fronts to their bands.

T. S. MONK

You know what made it so great? It was the spontaneity. Mingus was in from the West Coast and didn't know a lot of the music, and Dizzy suggested we try this tune and that tune; and when we hit, it was the most marvelous spontaneity I've ever heard.

MAX ROACH
about the peak period of membership
in Charlie Parker's quintet

Behind the clownish demeanor was a superb innovator and composer, a composer whose tunes such as "A Night in Tunisia," "Manteca," and "Salt Peanuts," are standard fare in the jazz canon.

HERB BOYD
Jazz Aficionado, in Emerge *magazine*
about Dizzy Gillespie's contribution to bebop

When you put your personality into your music, your personality will shine through. Once the personality has been identified, everything opens up.

BETTY CARTER, *Singer*

One of the guiding philosophies of music is to find your own voice.

T. S. MONK

I continue to choose the path I take musically. And it's not motivated by becoming famous or having a lot of money, or any other pop aspiration.

CASSANDRA WILSON, *Jazz Singer*

It don't mean a thing if it ain't got that swing.

DUKE ELLINGTON

I'm a jazz singer, there's no doubt about it. I reach and I take liberties. I do a lot of stuff—and it's *mine*. What you hear is me and my thinking at that moment *and* the musicians behind me. They're reaching and growing at the same time. There's a real energy that these young kids have and *want* to have. There's a real camaraderie between the audience and these young musicians that bounces off me. I really do *feed* off these kids.

BETTY CARTER, *Singer*

She [Betty Carter] doesn't have a format when she sings. She improvises and demands that spontaneity from the people she's with. She expects a serious contribution from everybody and draws it out of them. She gets right in your face when she sings. She comes right up and sings into your bass! It's real communication. It's a real *band*.

DAVE HOLLAND, *Bassist*

On top of playing our asses off we [jazz musicians] have got to get sensational about it.

T. S. MONK

Remember, a written note of music from the kora is but an approximation of the actual sound.

HERB BOYD
African History for Beginners

My mother still thinks I should go out and get a real job.

MARION MEADOWS, *Saxophonist*

Nobody in jazz retires. We play until we can't anymore. As long as I'm healthy, I'll be out there.

BETTY CARTER, *Singer*

My all-time favorite non-Motown singer is Aretha Franklin.

BERRY GORDY

The best thing about being Luther Vandross is that I was never burdened with a label of being the new Sam Cooke or the new Otis Redding, Joe Tex or Teddy Pendergrass. I was Luther from day one. Now I've seen a lot of other singers come along being tagged the new Luther, but I was never the new anybody.

LUTHER VANDROSS

This time I told Gerald to hell with the meter, let's let it all hang out.

ANITA BAKER
about Rhythm of Love

In the emergence of the blues in the South there were really three stylistic areas. One was the Piedmont area, or really the entire Eastern Seaboard. The second was that whole South Central region that is centered around the Delta. And the third one is in the Southwest, especially Texas, parts of Arkansas, Oklahoma, where there was a style that was very much its own.

GLENN HINSON
Professor of Folklore

Yo feets too big for de bed.

FATS WALLER

The blues is an impulse to keep the painful details and episodes of a brutal experience alive in one's aching consciousness, to finger its jagged grain, and to transcend it, not by the consolation of philosophy but by squeezing from it a near-tragic, near-comic lyricism.

RALPH ELLISON

Black folk songs exerted a particularly strong influence on American music. The musical culture of the Afro-American originated in the old culture of Africa.

PAUL ROBESON

The best way to explain rap is that it's a conversation going on between two people from the same neighborhood. I rap to someone who has the same lingo as me and the record buyer is tapping into our phone line.

ICE T

Rappers are saying, "Look at my life, look at what it's become." Kids have something to say, and we should listen. Rap is to Black music today what [spirituals were] to slavery. I won't dump on rappers. They're doing the best they can with what they have to work with.

NIKKI GIOVANNI

Many of the black critics of gangsta rap are not interested in critiquing patriarchy or sexism. They're really interested in checking black folks who aren't worried about whether white people see them as "jungle bunnies."

BELL HOOKS

Black rap music recovers and revises elements of black rhetorical styles—some from black preaching—and black rhythmic drumming.

CORNEL WEST, *Theologian*

I think American rap music is very strong. Rappers talk about many things; it's the next griot family.

SALIF KEITA, *Singer*

Probably one of the most amazing aspects of the rap music explosion was that it managed to sell to millions of fans with relatively little radio play for a long time. In this respect, rap's commercial growth continued the "word of mouth" tradition that had given birth to it.

K. MAURICE JONES
Say It Loud

With the emergence of hip-hop as a billion-dollar industry ... Rap music has reinvigorated the spoken word and redefined its possibilities.

MICHAEL ROBINSON
Writer and Independent Music Publicist,
about the revival of black poetry and its new flamboyance

I just listen to jazz. I don't listen to ... hip-hop at all ... I give them respect, because they have given us an audience.

REG E. GAINES
about the musical muse behind his poetry

Some rap songs I just don't understand. I don't know what they mean. But there are songs that are so clever I find myself saying: "Oh, the mind of this kid! I want to find this kid. I want to talk to this kid."

BERRY GORDY

All music is folk music; you ever heard a horse sing?

LOUIS ARMSTRONG

The folks used to come out to the Apollo to see the Ward Singers dress. A group might outsing them, but they couldn't outdress them.

THURMAN RUTH

The Motown sound was a young sound created by a bunch of young people at a certain place in time.

BERRY GORDY

Berry Gordy ran a tight ship. I marveled at the amount of music that was produced in his house. There was never any drinking or horsing around, and I never smelled alcohol or knew of any drugs in the establishment. People suddenly became very businesslike whenever Berry showed up to check out his facility and the activities that transpired.

MARTHA REEVES
Lead Singer, Martha and the Vandellas

Never sing a song unless you mean it from your heart.

RUBY LEE REEVES
Mother of Martha Reeves

Della Reese had inspired me when I saw her at New Liberty Baptist Church, and my soul was blessed. She had sung the most beautiful rendition of "Amazing Grace," and then the next day I saw her singing "Don't You Know" on network television. In my mind, she could do it all—church and popular music. She was also one of Mr. Gordy's associates from his Flame Show Bar days. She was one of Detroit's finest, and one of the most beautiful performers when she was on stage. I felt that the association with her name would bring us luck, so I decided to go for it. The "Della" in Vandellas comes from her name.

As for the "Van," I lived in my parents' house, which is still our home, near Van Dyke Street. It would always identify us with Detroit, for it's a street that goes from east to west and connects you to north and south as it curves and winds through the heart of my neighborhood. So the name Vandellas was derived more or less right on the spot. It had a certain ring to it.

MARTHA REEVES
about naming the Vandellas

The greatest part of being a conductor is expressing my feelings about what a particular composer has to say. Being able to reach down inside the players and try to draw the music from them.

ANDRÉ RAPHEL SMITH, *Conductor*

Being around Coltrane and Parker and Davis and all these cats, what I learned was the philosophy behind the music, which I think is the singularly most missing ingredient in most of the young lions that we have today ... Guys that have a lot of chops but don't play a story. That's because what couldn't be written down, what could only be conveyed through hands-on contact with the masters themselves, was the philosophy. To play a solo and make sense, to play an ensemble and make it sound like it's a million years old—that has to do with respect for the history and tech that played that music.

T. S. MONK

You [jazz drummers] try to provide an overall musical statement so that there is no doubt that without what you did, no one would play as effectively on either an individual basis or as part of the group. You're the spoon that stirs the soup.

BILLY COBHAM

James Carter is the man. He's the tenor player of the future. I haven't heard anyone who can touch him.

LESTER BOWIE

I'm just glad I'm able to make sense out of all the various eras. What I've done is live up to what the music is supposed to be about—ever-evolving but still having a reverence for the past.

JAMES CARTER, *Saxophonist*

As far as the real music, I mean the masters, I have to give it up to them. Sometimes, when I'm feeling really good about myself, I pop in a Trane record . . . and that really puts me back in perspective.

STEVE MONROE, *Saxophonist*

We're trying to make a big midcourse correction in jazz education and involve the masters that we have left in new curriculum development, and turn jazz education into what it should be: a springboard for jazz performers and not music teachers.

T. S. MONK

I find that a whole lot of musicians only go down to a certain level in the musical bag of history, and it's sad, especially among people my age who are supposed to be continuing the tradition. As soon as you feel like you've conquered the music by labeling it and saying it doesn't swing or it's avant garde, you get away from what you're supposed to be listening to the music for, which is enlightenment—you know, being lifted up spiritually. A lot of cats say that certain avant-garde players don't listen to what has come before them, but you can look at bop in that sense. During the time it was going through its revolutionary process, they weren't saying that they've thrown out what Louis [Armstrong] and all the swing cats have done previously. That's the thing about it—it's a continuum.

JAMES CARTER, *Saxaphonist*

I want to keep time *behind me* and not let it catch up. When time catches up with you, you become passé, so I am striving to keep time behind me.

PHILLY JO JONES

The thing that has affected my stamina is the fact that I just turned sixty-six. My mind is as strong as if I were twenty-one. But once in a while I notice that my body don't match, you know?

HORACE SILVER

At the bottom of it, music experience is bringing us all together. My teacher always tells me, "Study the music, study the music, study the music. Keep your eyes on the prize." And for people to say to me, "I've enjoyed your music. I've enjoyed where you're coming from. I really hear the tradition in you, but I also hear you in it, as a part of that tradition"—that's the prize itself, and I'm glad I got a hold of it.

JAMES CARTER, *Saxaphonist*

I've got so many musical goals that I want to achieve before I leave this earthly plane. I was just praying that the good Lord would spare me so I can stay here long enough to complete my musical dreams. Then I'll be ready to go.

HORACE SILVER

People come up to me all the time and ask me how I feel now that jazz is back ... It's as if the music went somewhere—when in fact, if anything, it was the audience that left and came back.

GROVER WASHINGTON JR.

A friend told me he'd risen above jazz. I leave him there.

AKINSHIJU OLA

Her [Roberta Flack's] voice touched, tapped, trapped and kicked over every emotion I'd ever known. I laughed, cried, and screamed for more. When she sang a love song, I was in love, we all were in love, we all were singing, singing our love; but she alone had the voice.

LES MCCANN

I've been singing since I was three. I sang gospel. You see, my mother grew up on Aretha Franklin ... The first album she gave me was Aretha Franklin's *Amazing Grace* when I was five ... Singing is all I know ... I just love to sing and I always will.

TEVIN CAMPBELL

Sometimes I find black music so disturbing. I find it resonating with the disturbances of our souls. The great disturbance we feel over the unfair treatment that whites consistently extend.

MILDRED GREENE

I never listen to "Roll Jordan Roll" without seeming to hear, almost to feel, the rolling waters.

CHARLOTTE FORTEN GRIMKE

The blues always impressed me as being very sad, sadder even than the spirituals, because their sadness is not softened with tears, but hardened with laughter.

LANGSTON HUGHES

The blues are the songs of despair; gospel songs are the songs of hope.

MAHALIA JACKSON

The blues that are genuine are really folk songs.

W. C. HANDY

We've had flops before. We like to call them experiments. Some of our artists got lost in music business politics and sometimes the timing just wasn't right. See, we aim to be the most *original* producers out there, not the best.

DENZIL FOSTER AND THOMAS MCELROY
Music Producers

... these days, your market, no matter if your product is rap or old school, or whatever, is an international market.

CHARLES UNDERWOOD
Independent Music Mogul

What's black? I've been trying to figure this out since I've been in this business. I don't know how to sing black—and I don't know how to sing white either. I know how to sing. Music is not color to me. It's an art.

WHITNEY HOUSTON

Into our singing, we have forged the sounds of a people of resolute spirit and fortitude in this land that debated our worth as human beings. Our singing tradition announces the presence of our community. It is a way in which we nurture and heal ourselves. It is an offering to the celebration of life and the lifting of the spirit.

BERNICE JOHNSON REAGON

Community, Family, and the Healing Power of Responsibility

A child is raised by the village.

African proverb

We were very sheltered in many ways in Boley. All the adults monitored the children. Any adult could come and tell my parents about what I had been doing ... well, any adult except the rogues and thieves and whore mongers. The town had a very strict marshal on the street, and he kept children away from the liquor places and other bad spots.

VELMA DOLPHIN ASHLEY
eighty-five year-old citizen of Boley,
one of seventeen former all-black towns in Oklahoma

Your family is my family.

Traditional wisdom

The family is the basis of society, the nation and civilization.

RUBY DEE

72

The ruin of a nation begins in the homes of its people.

Ashanti proverb

We don't do drugs, drink or use profanity. Instead we instill morals and values in my boys by raising them with a love of God and a love and respect for themselves and all people.

ANITA BAKER

I got out of comedy because I saw a conflict in saying to young folks that drugs and alcohol are bad and then coming to a nightclub and having a taste. I decided I would not do an anti-drug commercial unless you hook a whiskey commercial with it.

DICK GREGORY

Be generous as long as you live. What goes into the storehouse should come out. For bread is made to be shared. Those whose bellies are empty turn into accusers and those who are deprived become opponents. See that none such as these are your neighbors. Generosity is a memorial for those who show it, long after they have departed.

Sacred wisdom of ancient Egypt

Service was as much a part of my upbringing as eating breakfast and going to school. It isn't something that you do in your spare time. It was clear that it was the very purpose of life. In that context, you're not obligated to win. You're obligated to keep trying, to keep doing the best you can every day.

MARIAN WRIGHT EDELMAN
I Dream a World

Everybody can be great because anybody can serve.

DR. MARTIN LUTHER KING JR.

She kept Vivian and she didn't charge me nothin' either. You see, people used to look after each other, but now it's not that way. I reckon it's because we all was poor, and I guess they put theirself in the place of the person that they was helpin'.

A SOUTHERN DOMESTIC WORKER
Doublestitch: Black Women Write About Mothers and
Daughters

Help others and you help yourself.

DAVE DINWIDDIE, *My Father*

I can well understand what Langston Hughes said ... that he would never live outside the Negro community. Because this was his life ... his sustenance.

JACOB LAWRENCE, *Painter*

When you put out a record like that, are you thinking, "I'm just going to get paid and sell records," or "What do those lyrics really mean?" Wave your guns in the air? When there's already a mad, crazy abundance of weapons?

SPIKE LEE
a question to Russell Simmons of Def Jam fame

We who minister to people must listen carefully to hear what is being said, to catch the words of truth uttered in the excessive rhetoric of violence of so many of our best young minds.

GARDNER C. TAYLOR
Pastor Emeritus, Concord Baptist Church of Christ

Evil enters like a needle and spreads like an oak tree.

Ethiopian proverb

What's right ain't always popular and what's popular ain't always right.

African-American folk saying

... this is *our* moment. I honestly wouldn't be anyone but a Black woman in America right now. I feel that this is *our* time to break new ground, to make statements. But first we have to do something about the guns and drugs in our communities. We have to find the outlets for our frustrations. One thing we can do is to stop, as African-Americans, supporting these shoot-'em-up, gang-banging films. We have to prove to Hollywood that we can support films that show us as something other than pimps, prostitutes and kids in gangs. We have to see films like *Daughters of the Dust* again and again. Just like White people see *The Silence of the Lambs* five times. We have to see a *Daughters of the Dust* five times. We have to make meaningful films with all-black casts that do well at the box office. It all boils down to money. We have to put our money where our visions are.

HALLE BERRY, *Actress*

I wanted to invest in the black community and keep money in the black community, live among black people and work among them.

DR. J. R. TODD
discussing his choice of rural practice in Mississippi
over a big city practice where the money is

No one family form—nuclear, extended, single-parent, matrilineal, patrilineal, fictive, residential, nonresidential—necessarily provides an environment better for humans to live or raise children in. Wife beating, child abuse, psychological terror, material deprivation and malnutrition take place in each of those family forms. And our responsibility, whether single parents or coparents or no parents at all, is to do all in our power to help create a healthy nonoppressive family environment for every living human being.

DR. JOHNETTA B. COLE

If relatives help each other, what evil can hurt them?

Ethiopian proverb

We have to be elders because the tribe needs its elders.

RUBY DEE

If I can inspire one of these youngsters to develop the talent I know they possess, then my monument will be in their work.

AUGUSTA SAVAGE, *Artist*

Her [Augusta Savage] interest was a peak experience in my life because, you know, she didn't forget ... I got most of my encouragement from Charles Alston and Augusta Savage. And, you just have to believe that what you're doing has value and that's it.

JACOB LAWRENCE, *Artist*

... the diffusion of knowledge, the suppression of vice and immorality, and for cherishing such virtues as will render us happy and useful to society.

ORGANIZING PRINCIPLES
African-American-Female Intelligence Society, 1830

We stood by each other through many a storm. Praise the Lord! It was her turn that afternoon to open the meeting. We generally took turns about; one would open by giving out a hymn, reading a chapter and then praying. Then we would tell each other our joys or sorrows, our victories and defeats, if we had any, and if Satan had buffeted us, how we bore up or if we yielded under the pressure, etc., and then we would advise each other and pray for each other.

AMANDA SMITH (1837-1915), *Evangelist*
writing about her women's group

If you watch your pot, your food will not burn.

Mauritanian proverb

The Birthing Project draws on many of the inherent strengths in the African-American community, including the extended family, the wise woman or "big mamma" concept, creative visualization and community wisdom. The project is based on the premise that the black community has the strength and ability to grow healthy babies. We attempt to heal the sometimes disheartened spirit of our community by reminding ourselves that the babies are all of our babies and we must reclaim and celebrate each life.

KATHRYN HALL
Executive Director and Founder
The Birthing Project, Berkeley, California

We all have a role in combating teenage pregnancy: the churches, the schools, the community.

DR. JOYCELYN ELDERS

Teenage pregnancy and parenting is both a cause and a consequence of poverty.

DR. JOHNETTA B. COLE

We must face up to the fact that the phenomenon of out-of-wedlock births has reached epidemic proportions and is undermining the viability of our community. We've simply got to persuade our young people that they ought not to bring their own flesh and blood into this world unless they are fully prepared to love, nurture and provide for them.

If they aren't ready and willing to assume full responsibilities of parenthood, then this is an almost surefire prescription for poverty for their own flesh and blood. They owe their children and our people a better shot at success in life.

HUGH PRICE
President, National Urban League

... The Murphy Browns of American are not the problem: It's the young, undereducated women who cannot care for themselves or their children who give us good reason to worry. And we must help them break the cycle.

AVIS LAVELLE, M.S.W.

Like every man, every woman must decide whether she will walk in the light of creative altruism or the darkness of destructive selfishness. This is the judgment. Life's most persistent and urgent question is, what are you doing for others?

MARTIN LUTHER KING JR.

It is a burden of black people that we have to do more than talk.

BARBARA JORDAN

As a performer, I feel a responsibility to provide a good example and address issues that people, especially young people, must deal with.

QUEEN LATIFAH

I would unite with anybody to do right and with nobody to do wrong.

FREDERICK DOUGLASS

Families are the conduit of values, discipline and the belief in ourselves. You cannot build the family on poverty. We need to find jobs. We have to achieve the reconstruction of the black community.

ROGER WILKINS
Author, Professor

If you pay attention to the futurists and their trend analysis you know that the dividing line between the "haves" and the "have nots" separates those who have skills and knowledge from those who are unskilled and unlearned. What is overlooked, however, is the role the family, church and community play in imparting knowledge from one generation to the next. I know that education is the key to success in the twenty-first century. I do not believe, though, that we can access a quality education for the majority of our children without a healthy family and community.

DR. BESSIE W. BLAKE, *Dean*
College of New Rochelle, School of New Resources

The cattle is as good as the pasture in which it grazes.

Ethiopian proverb

I made a decision to focus on my home and family . . . Because when the lights go out, and you have to go home, the most important thing in the world is your family.

SHIRLEY HORN, *Jazz Singer*
about her twenty-five year
hiatus from the music industry

Black folks have never been particularly friendly to me, career-wise or otherwise.

WHOOPI GOLDBERG

I couldn't laugh; I didn't find it funny. And as a Black woman who struggles with racism every day, who has White men tell me to my face they won't see me for a role because I'm Black, I couldn't find it in myself to sit there and pretend to find it funny.

I didn't want to speak out about it because the last thing I want to do is tear down another Black woman. But I can't ignore how it made me feel. Just as I respect Whoopi as a Black woman, I have to respect myself as a Black woman. And that means standing up for what I believe to be right. That night, I said what's right for me is to get the hell out of here.

HALLE BERRY
about the infamous Whoopi
Goldberg Friars Club Roast

When the bee comes to your house, let her have beer; you may want to visit the bee's house some day.

Congolese proverb

I regret very much that some of our people are in such a mental state that they would hurt and rob an older person.

ROSA PARKS

Anytime we can't protect our great leaders, we're in trouble.

MOSES MILES
Detroit resident about the robbery of Rosa Parks

A flame burns best when it is passed on.

African proverb

Our elders give us a path, a way to go. Respect them.

ANONYMOUS

Let him speak who has seen with his eyes.

Congolese proverb

Always keep the flame in your father's house burning.

African proverb

Unfortunately, in many circles, the term "Black community" has become shorthand for high crime, poor schools, unemployment and drug abuse.

JOHNETTA B. COLE

Southeast [Washington, D.C.] is a place, some say in speeches, where no human being should have to live in such conditions. But I have lived there and flourished.

RALPH WILEY

A good deed is something one returns.

Guinean proverb

We need the doers. I think that the unrewarded doers are the community workers. They never get recognition, and they contribute a lot.

CAMILLE COSBY

Most people leave their original base of operation when they get successful and go to the affluent section. That's something I refuse to do. We are part of the community.

ARTHUR MITCHELL
Choreographer and Founder of Dance Theatre of Harlem

I had acceptance at a very early age from the community, and that does a lot. The people that accepted me didn't necessarily know about art, but they encouraged me.

JACOB LAWRENCE, *Painter*

She [Betty Carter] goes around scouting talent because she wants to give something back to the community.

JACK DEJOHNETTE, *Drummer*

I feel strongly that we have to make the orchestra more accessible to the African-American community. Traditionally, African-Americans have not felt welcome in concert halls. [Symphony] Orchestras haven't done enough to address these needs ... I want children to get to know various dimensions of the orchestra. We often underestimate kids. They can understand many of these concepts.

ANDRÉ RAPHEL SMITH, *Conductor*

When you have opportunities in life, you are obligated to give something back.

PATRICIA IRVIN
Wall Street Attorney

The domestic neocolonialist relationship between the nation's largest civil rights organization and white foundation funds is tragic, and debilitating to the movement for social change. We must be in control of our movements for change, in order to be in control of our destiny.

AKINSHIJU C. OLA, *Journalist*

The agenda of the civil rights movement in recent years has tended to favor the interests of the haves over those of the have nots.

DON ROJAS
Journalist, Activist

Rain does not fall on one roof alone.

African proverb

The four billion dollars African Americans spend don't go to the Black Community. We tend to underestimate what we have in our hands. We need to understand that at this point in our history, self-sufficiency is our best means to economic development and empowerment. We need a fund that is funded by us!

DR. BENJAMIN CHAVIS, *Activist*

Everybody wants you to take on people but they don't want to give you the funds to take them on with.

THE REVEREND AL SHARPTON

The difficulties of life will not be solved by absolutes, but will be solved in the tough engagement of relating one to another, whether it is a family or in a community or in a church or in the world.

BISHOP STITH
Pianist, Jazz Innovator, Teacher

African-American leaders have now taken hold of the concept that we need to be responsible for what goes on in our own backyard. In terms of solutions we need to look inward . . . we need to do a better job of parenting. We need to create extended families. We need to create our own economic institutions. We need to take responsibility for what goes on in our communities, in our families.

BILL NABOR
Southfield, Michigan

When the ax entered the forest the tree said "the handle is one of us."

African proverb

Approximately 65 percent black and 10 percent Hispanic, D.C. exemplifies the extremes of African America. The largest percentage of black college graduates coexist with the highest murder rate and a huge black prison population.

PAUL RUFFINS
Writer, Environmentalist

For all my ambiguities and oddness, I'm claimed. That's what I love about the black community. They'll say, "Well, you know, we don't know how we feel about that homosexuality thing, Junior. But take off that dress and come on in."

GEORGE C. WOLFE, *Producer*

When we pit our family and our base community against the larger society, it is our very soul that suffers. It is our task to find ways to maintain our biculturalism, to move comfortably in both worlds.

JOHNETTA B. COLE

Where elephants fight only the grass suffers.

African proverb

In our eagerness to decode the laws and legends of the majority community—necessities for sure in this world—many of us have either abandoned or taken for granted those aspects of our African heritage, our African-American culture that are worth nurturing and preserving. The ultimate consequence of such abandonment is that we will become strangers to ourselves and to each other. We have had different experiences, and come from varied backgrounds, but as African Americans, we all share to some degree in an African cosmology that binds us all and that influences all who come in contact with us. This is the sense in which much of the culture of American is itself deeply African.

JOHNETTA B. COLE

When you follow in the path of your father, you learn to walk like him.

Ashanti proverb

It is my responsibility to be a role model.

EDDY L. HARRIS, *Author*

Being a change agent in people's lives, that's the gospel of Jesus Christ.

LT. JOHN DUCKSWORTH
Minister, Salvation Army

African American churches have forgotten the poor.

THE REVEREND TIMOTHY MITCHELL

The best thing you can do for a poor person is not to be one.

REDD FOXX

My mission is to demonstrate that the church as a community-based organization can be a major player in the liberation and advancement of the people who live around it.

THE REVEREND M. WILLIAM HOWARD JR.
President, New York Theological Seminary

We've got to lift the name of Jesus; yes, that's No. 1. But it's also got to be shown that we're about the business of turning our communities around. We're going to have to take back our streets and our neighborhoods.

DR. HENRY J. LYONS
President, National Baptist Convention, USA, Inc.

Every little hurt counts.

ANONYMOUS

This is not to deny that the severe problems that plague poor Black youth have led some of them to become predators—predators who must be stopped and saved, for their sake and ours. It is to declare, first, that we should recognize that they have become predators precisely because Black people continue to be victimized by the systematic violence directed against all of them, especially those trapped in ghettos, and secondly, that even as we mount programs to reduce all forms of violence in Black communities, we should resist thinking of this as a "Negro problem." Today's evidence that the "mean streets" produced by America's violent culture can be anywhere is too overwhelming.

LEE A. DANIELS
Journalist, Scholar

Eat not bread while another stands by without extending your hand to him or her. As for food, it is always here; it is man and woman who do not remain.

Sacred wisdom of ancient Egypt

Our Children, Ourselves, or Parents and Children

The father and his worship is Asia; Europe is the precocious, self-centered, forward-striving child; but the land of the mother is and was Africa.... Isis, the mother, is still titular goddess, in thought if not in name, of the dark continent. Nor does this all seem to be solely a survival of the historic matriarchate through which all nations pass—it appears to be more than this—as if the great Black race in passing up the steps of human culture gave the world, not only the iron age, the cultivation of the soil, and the domestication of animals, but also, in peculiar emphasis, the Mother idea.

W. E. B. Du Bois

What your mother tells you now, in time you will come to know.

Gloria I. Joseph, *Educator*

A child who requests help and is ridiculed will increasingly withdraw from seeking assistance.

Carol E. Bonner, *Psychologist*

All of us need people we can open up to, not only to show our strengths, but to show our weaknesses. Children need that as well as adults.

EVELYN MOORE
Executive Director, National Black Child Development Institute

I figure that by laying the groundwork early, with honest and nonjudgmental answers to my daughter's preadolescent questions, she'll confide in me when she hits those dreaded teenage years.

ANGELA DUERSON TUCK

Advise and counsel him; if he does not listen, let adversity teach him.

Ethiopian proverb

There are so many Mr. Browns out there who do their damndest to teach the Nathan McCalls that there is a right way and a wrong way, a good way and a bad. And there are far too many Nathan McCalls who simply must learn the hard way.

NATHAN McCALL
Makes Me Wanna Holler: A Young Black Man in America

Seeing is different from being told.

Kenyan proverb

Do what parents used to do a long time ago. Parents wanted to know, "Who is this person? Who are his parents? What kind of work do they do? Does he go to school?" ... I think we really have to get back to some of the basics.

DR. SHIRLEY B. WILSON
Pediatric Psychologist

You are judged by the company you keep.

Traditional wisdom

Association brings about assimilation.

ARTEMISA ELIZABETH DINWIDDIE
One of my mother's favorite admonitions

The company you keep will reflect in your language, behavior and actions.

VICTORIA JOHNSON, *Author*

Know who your kids are running with. Because if you don't know who they're running with, how are you going to know when they're running with the wrong people?

JAMES PARKER
Program Manager, Substance Abuse Treatment Facility

When you know who his friend is, you know who he is.

Senegalese proverb

A silly daughter teaches her mother how to bear children.

Ethiopian proverb

African-American boys need to be prepared for discrimination on a daily basis. Parents need to discuss the types of experiences they may encounter such as being followed by security while shopping in a store, having people cross the street when they see them and being indiscriminately stopped by police [when] in a car, particularly in predominately white areas. Through careful discussion with parents, boys can learn how to handle their behavior and their emotions in various situations.

CAROL E. BONNER, *Psychologist*

The parents of the children in my generation, veterans of lunch-counter sit-ins and the like, were simply not prepared to help us fight the invisible dragons created by integration. Our parents were too busy opening the doors to worry about what would happen once we got inside.

TERESA WILTZ, *Writer*

The whole gangster mentality, it's killing our youth. Black males, we're really just choking ourselves with this whole macho shit, where you can't show any tenderness, no vulnerability, no nothing. You have to be granite, 100 percent. And that's just not natural. And another thing: you have a hundred thousand black kids across this country failing classes on purpose because of peer pressure. And if you speak proper English, and you get straight A's in school, then you're considered a white boy or a white girl. But if you're hanging on the corner, scratching your nuts, drinking, then you're down. So, you know, the whole value system is fucked up; ignorance is being championed over intelligence.

SPIKE LEE

We had to learn to be men.

NATHAN MORRIS, *Boyz II Men*

Only men can develop boys into men.

JAWANZA KUNJUFU

Black women raise their daughters and spoil their sons.

African-American folk saying

Way down deep we feel it. The power of mother love. For centuries, it has been the glue that cemented the two things

Black folks have traditionally valued above all others: our families and our faith.

LAURA B. RANDOLPH, *Writer*

He said I could move with him, but I'm staying right here. This is home. Our home. He said he would like to build me a new house here, and that is fine, but I'll still keep this one, fix it up and let others in the family use it. None of us will change. Money won't change love. I firmly believe what I have taught Steve and all of my boys—cherish the bridge that brought you across.

LUCILLE MCNAIR
Mother of Pro Football's Steve McNair

I saw my mother wear cardboard in her shoes, just so each of us could have a good pair. . . . I can never repay her.

KARL MALONE

It's a bad child who does not take advice.

Ashanti proverb

If your son laughs when you scold him, you ought to cry, for you have lost him; if he cries, you may laugh, for you have a worthy heir.

Senegalese proverb

A bad son gives a bad name to his mother.

Ivory Coast proverb

My mother would always go into the bathroom to pray. One day, when I was about ten years old, while she was in the bathroom praying, I walked in just as she was calling my name in prayer. That experience had such a tremendous impact on my life because from that moment on, I knew that no matter where I went in the world, or whatever circumstances I found myself in, my mother was praying for me!

THE REVEREND RODNEY T. FRANCIS

Just because you are in hell does not mean you should act like a devil.

KATHERINE BROWN
and legions of other mothers

When I am feeling paralyzed by a task that seems too difficult, I remember the love that lies at the core of my family and their legacy to me. The love gives me strength and I can go on.

JONAH EDELMAN
Son of Marian Wright Edelman

Society pushes this idea that women can't raise children without a man. But children need men in their lives—not necessarily in their homes.

MARITA GOLDEN, *Author*

Mother to Son:

"I carried you until you took that first step,
But you don't ever have to stand alone."

BURNECE BRUNSON

They [mothers] were the only figures, most of our years anyway, the ones who taught us how to respect girls. My mom told me to open doors for girls and pull out their chairs. I never understood why until I started doing it and saw that it made them feel nice.

SHAWN STOCKMAN, *Boyz II Men*

The family is an important source of emotional support and love given in an unconditional and consistent manner. Additionally, a conscious effort should be made to assess your parenting skills and determine the degree to which we place emphasis on our child's positive qualities rather than his shortcomings.

CAROL E. BONNER, *Psychologist*

When we in this house had to face very grave issues with our children, it usually took place at the dinner table. The dinner table was a place where much more than food was being exchanged. We learned our history, and we learned the values, attitudes and propositions of the past.

OSSIE DAVIS

It is popular today to say that we have to find the child within us. For men, this would be a short search.

BILL COSBY

There is something systemic, however, between the environments in which young black males are reared and incarceration rates.

RONALD B. MINCY

Young men who are tutored in a moral and spiritual foundation cannot help but become productive positive men.

CLIFFORD B. SIMMONS

Sometimes it is hard to tell the baby gunmen from the kids just trying to grow up without getting shot. Often the basketball players or the kids on the Thomas Jefferson High School debate team, kids who haven't had the heart cut out of them by the relentless violence in their neighborhoods, dress just like the killers, so they won't become victims themselves.

GREG DONALDSON, *Author*
about life in the Brownsville section of Brooklyn

Youth development programs meet the needs of these youth for security and affiliation by providing safe places for them to assemble and peer groups that are open to guidance by adults and positively-oriented older males. Such programs become focal points to create positive peer pressure, so that young people begin processes of self and group exploration and values clarification that can support choices to stay engaged in school to value academic achievement, to contribute to their communities, and to meet other basic needs of preadolescents. The criminal justice approach ignores most of these basic needs and competencies.

RONALD B. MINCY
Nurturing Young Males

Millions of our children are doing the right thing every day. They deserve our full support so that they stay the course. Their story goes so unreported in the media that the broader society is losing sight of the fact that our children are an asset, not a liability, to society. We owe it to these youngsters to tell their story, loudly and relentlessly, until their accomplishments are widely acknowledged.

HUGH PRICE
President, National Urban League

A vast number of black and Latino youths in the inner cities are trying desperately to make some sense of their lives. But they are caught in a crossfire between a small group of sociopaths in their midst and the larger society that ignores their potential and has written them out of the future.

Every time a delivery man is murdered, a drama teacher shot

off his bike in the park, public opinion hardens against taking steps to remedy the desperate condition of urban youth including those who carry dreams instead of guns . . .

Trapped between the shooters in their neighborhood and a society that fears and quarantines them, a generation of city teen-agers is turning inward, away from counsel from the old heads in their community and communication with the larger society.

GREG DONALDSON, *Author*

Only when you have crossed the river can you say the crocodile has a lump on his snout.

Ashanti proverb

With black boys especially, we are dealing with the products of a broken patriarchy. In a patriarchal racism, it is the male who poses the primary threat to the ruling male, who in his mind can take his place in the bedroom and the boardroom. Hence a white oppressor must take special pains to suppress the black male. If you kill the male, you do not have to worry about the female and the children, as they are bound to wither away. This is not sexual chauvinism but a biosocial reality.

NATHAN HARE AND JULIA HARE
The Miseducation of the Black Child

We had to protect our men. If my husband had been in my place, he would not have made it, 'cause the black man has always been the target.

WINSON HUDSON

Children should be taught to save money.

W. A. LEWIS
Writer, Activist

Some people marry their cross. Some people give birth to their cross. And some people put their cross in a nursing home.

THE REVEREND JAMES A. HOLMAN

I don't think every athlete is a role model. I have played with and against a lot of athletes I wouldn't want any of my kids to be like. On the other hand, there are other athletes who are great role models. Being an athlete and being a role model do not go hand in hand. I think it is up to kids to look a little farther.

AHMAD RASHAD

The media portrays our celebrities as role models, but we have to really look around us and determine who our role models are. I have never read an article about a white celebrity that portrayed him or her as a role model for white people. But when you read about black role models, they are either entertainers or athletes.

CAMILLE COSBY

Everybody is looking for role models for their kids on television, but the positive role models should be right there in the home.

KEVIN TERYL

It was stunning, the realization of how poorly my generation of middle-class African-Americans had managed the rearing of our children. In my group, most had delayed marriage and children until after college graduation and career paths were well established. We were too smart for the old values, we had it made. But as I listened to the two young people in my kitchen at 10:00 A.M. one Sunday morning going through the newspaper and discussing what they would buy if they had more money I realized that we had somehow missed the boat. Here they were eighteen and nineteen, male and female cousins, discussing the value of a dollar (or of a consumer-oriented society) when our failure shown crystal clear. Our children were having this conversation at a time when they should have been in Sunday School (or Church School, if you prefer) learning the value of high ideals and principles of living right.

A FORTY-EIGHT-YEAR-OLD MOTHER
Summer 1994

As a mother you try to give your child the best that you can and the best thing I can give Bobbi Kristina is the love of God, and to teach her the way I was taught. Whatever you do, train a child up in the way of God, no matter what.

WHITNEY HOUSTON

If you are a parent of worth and wisdom, train your children so that they will be pleasing to God.

Sacred wisdom of ancient Egypt

[Parents] *should* be concerned about the negative influence your state of mind might have on your [children]. We learn many of life's lessons from watching our mothers, including how we see and treat others.

DR. GWENDOLYN GOLDSBY GRANT, *Psychologist*

I believe that we're all born with enough personal self-esteem messages to last us a lifetime. But when these messages don't get nurtured when we are children, they become almost nonexistent when we are adults. Just as our infant and childhood bodies need care, nurturing, and stimulation in order to help us grow into healthy adults, our self-esteem needs the same type of care in order to remain a healthy part of our lives.

JULIA BOYD

Single parents should be aware that their behavior and attitudes concerning intimate relationships may be especially influential for their adolescent children who are engaging in similar behavior.

Report from the CENTER FOR FAMILY RESEARCH

Our children are in trouble because we adults are in trouble.

CAMILLE YARBOROUGH, *Author*

I tell my kids and my players, "The same things I tell you now, I used to rebel against." You have to learn from your mistakes.

JOHN LUCAS, *NBA Coach*

A cow gave birth to a fire: she wanted to lick it, but it burned; she wanted to leave it, but she could not because it was her own child.

Ethiopian proverb

When we were growing up, we didn't watch that much television. We were all encouraged to read and made regular visits to the library.

RITA DOVE
Poet Laureate of the United States

Good behavior reflects good background.

Ugandan proverb

We have fallen out of forcing our children to read. Knowledge is power and power is the key to changing society.

JILL NELSON, *Author*

My father impressed me with his ability to repair watches and clocks and even to build in the 1920s a crystal radio set. My mother always bought me toys that I could assemble or operate—train sets, windmills. She, moreover, sacrificed to buy expensive building erector sets and freight and passenger cars for my railroad train sets.

At twelve I became a boy scout. Explorations by pioneers who opened up the Western United Sates—land surveyors—had my rapt attention. I learned to read maps, make field sketches, and plot directions from compass readings while walking through the woods with maps.

BENSON L. DUTTON
*First Black Civil Engineer to graduate
from Pennsylvania State University, 1933*

When [my daughter] reads a book that I think is too fanciful, I try to remember that no one stopped me from reading fairy tales, comic books or anything else.

RITA DOVE, *Poet Laureate of the United States*

Providing children with experiences related to their expressed curiosities helps expand their thinking.

MURIEL WHITSTONE, *Educator*

Sometimes we get so caught up in looking for the big example, we lose sight of people who, in their daily lives, stand up for what they believe. My parents were just ordinary people, but in their convictions, their efforts, they were people of real conscience.

ALAN C. PAGE
*Associate Justice, Minnesota Supreme Court
NFL Hall of Famer*

My parents inspired me like no one else in my life. They believed fervently in the value of education.

D. ANTOINETTE HANDY
Classical Flutist, about her parents

[My mother's support] manifested as the key element that was a constant for me, to go ahead and do what I wanted to and do my best. She completely supported me throughout all of the crises that I faced: dropping out of school, going to work in a Manhattan disco, moving to Detroit to work for Motown.

SUZANNE DE PASSE

My parents always believed that the pursuit of excellence knows no color and knows no class. They believed that whatever you do, you did it well. No shortcuts. They believed in standards, but that you should set your own personal standards.

D. ANTOINETTE HANDY

I was extremely fortunate that I had special parents. They impressed on us the importance of honest, hard work, education in a personal way.

ALAN C. PAGE
Associate Justice, Minnesota Supreme Court
NFL Hall of Famer

Young lady, God's not through with you yet.

MOTHER *to a young but successful executive daughter*

He who is free of faults will never die.

Congolese proverb

When a woman is hungry, she says, "Roast something for the children that they may eat."

Ashanti proverb

[My mother] would always say "Don't waste your time being disappointed with people, being envious or jealous."

EDDIE BERNICE JOHNSON
U.S. Representative, Texas

My mother believed it was vital to have a certain amount of confidence in yourself and to believe in your ability to do whatever it is you want to do.

JAMES H. WILLIAMS
Professor, Mechanical Engineering, MIT

[My mother] often recited this bit of poetry: "Once a task has begun, never leave it till it's done. Be the labor great or small, do it well or not at all."

EDDIE BERNICE JOHNSON
U.S. Representative, Texas

He has to go to school or he has to work.

Axiom

One of the things that brought me an enormous amount of pleasure when I was a kid, was simply to bring my report card home to my mom, and watch her face, just to see her smile.

JAMES H. WILLIAMS
Professor, Mechanical Engineering, MIT

I loved math and applied myself diligently. My mother always made me feel that she took pride in my accomplishments. When I entered Penn State as a civil engineering freshman in 1929, she was proud and happy that I had found my "calling."

BENSON L. DUTTON
*First African-American Graduate
from the College of Engineering,
Pennsylvania State University, 1933*

I have answered many difficult questions in my life, some of them posed by hostile reporters, some by policemen, some by lawyers and judges, some even by jailers. But the hardest questions I have ever had to answer have come from my own children.

THE REVEREND RALPH DAVID ABERNATHY

It is the duty of children to wait on elders and not the elders on children.

Kenyan proverb

Children are the reward of life.

Congolese proverb

When I was eight, Thelonious was on his way to Europe and we were out at Idlewild Airport. He took me to one end of the terminal, turned and said, "I don't care what you do in life. And don't let anybody tell you that you have to be or do anything. I am me and you are you, and don't let anybody worry you about it." He had released me from the shadow in a fashion that most famous people don't take the time to do with their kids. That took all the pressure off of me, and I didn't start thinking about music until I was thirteen or fourteen.

T. S. MONK

The federal system has created the original ghost dad.

MICHAEL O'NEIL
Founder, Fathers Inc.

Starting out as a father, it was frightening at first. I didn't know what fathers did. I found out in the end that you do the best that you can. No one really has the corner on [fatherhood.]

DICK ANTHONY WILLIAMS, *Actor*

I found out about the Georgia Peach Program last year. The Peach Program helps single parents. I went down there trying to get information, and they were so busy asking where is the mom. I had to tell them I am the mom. I'm Mr. Mom.

BRYAN ELMORE, *Single Parent*

If you choose to have that baby, then choose to take care of it. Kids are our future. We need to prepare them for their future. It's up to us no matter what. We gotta take our kids and lead them up right.

MICHAEL MOSES SR.

I struggle on a daily basis with how to raise my children, how to teach them about the world and how it works. I try to explain race to them in such a way that it doesn't blind them to other people's humanity or cripple them in such a way that they cannot appreciate their own cultural roots.

E. ETHELBERT MILLER, *Writer*

One seldom hears a child cry in Africa. No matter the economic status of the mother, she seems to rear her children with such a precise balance of indulgence and discipline that they have no need, or desire, to pierce the air with public complaint.

PAULA GIDDINGS, *Author*

... Work for Black women has been an important and valued dimension of Afrocentric definitions of Black motherhood.

PATRICIA HILL COLLINS
Professor of Sociology,
University of Cincinnati

What these mothers passed on would take you anywhere in the world you wanted to go.

MARY HELEN WASHINGTON
Professor, University of Maryland, College Park

I grew up among poets. Now they didn't look like poets ...
They were just a group of ordinary housewives and mothers,
my mother included ... Nor did they do what poets were supposed to do ... they never put pen to paper ... For me sitting
over in the corner ... it wasn't only what the women talked
about—the content—but the way they put things—their style.
The insight, irony, wit and humor they brought to their stories
and discussions and their poet's inventiveness and daring with
language ... They had taken the standard English taught them
in the primary schools ... and transformed it into an idiom,
an instrument that more adequately described them—changing
around the syntax and imposing their own rhythm and accent
so that the sentences were more pleasing to their ears. They
added the few African sounds and words that had survived ...
And to make it more vivid, more in keeping with their expres-
sive quality, they brought to bear a raft of metaphors, parables,
Bible quotations, sayings and the like . . . using everyday
speech, the simple commonplace words—but always with imagination and skill—they gave voice to the most complex ideas.

PAULE MARSHALL
"From the Poets in the Kitchen"

It is critical that we do not romanticize the struggles of Black
mothers by failing to acknowledge and understand fully the
psychological and physical costs of their survival.

BEVERLY GREENE

Double the gifts your mother gave you and care for her as she
cared for you.

Sacred wisdom of ancient Egypt

You should not confuse [spoiling] with the love, warmth and
comfort that an infant really needs, particularly during those
early, early months.

DR. TRUDDIE E. DARDEN
Associate Professor, Morehouse School of Medicine

Parents should be more concerned with bonding with their newborns than they are with spoiling them.

MURIEL L. WHITSTONE, *Writer*

I learned the most basic lesson of parenting from my mother: No child is ever spoiled by too much attention. It is the lack of attention that spoils. The time we spend with children is far more important than any other gift. It lets them know that we love them, that we place them ahead of other commitments, and that they can turn to us amidst the turbulence of growing up. This basic principle worked for my mother. It has worked for my husband and me. And I am sure it will work for my son and daughter-in-law.

DR. BESSIE W. BLAKE, *Educator*

Our Leaders, Leadership, and Accountability

If you are a leader see that the plans you make are carried out.

Sacred wisdom of ancient Egypt

Leaders are like eagles. They don't flock, you find them one at a time.

ANONYMOUS

He leads best who leads least.

Saying

Leadership is a process of morality to the degree that leaders engage with followers on the basis of shared motives and values and goals—on the basis, that is, of the followers' "true" needs as well as those leaders': psychological, economic, safety, spiritual, sexual, aesthetic, or physical. Friends, relatives, teachers, officials, politicians, ministers, and others will supply a variety of initiatives, but only the followers themselves can ultimately define their own true needs.

HAROLD CRUSE

We need leaders . . . who do not abuse the privileges that come with leadership.

MYRLIE EVERS-WILLIAMS

. . . a good leader is someone who can bring together people of different views and persuasions.

MARY HATWOOD FUTRELL

Most of our leaders are picked by the very enemy we are trying to get free of. Our leaders are not connected to the black masses.

LOUIS FARRAKHAN

If you are a leader, be courteous and listen carefully to the presentations of petitioners.

Sacred wisdom of ancient Egypt

It is better to be part of a great whole than to be the whole of a small part.

FREDERICK DOUGLASS

Medgar Evers was a very strong man, a man who wanted to see his people enjoy the same rights and privileges that all other people who live in the United States enjoy. He was a very good husband to me. He was a wonderful father who took time with his three children to explain to them why he was working so hard and why he dedicated his life to making things better for all parents and their children, both black and white.

MYRLIE EVERS-WILLIAMS

We're looking for moral leadership. We're looking for a president who's not afraid to talk about race in a public forum. The entire country is running from this problem.

LANI GUINIER

If the association must steer clear of the vital issues that mold
the lives of most black people . . . NAACP will stand for the
national association for the advancement of corporate privilege,
comfortable positions and complacent policies.

MICHAEL ERIC DYSON
Professor, Author

If our leaders create their own nightmares, then they belittle
our character by implicating us in a race issue that does not
exist. If we support them simply because we are angry with
"the system," then we are mindless fools, not free-thinking
citizens.

DIANA BEARD-WILLIAMS
Consultant on black leadership
for the UCLA School of Education

He who conceals his disease cannot expect to be cured.

Ethiopian proverb

He never admitted to substance abuse, although he was caught
in the act on videotape. There was never the candor of sharing
points about recovering. That would have been the moral way
to begin reestablishing his public life.

K. MAURICE JONES
Poet, about the reelection of
Marion Barry and the public trust

Where there is no shame, there is no honor.

Ethiopian proverb

After a foolish deed comes remorse.

Kenyan proverb

[Marion] Barry has wrapped himself in black America's two most compelling cultural values: resistance to white power and a belief in the possibility of redemption.

PAUL RUFFINS
Writer, Environmentalist

... in order for us to be effective political people, we must be in control of the personal.

TONI CADE BAMBARA
Activist, Novelist

Malcolm X is the Elvis Presley of race politics, a pop black power icon mistaken for a serious thinker.

STANLEY CROUCH, *Author*

Malcolm's lasting contribution to the struggle of Black people—and to the possible rescue of America—is his analysis of the destructive power of American racism. Malcolm did not live long enough to change Americans himself, but his analysis of racism gave Black folks the cultural and intellectual keys to re-create ourselves and redefine America.

WILLIAM STRICKLAND
Writer, Professor

I know often when people talk about Malcolm X, they make him seem larger than life, and that's dangerous—because young people, hearing about him—this-larger-than-life person—will be led to think they could never be like him, you see. He's not accessible, then. The truth is, the man was as large as life, a man of great profundity, with a wonderful sense of humor and a loving sense of his people.

MAYA ANGELOU

First, I don't profess to be anybody's leader. I'm one of 22 million Afro-Americans, all of whom have suffered the same things. And I probably cry out a little louder against the suffering than most others and therefore, perhaps, I'm better known. I don't profess to have a political, economic, or social solution to a problem as complicated as the one which our people face in the States, but I am one of those who is willing to try *any means necessary* to bring an end to the injustices that our people suffer.

MALCOLM X

Where King advocated redemptive suffering for blacks through their own bloodshed, Malcolm promulgated "reciprocal bleeding" for blacks and whites. As King preached the virtues of a Christian love, Malcolm articulated black anger with unmitigated passion. While King urged nonviolent civil disobedience, Malcolm promoted the liberation of blacks by whatever means were necessary.

MICHAEL ERIC DYSON, PH.D.

It means creating an environment where people understand my father's message, that first and foremost he was a man of God.

DEXTER SCOTT KING

... It's almost like black people have been *duped* into thinking that black masculinity is not nuanced or complex.

It's a black culture that can't see a difference between Malcolm X and Farrakhan. One of the deepest differences between them is that Farrakhan is completely procapitalist. Part of why he can be less of a threat to the American government and the American way of life is his total investment in the free enterprise system. Malcolm X was really calling that system into question and allying himself with global struggles against imperialism and colonization.

BELL HOOKS

It was Malcolm's unique ability to narrate the prospects of black resistance at the edge of racial apocalypse that made him both exciting and threatening.

MICHAEL ERIC DYSON, PH.D.

I tried my best to faithfully reproduce Malcolm in my work, to show Malcolm as a human being, to show the human side of him that the press never projected.

ROBERT L. HAGGINS, *Photographer*

What about the gold-decorated set of chinaware commemorating black leaders? Will the china ever be used or can it be easily destroyed like Medgar Evers, Malcolm X, Muhammad Ali and Martin Luther King Jr., experiencing a Humpty Dumpty fate without even the Krazy Glue of Khalid Muhammad able to patch them together?

MEL TAPLEY, *Art Critic*
reviewing a Black Male exhibit at
the Whitney Museum in New York

People who want to lead should acquire more knowledge than those they lead.

ALTON MADDOX

The time has come to admit that African-American leaders must be put to the same credibility test that we say we want all leaders measured by. Disagreeing with, condemning or not supporting an African-American leader is not an indictment of our "blackness" or sense of community.

DIANA BEARD-WILLIAMS
Executive Director, Coalition for the
Empowerment of Children and Families

I am not a perfect servant. I am a public servant.

JESSE JACKSON

The board of [directors] of the NAACP questioned Chavis and found it imprudent to let him continue as director—really it found a man too hollow morally to say "I'm sorry."

EWIN JAMES, *Writer*

Ben Chavis has shown no remorse and has not been the least bit contrite about his fall from grace, fiercely adamant in his denial of any wrongdoing. It might have helped his cause, some pundits submit, if he had confessed an error of judgment in handing over the first payments of a rumored $332,000 settlement with the accuser Mary Stansel.

HERB BOYD
Journalist, Amsterdam News

Dr. Chavis failed to heed the advice of his most trusted colleagues. And leaders must listen to not only their advisors, but the people. Furthermore, he needed to subsume his ego and to have made himself more accessible to those who had his best interest in mind.

UTRICE LEID, *Journalist*

We must not be pawns in the race-card game when our leaders have betrayed our trust, when money and power—not "the system"—is their shortcoming.

DIANA BEARD-WILLIAMS

We should not point a finger and cast blame on who lost the NAACP. What we have all lost is a once in a lifetime opportunity to transform the NAACP into an effective fighting instrument for social change.

DON ROJAS, Activist, Journalist

Dr. Ben Chavis appeared like a hopeful meteor on the civil rights horizon, promising so much but burning out before completing his mission. There are some painful lessons to learn from this debacle, and Dr. Chavis would do well to stop and reflect on the last year or so. When you are entrusted with such an awesome responsibility of leadership, it is arrogant and foolish to think you have all the answers. Good leaders listen, particularly to those they have hired to help them accomplish their goals.

Yes, we have lost a crucial battle, but the war continues, and the NAACP for all its shortcomings is here to stay, and if Dr. Chavis will own up to this personal tragedy, seek counsel for his various excesses, and apologize to his comrades he may continue as a potent and valuable player in the struggle for civil and human rights.

HERB BOYD
Journalist, Amsterdam News

The NAACP . . . through the years, the oldest, largest, most consulted, most feared, most respected and most effective civil rights organization, has been a beacon in the continuing struggle for freedom.

BENJAMIN HOOKS

I've always tried to practice what I preach to students—namely, that beyond a reasonable tolerance they should not take a lot of nonsense from people just because they're in authority positions.

DERRICK BELL

The Nation of Islam is a puritanical cult that very, very few of those Negroes, wearing their caps sideways and backward, their tennis shoes untied and their pants nearly sliding off, could stomach for more than a few hours. They will never trade their decadent, all-American hedonism for a religious cult opposed to partying, alcohol, promiscuity, dancing, pork and sports. And those successful Negro women shouting and clapping for Farrakhan . . . wouldn't think a second about accepting the position females have in his cult.

STANLEY CROUCH, *Author*

Minister Farrakhan gives us hope because he is getting our young men off dope. And he is the only leader who stands up and tells the white man exactly how we feel, he don't shuck and jive like the rest of them.

AN ANONYMOUS BLACK MAN *speaking to journalist Playthell Benjamin about his attendance at a Louis Farrakhan rally in New York City*

We should really appreciate the Louis Farrakhans and Khalid Muhammads while we've got them. While these guys talk a lot, they don't actually *do* anything. The new crop of leaders are going to be a lot more dangerous and radical, and the next phase will probably be led by charismatic individuals, maybe even teenagers, who urge that instead of killing each other, they should go out in gangs and kill a whole lot of white people. And hell, it's not just going to be the whites who get killed. I'm sure that we black tokens are going to be the first to go.

DERRICK BELL

Just because we disagree don't mean we goin' to fall out.

THE REVEREND AL SHARPTON

Envy is the mother of murder.

MINISTER LOUIS FARRAKHAN

Kingdoms rise and fall based on words.

REVEREND HERB DAUGHTRY

Some people want to take curtain calls without being involved in the performance.

ALTON MADDOX

We ought to learn what we can from our national leaders. We pay very high prices for the lessons they inflict.

OCTAVIA BUTLER

Honest and earnest criticism from those whose interests are most nearly touched—criticism of writers by readers, of government by those governed, of leaders by those led—this is the soul of democracy and the safeguard of modern society.

W. E. B. DU BOIS

There would never be any role for me in a leadership capacity with SCLC. Why? First, I'm a woman. Also, I'm not a minister. And second ... I knew that my penchant for speaking honestly ... would not be well tolerated. The combination of basic attitudes of men, and especially ministers, as to what the role of women in their church setups is ... that of taking orders, not providing leadership and the ... ego problems involved in having to feel that here is someone who ... had more information about a lot of things than they possessed at that time ... This would never have lent itself to my being a leader in the movement there.

ELLA JO BAKER

Your job is to help somebody.

THE DELANY FAMILY MOTTO

Leadership, Spelman sisters, leadership is, at its very core, service to others.

Dr. Johnetta B. Cole
President, Spelman College

Service is the rent you pay for room on this earth.

Shirley Chisholm

My mother instilled a love of community. She taught me that each individual is obligated to continuously work toward the improvement of the world in which we live.

John W. Rogers Jr.
Financial Analyst

In a very deep sense she [Nomzamo Winnie Mandela] qualifies for the title of being "the Mother of Black People." If anyone is in doubt of Nomzamo (Winnie) Mandela's love for her people and for South Africa as a whole let him look at what she has endured.

Bishop Manas Buthelezi
Lutheran Church of South Africa

Winnie Mandela isn't a leader because she confronts and challenges apartheid in the interest of her own dignity. Winnie Mandela isn't a leader because she speaks for the freedom of Nelson Mandela. To do so is to be alive in South Africa. Winnie Mandela is a leader because her efforts, her work, her organizing is for the basic human rights of a people.

Dr. Johnetta B. Cole

Count the cost.

Adage

To be the father of a nation is a great honor, but to be the father of a family is a greater joy. But it was a joy I had far too little of.

NELSON MANDELA
Long Walk to Freedom

Perhaps someone may be surprised why I lay so much emphasis on the aspect of suffering in Mrs. Mandela's life. I do so because there are many people who do a lot of talking without counting the cost they may be called upon to pay as a consequence. Very often when such people are confronted with the reality of the stand they have taken they quaver and quiver to the point of marching right about turn. Mrs. Mandela stuck to her guns to the end.

BISHOP MANAS BUTHELEZI
Lutheran Church of South Africa

There is no free lunch.

Adage

You never get something for nothing. A cause that fails to produce leaders of the stuff martyrs are made of cannot hope to achieve its aims. It is only great religions which have produced leaders of such high moral integrity that they were able to endure the test of the fire of persecution at the hands of their enemies and detractors.

Mrs. Nomzamo (Winnie) Mandela should be counted among such great heroes.

BISHOP MANAS BUTHELEZI
Lutheran Church of South Africa

Racism

If all God's dangers ain't the white man, all God's dangers ain't the black man either.

AN EX-SLAVE

The problem of the twentieth century is the problem of the color line—the relations of the darker to the lighter races of men in Asia, Africa, in America and the islands of the sea.

W. E. B. DU BOIS

Nowhere in the civilized world, save in the United States, do men go out in bands . . . to hunt, shoot, hang or burn to death, a single individual, unarmed and absolutely powerless.

IDA B. WELLS

Fight back!

RACHEL ROBINSON

Black people will never gain full equality in this country. Even those herculean efforts that we hail as successful will produce no more than temporary "peaks of progress," short-lived victories that slide into irrelevance as racial patterns adapt in ways that maintain white dominance. This is a hard to accept fact that all history verifies. We must acknowledge it, not as a sign of submission, but as an act of ultimate defiance.

DERRICK BELL, *Lawyer, Author*

It's twenty-four hours a day. I don't care who you are—you can be Reginald Lewis, Bill Cosby. You ask any of them. It is a problem. It is something you have to plug into your daily computer and figure now how am I going to work around this today?

ARTHUR ASHE

The civil rights movement's success in changing racist laws did not automatically lead to changed racist attitudes among a majority of White Americans. New, subtle and insidious forms of racism have emerged to replace the blatant and vulgar manifestations of Jim Crow segregation.

DON ROJAS
Activist, Journalist

Rain beats a leopard's skin, but it does not wash out the spots.
Ashanti proverb

On the opening day of school in the fall of 1964, school after school was integrated in Jackson, Mississippi, without any kind of incident. The same day in Jackson Heights, Queens, in liberal old New York City, sixty-five screaming white mothers, with their babies in their arms, were arrested for opposing the new school integration plan.

DICK GREGORY

What integration achieved for me and my peers was the subtle (and sometimes not-so-subtle) daily reinforcement of the notion that being Black means being inferior.

TERESA WILTZ, *Writer*

The leaky house can fool the sun, but it can't fool the rain.
African proverb

Racism in America is much more complex than either the conscious conspiracy of a power elite or the simple delusion of a few ignorant bigots. It is part of our common experience, therefore, a part of our common culture.

CHARLES LAWRENCE

The American people have this to learn: That where justice is denied; where poverty is enforced; where ignorance prevails, and where any one class is made to feel that society is an organized conspiracy to oppress, rob, and degrade them, neither person nor property will be safe.

FREDERICK DOUGLASS

Wood already touched by fire is not hard to set alight.

Ashanti proverb

Whatever future America will have will be directly related to the solving of its racial dilemma, which is a human dilemma.

JOHN A. WILLIAMS, *Author*

Hatred never failed to destroy the man who hated. And this is an immutable law.

JAMES BALDWIN

I'm tired of being sick and tired.

FANNIE LOU HAMER

What the child says, he has heard at home.

Nigerian proverb

If you fill your mouth with a razor, you will spit blood.

Nigerian proverb

For the majority of nonblack Americans, accepting the Negro's humanity would have meant acknowledging their own callousness and barbarity—an admission of venality and hypocrisy belying nearly all the democratic principles on which the nation was founded.

MEL WATKINS

Hunger is felt by a slave and hunger is felt by a king.

Ashanti proverb

To kill a dog you must call him crazy.

African proverb

The first thing immigrants learn is nigger, nigger, nigger.

RICHARD PRYOR

In race talk the move into mainstream America always means buying into the notion of American blacks as the real aliens. Whatever the ethnicity or nationality of the immigrant, his nemesis is understood to be African American . . . It doesn't matter what shade the newcomer's skin is. A hostile posture toward resident blacks must be struck at the Americanizing door before it will open.

TONI MORRISON

White racism is being replaced by a brown and yellow racism, that may prove to be worse.

ISHMAEL REED

The road to acclaim and recognition is so clear. All you have to do is get up in a public place and say: It's all black folk's fault.

DERRICK BELL

[Booker T. Washington's] doctrine has tended to make the whites, North and South, shift the burden of the Negro problem to the Negro's shoulders and stand aside as critical and rather pessimistic spectators; when in fact the burden belongs to the nation, and the hands of none of us are clean if we bend not our energies to righting these great wrongs.

W. E. B. DU BOIS

The destructive and aggressive behavior patterns displayed throughout the world by white peoples toward all nonwhite peoples is the evidence of inner hate, hostility, and rejection they feel toward themselves ...

DR. FRANCIS CRESS WELSING

Sometimes white acts of racism are so ridiculous ...

DR. LONNIE BRISTOW
First Black President of the
American Medical Association

You can't expect white kids to be the same after they get to be twelve and thirteen ...

A BLACK MOTHER *preparing her daughter*
for the reality of racism in America

... AIDS isn't the heaviest burden I have had to bear ... being black is the greatest burden I've had to bear. No question about it. Race has always been my biggest burden. Having to live as a minority in America. Even now it continues to feel like an extra weight tied around me.

ARTHUR ASHE

What I have learned reinforces something I have always known—that being a black man in this society is one of the most difficult tasks anyone must face. Black women often forget this reality or too quickly dismiss it.

AUDREY B. CHAPMAN
Wild Women Don't Wear No Blues

I hope the day will come when America no longer has to worry about the first black this and the first black that.

DR. LONNIE BRISTOW
*First Black President of the
American Medical Association*

If folk can learn to be racist, then they can learn to be anti-racist. If being a sexist ain't genetic, then, dad gum, people can learn about gender equality.

JOHNETTA B. COLE

Racially offensive remarks are not the fuel for progress.

JESSE JACKSON

[George Wallace] came up North and proved to Northerners what Negroes have known all their lives and been afraid to say. He proved to the nation that the system of oppression over black people does not begin south of the Mason-Dixon line. It really begins south of the Canadian border.

DICK GREGORY
The Shadow that Scares

If you are going to hold someone down, you're going to have to hold on to the other end of the chain. You are confined by your own system of oppression.

TONI MORRISON

You gotta say this for whites, their self-confidence knows no bounds. Who else could go to a small island in the South Pacific, where there's no crime, poverty, unemployment, wary or worry—and call it a "primitive society"?

DICK GREGORY

While African Americans are still exulting over Maya Angelou's poem at the inaugural, and four black Cabinet officers, bank practices and mortgage lenders keep discriminating against African Americans, police brutality and hate crimes increase. Shoney's and Denny's and other restaurants, and public accommodations that care to exclude or decline to serve African Americans; . . . the absence of drug treatment facilities, bad housing, unemployment, glass ceilings in employment, racial intolerance on campus, all continue to thrive. The slap at Lani Guinier was just another reminder of the racial problems that demand our attention.

MARY FRANCIS BERRY
Author, Historian

[African-Americans] are very good at reacting to something we perceive as disrespectful, but less good at articulating an analysis of why that particular action occurred in the first place and what can be done to prevent it in the future.

LANI GUINIER

Ultimately, it's men, white men, that make the decisions about who's going to be cast in the sexy lead role or the supporting role. We [black people] are not seen as having the world as our arena. We're not seen as having the intellect or complexity of other people.

DANNY GLOVER

Maybe it's because his looks are not just a blacker shade of pale that Danny Glover might be more than Hollywood is ready to handle.

KEVIN POWELL, *Writer*

We see black men who have families and who express love, but what we don't see is the fantasy of falling in love, of romance. So many of our references to those things are simply what we see whites do in the movies, and so it's a way of denying our humanity.

DANNY GLOVER

I still think today as yesterday that the color line is a great problem of this century. But today I see more clearly than yesterday that back of the problem of race and color, lies a greater problem which both obscures and implements it: and that is the fact that so many civilized persons are willing to live in comfort even if the price of this is poverty, ignorance and disease of the majority of their fellow men; that to maintain this privilege men have waged war until today war tends to become universal and continuous, and the excuse for this war continues largely to be color and race.

W. E. B. DU BOIS

See, when white folks reach what they consider their mountain top, they don't want to look over and see us. How can they have achieved as much as they think they have if they look up and see some black folks there doing the same thing? The neighborhood can't be that good if we're there. The country club can't be that exclusive. And my God, if one of us has the same job, well they must not be as smart as they think they are.

BEBE MOORE CAMPBELL
Brothers & Sisters

I been to the mountain top, too, and what did I see? Mo' white folks with guns.

RICHARD PRYOR

When a white man sits on a subway train, feet stretched out into the aisleway and refuses to move his feet out of the aisle when a black man passes, albeit micro, that is an act of hostility.

LAVERNE MARKS, *Social Worker*

Just how badly am I going to feel if I tolerate this particular instance of disrespect or bad behavior?

SUSAN L. TAYLOR AND AUDREY EDWARDS
*about choosing when to confront
micro and macro racism*

Black women know that white women have benefitted, and continue to benefit, from black female oppression.

KESHO YVONNE SCOTT
The Habit of Surviving

We first have to understand that racism is permanent, and then we have to take a stance similar to that of Mrs. Biona MacDonald, the Black lady down in Mississippi who once said to me, "Derrick, I live to harass White folks!" The point here is that even though this woman had no money, had no gun, she was still going to be on the case as long as she lived. She was always going to fight. At that point she had triumphed over them.

DERRICK BELL

Now they want me to go to New Orleans . . . It'll be Old Orleans 'fore I get down there. The Greyhound ain't goin' take me down there and the bloodhounds run me back . . .

MOMS MABLEY, *Comedian*

When America becomes truly attentive to the supplication voice of the black ghetto and removes the log of indifference and judgment from her own eye, she will be able to see clearly to remove the speck of suffering from the eye of the ghetto. Until relief from oppression is granted, the only appropriate name for America is "you hypocrite"!

DICK GREGORY

This is our task: Celebrate our diversity! Value our uniqueness! Share our faith stories!

BISHOP STITH

. . . White hoboes from Arkansas and Oklahoma were friendly enough individually, but I knew as a group they were dangerous.

NELSON PEERY
Black Fire: The Making of a Revolutionary

You never get away from the question of race in America, and certainly in New York State that has a major impact on who goes to prison. The overwhelming number of people who use drugs in New York State are not the people you see on the six o'clock news. The overwhelming majority are not black and Latino. The majority of those who sell and use drugs are white, middle income, well-educated persons according to the Drug Enforcement Agency. But when we look at who goes to prison, what we see are poor people, blacks, Latinos, Asians, people of color. We would get the idea from the media that these people were, in fact, the major users and sellers of narcotics in New York State. This simply isn't the case.

EDDIE ELLIS
Former Black Panther

. . . [we] are treated worse than aliens among a people whose language we speak, whose religion we profess, and whose blood flows and mingles in our veins.

FRANCES ELLEN WATKINS HARPER
Abolitionist, Poet

The Negro is America's metaphor.

RICHARD WRIGHT

You know the definition of a Southern moderate. That's a cat that'll lynch you from a low tree.

DICK GREGORY

In time I would come to see that black nationalism almost inevitably leads to a kind of cultural chauvinism indistinguishable from racism, the very thing I thought I was fighting.

ITABARI NJERI

Identity, Self-Actualization, and the Irksome Question of Color

We know that we are beautiful.

LANGSTON HUGHES

Look at me. I am black. I am beautiful.

MARY MCLEOD BETHUNE

Especially do I believe in the Negro Race: in the beauty of its genius, the sweetness of its soul.

W. E. B. DU BOIS

This color seems to operate as a most disagreeable mirror, and a great deal of one's energy is expended in reassuring white Americans that they do not see what they see.

JAMES BALDWIN

The black man's is a strange situation; it is a perspective, an angle of vision held by oppressed people; it is an outlook of people looking upward from below.

RICHARD WRIGHT

129

Black and white Americans are stuck with each other, for better or worse. What all of us need to know is the extent to which we are, and have been, bound together down the glory road. Deny it though we may, black and white Americans have experienced such a seamless relationship during nearly four hundred years of contact in this land that it is often difficult to determine where European culture ends and African culture begins.

HERB BOYD
Down the Glory Road

I am a Negro. My skin is white, my eyes are blue, my hair is blonde.

WALTER WHITE
Executive Secretary, NAACP

This mixing was so common then that there was a saying among poor whites. They used to say, "Takes a little bit of nigger blood to bring out the beauty."

SADIE AND BESSIE DELANY
Having Our Say: The Delany Sisters' First 100 Years

We will never feel psychologically whole until we are able to call ourselves Africans. To call Africans in America "blacks" is like calling Asians in America "yellows."

NATHAN HARE AND JULIA HARE
The Miseducation of the Black Child

Soul is the reaffirmation of the black man's estimate of himself. It is the connective skein that runs through the totality of the black experience, weaving it together and infusing it with meaning.

C. ERIC LINCOLN

I realized that the only way this society was going to view my calling myself a mulatto was as a rejection of my blackness, which is certainly not the case. I'm proud of my black heritage, and I'm proud of my white mother, too.

LONETTE MCKEE, *Actress*

Wood may remain ten years in the water, but it will never become a crocodile.

Congolese folk saying

People usually don't have a problem with me being black. That's just who I am. Black people know we come in all shades. I was raised by my mother, who is black, and maybe because of that I never had any confusion over who or what I was.

SALLI RICHARDSON, *Actress*

Color is not a human or a personal reality; it is a political reality.

JAMES BALDWIN

When I was growing up my mother taught me and my two sisters that we had the best of both worlds, the opportunities and advantages of both races. But, in retrospect, that was idealistic of her. Now I'd tell kids from a mixed background, "Remember your roots and be proud, but don't be fooled. If you have black blood, in society's terms you are black, and you will be treated as such."

LONETTE MCKEE, *Actress*

If you burn a house, can you conceal the smoke?

African folk saying

As a people we need to know of our historical connection to the continent of Africa, as well as its true place in the sphere of humankind as the home of all mankind.

LOUISE SPENCER-STRACHAN
Color Crisis

> *If you're white, you're right,*
> *If you're yellow, you're mellow,*
> *If you're brown, stick around,*
> *And if you're black—get back*

African-American ditty

A poor mulatto is a black man, a rich black man is a mulatto.

Haitian proverb

A long view of the portrayal of Black Americans in our cinema indicates that, as James Baldwin once implied, not everyone in the interracial melting pot of America has the intention of being melted.

ALBERT JOHNSON

I believe the individual is as important as the group. And the only category I allow people to lump me in with is "American." This is mine, the culture that is here. From *I Spy* to Thomas Jefferson and Sally Hemings, to the Underground Railroad and the above-ground railroad, to all the Chinese people who've been here for generations and the indigenous people who intermarried . . . This is mine. And y'all who came over in 1940, 1915—y'all are the new ones. I was here when y'all got here.

WHOOPI GOLDBERG

I have an assuredness of myself.

JACOB LAWRENCE, *Painter*

Oneself is bound up with the needs and aspirations of one's people.

SARAH WRIGHT, *Novelist*

I am the greatest! I am the king!

MUHAMMAD ALI

No one can figure out your worth but you.

PEARL BAILEY

Less than one percent of all the people in the world ever reach their full potential. I created that statistic.

BERRY GORDY

What is inflated too much, will burst into fragments.

Ethiopian proverb

The frog wanted to be as big as the elephant, and burst.

Ethiopian proverb

I am an incurable activist.

ALTHEA SIMMONS

What am I too a tornado?

JUDY DOTHARD SIMMONS, *Poet*

Often light-skinned African Americans are considered more at-tractive than those with the blackest skin colors. We have shunned each other as reminders of our alleged inferiority. And in doing that, we guaranteed our continued enslavement.

GEORGE FRASER

Fine clothes, good looks, or the color of the skin does not make the man.

W. A. LEWIS
Writer, Activist

Nobody takes a picture of me without my makeup. This is why writers are so boring. They think they're so intelligent they don't have to bother making up their face. I know better because I'm an actress.

NTOZAKE SHANGE

Unlike many African-American pop musicians, most rappers expressed no desire to cross over to fame in mainstream—which to some meant white—America. Nor did they attempt to imitate mainstream codes of dress and demeanor once they became successful.

K. MAURICE JONES, *Poet*

When a man is wealthy, he may wear an old cloth.

Ashanti proverb

I was a nigger for twenty-three years. I gave it up, no room for advancement.

RICHARD PRYOR

I want to feel that I made choices that empowered me and substantiated me as a human being. My career is going to be here and gone. But I'm always going to be a human being. And

I want to look myself in the mirror and say that I was the human being I wanted to be.

DANNY GLOVER

Individuals are often not assertive because they don't believe they have the right to be or because they view the word as negative. To be assertive is to have the ability to stand up for your basic rights and express yourself honestly without savaging those around you.

LAVERNE MARKS, *Social Worker*

A too modest man goes hungry.

Ethiopian proverb

Unless you call out, who will open the door?

Ethiopian proverb

If you have no confidence in self, you are twice defeated in the race of life. With confidence you have won even before you have started.

MARCUS GARVEY

MY POETRY is whatever I think I am.... I CAN BE ANY-THING I CAN. I make poetry with what I feel is useful & can be saved out of all the garbage of our lives.

AMIRI BARAKA

I just think that so many . . . of them are bordering on being minstrel shows, and we might as well bring back *Amos 'n' Andy*.

And there was always this thought that, well, once we get into the industry, and once we start being in front of the camera, when we start writing, directing, producing our own shows, things will be different. But we're writing these things ourselves. So there's never going to be a guarantee, just because somebody's black, that it's going to be righteous.

SPIKE LEE *on Black sitcoms*

It's really tough to explore and understand our individual identities when we continually receive messages from our parents, relatives, friends and mainstream society about who we're suppose to be as Black women.

JULIA BOYD

The problem with the image of Black women as *the* nurturers is the implication that Black men are incapable of being caring souls, loving parents, warm human beings.

JOHNETTA B. COLE

Our [society's] idea of beauty and sexuality has nothing to do with someone who looks like me. The mulatto is something you can bring home now and get over with it. I'm a little harder to explain, because I don't fit the criteria. The nose is too wide, the skin is too dark, the hair is too nappy.

WHOOPI GOLDBERG

The truth is, son, I have never been the kind of person people would turn around and look at in the street. I'm just, well, what you might say drylongso. Neither ugly nor pretty, just drylongso.

RUTH SHAYS

I often say that I am a double minority, black and female, and it cuts both ways, Even when I'm accepted as a black, I have to fight the female portion. If you're female, you've got to be able to prove that once a month you're not going to go down the drain, that you're able to hold your own, and that's true within the race and outside the race.

ALTHEA T. L. SIMMONS

I don't know if I've been around here too long or won't be around here much longer.

MOMS MABLEY

After a period of time, the oppressed man begins imitating the behavior of the oppressor.

DICK GREGORY

The analogy I use is that of the kidnapped victim. Psychologists have done studies on kidnapped victims, and they've found one thing in common: In a lot of cases where a person has been held captive or hostage, they're usually in a very vulnerable, weak position. They feel helpless. They have no resources to fall back on. After a while, a strange psychic process begins to happen. They begin to identify with their captors.

I suggest this: I see a similar parallel with African Americans. Many African Americans over time have begun to identify, empathize and bond with white supremacy.

EARL OFARI HUTCHINSON

He who lives with an ass, makes noises like an ass.

Ethiopian proverb

I am not always clear on what I want, but I am very clear on what I don't want.

BUTCH HINES

I am what I am, not because of what I am, but in spite of it!

BERT WILLIAMS

When I was younger, living in an all-black neighborhood, the other kids thought I thought I was better than them because of my light skin and straight hair. But it was really, they thought I was better than them.

HALLE BERRY, *Actress*

I am a woman and I write from that experience. I am a Black woman and I write from that experience. I do not feel inhibited or bound by what I am. That does not mean that I have never had bad scenes relating to being Black and/or a woman, it means that other people's craziness has not managed to make me crazy.

LUCILLE CLIFTON

In Africa, there are no niggers; and I will die before I become a nigger for your entertainment.

VERNON REID

When I went to West Africa, I had the deep sense not only of belonging, but of possession. This was ours! The whole continent was ours!

NIARA SUDARKASA

You show me one of those people over here who has been thoroughly brainwashed and has a negative attitude toward African, and I'll show you one who has a negative attitude toward himself.

MALCOLM X

I've got to be a colored funny man, not a funny colored man.
DICK GREGORY

Too many blacks foolishly repeat this ultraracist term the "endangered species," and thus inflame in themselves the virus of self-hate.
JOHN WOODFORD, *Writer*

An overreliance on others is a mistake.
RALPH WILEY

He who does not cultivate his field, will die of hunger.
Guinean proverb

Instead of seeking true equality with whites, too many blacks sought acceptance. They fled their own communities to live instead among the whites, because they saw whites as successful and blacks as doomed. This is a manifestation of self-hatred that many believe is a far greater obstacle to African-American economic empowerment than racial hatred.
GEORGE C. FRASER
Success Runs in Our Race

The poor man and the rich man do not play together.
Ashanti proverb

White folks are some strange people. If the first black they met was a scholar, then all blacks were scholars ... At an early age I learned the game that becomes a serious part of every black person's social personality. We learned roles. One person with our peers, we become a totally different person around whites. It was impossible for them to know us, and this was our defense. I didn't know how our race could stay out of the schizo-phrenic ward, considering the split personalities they forced upon us.

NELSON PEERY
Black Fire: The Making of a Revolutionary

We fooled them, Lue, slavery was terrible but we fooled them old people. We came out of it better than they did.

Attributed to LUCILLE CLIFTON'S FATHER
Black Women Writers

Honey ... White boys can do lots of things that you can't ... You have to learn to conduct yourself so that everyone else forgets you're Negro. But don't you ever forget it ...

NELSON PEERY'S MOTHER
Black Fire: The Making of a Revolutionary

[T]he Negro is a sort of seventh son, born with a veil, and gifted with second-sight in this American world—a world which yields him no true self-consciousness, but only lets him see himself through the revelation of the other world. It is a peculiar sensation, this double-consciousness, this sense of always look-ing at one's self through the eyes of others, of measuring one's soul by the tape of a world that looks on in amused contempt and pity. One ever feels his two-ness—an American, a Negro; two souls, two thoughts, two unreconciled strivings; two war-ring ideals in one dark body, whose dogged strength alone keeps it from being torn asunder.

The history of the American Negro is the history of this strife—this longing to attain self-conscious manhood, to merge his double self into a better and truer self. In this merging he wishes neither of the older selves to be lost. He would not Africanize American, for American has too much to teach the world and Africa. He would not bleach his Negro soul in a flood of white Americanism, for he knows that Negro blood has a message for the world. He simply wishes to make it possible for a man to be both a Negro and an American, without being cursed and spit upon by his fellows, without having the doors of opportunity closed roughly in his face.

W. E. B. Du Bois

[Booker T.] Washington and [W. E. B] Du Bois are excellent examples of the ambivalence which afflicts middle-class black leaders. Du Bois once wrote that "The Negro group has long been internally divided by dilemmas as to whether its striving upwards should be aimed at strengthening inner cultural and group bonds, both for intrinsic progress and for offensive power against caste; or whether it should seek escape wherever and however possible into the surrounding American culture." This is because . . . the black middle class as a whole vacillates between the two approaches posited by Du Bois.

Robert L. Allen, *Sociologist*

. . . I will never again involve myself with what I call secondary consciousness. I will never again see myself, see other Black women, see Black men, and Black children secondarily, through the eyes of the oppressor . . . the slave master.

Toni Cade Bambara
Writer, Activist

Once a missionary told a cousin of mine this Ham story and my cousin, being the daughter of a very wise elder, informed the missionary that he was wrong: All men were originally black. But when Cain killed his brother Abel, and God shouted at him, Cain was so frightened that he turned white and his features shrunk up, making him the first white man.

Olagun, the Griot
African History for Beginners

Having soon discovered that to be great I must appear so, I studiously avoided mixing in society and wrapped myself in mystery.

NAT TURNER

It is perfectly true to say that Negroes do not sit around twenty-four hours a day, thinking, *I am a Negro*.

LORRAINE HANSBERRY

... "true women" did not work outside the home at a time when the majority of African American women were employed. And in that process ... African American women were forced to define themselves and to develop new definition of womanhood—those definitions coming out of the dialectics of their lives. African American women have lived lives filled with contradictions and have formed a meaning for themselves and their people out of those contradictions.

ELSA BARKLEY BROWN, *Scholar*

My color has never destroyed my self-respect nor has it ever caused me to conduct myself in such a manner as to merit the disrespect of any person ... I would not exchange my color for all the wealth in the world, for had I been born white, I might not have been able to do all I have done or yet hope to do.

MARY MCLEOD BETHUNE

ƒOLIDARITY IN ƒTRUGGLE

If there is no struggle there is no progress ... Find just what any people will quietly submit to and you have found out the exact measure of injustice and wrong which will be imposed upon them, and these will continue till they are resisted with either words or blows or with both.

FREDERICK DOUGLASS

Tell no lies and claim no easy victories.

AMILCAR CABRAL

One ought to struggle for its own sake. One ought to be against racism and sexism because they are wrong, not because one is black or one is female.

ELEANOR HOLMES NORTON
First Black Woman Mayor
of Washington, D.C.

The struggle is my life.

NELSON MANDELA

All I demand for the black man is that white people shall take their heels off his neck, and let him have a chance to rise by his own efforts.

WILLIAM WELLS BROWN, *Dramatist*

We must attack the system of overcrowding in the poor districts by urging our men to contend for laws regulating the number of people in one dwelling ... that people may not be crowded together like cattle while soulless landlords collect fifty percent on their investments.

REBECCA J. COTE, M.D. (1846–1922)
Significantly Unsung Pioneer Physician

Black liberation, however, will not come about solely through the activities of black people. Black America cannot be genuinely liberated until white America is transformed into a humanistic society free of exploitation and class division.

ROBERT ALLEN
Editor, Author

There is a great social revolution going on in America today. And the wonderful thing about this revolution is that it is not black against white. It is simply right against wrong.

DICK GREGORY, *1968*

Ice Cube wishes to acknowledge white America's continued commitment to the silence and oppression of black men.

K. MAURICE JONES

In an industry where success and fame seem also to confer the right to flaunt one's aloofness and inaccessibility like the Nobel Peace Prize, Danny Glover's social activism is legend. It is also for real.

KEVIN POWELL, *Writer*

Very few people remember the names of the four little girls killed in the cowardly bombing of the Sixteenth Street Baptist Church in Birmingham, Alabama on September 15, 1963. Sometimes reporters and historians cite the wrong number killed or mistake the date, or debate whether they should be listed with other victims of Jim Crow. Carole Robertson, Cynthia Wesley, and Addie Mae Collins, all fourteen years [old], and eleven-year-old Denise McNair are as much martyrs of the civil rights movement as any of those dedicated fighters who gave their lives.

HERB BOYD
Down the Glory Road

Don't buy where you can't work!

ADAM CLAYTON POWELL JR.

When the millions of poor working people recognize that the interest of one poor man is the concern of all, and that a blow struck at the Negro's progress affects the entire working class; when they agree to stand for one object, and let the object be better conditions, racial troubles will be reduced to the minimum.

JAMES S. WALLACE
*member of the integrated New York
City Union of Street Pavers, 1906*

I consider the fight for the Negro masses the greatest service I can render to my people, and the fight alone is my complete compensation.

A. PHILLIP RANDOLPH

Aboard a recent luxury train ride with my wife and children to my boyhood home in Florida I asked a young conductor about A. Phillip Randolph, the organizer of the Brotherhood of Pullman Porters, a union which raised black railway men from the status of exploited servants to empowered workers. The twenty-eight-year-old who had no idea that his job once had been reserved for white men only, greeted my inquiry with a blank stare that reminded me of the looks I've seen on the faces of young black professional baseball players who don't recognize the name of Jackie Robinson. And it's just as appalling. Both reflect the loss of public school teachers who are informed about African-American history and culture.

PLAYTHELL BENJAMIN, *Journalist*

If there is nothing worth dying for there is nothing worth living for.

DR. MARTIN LUTHER KING JR.

The free man is the man with no fears.

DICK GREGORY

I ask you, had you not rather be killed than be a slave to a tyrant, who takes the life of your mother, wife, and dear little children?

DAVID WALKER

I have heard their groans and sighs, and seen their tears, and I would give every drop of blood in my veins to free them.

HARRIET TUBMAN

Harriet Tubman wasn't a leader because she struggled and fought for her own freedom. Harriet Tubman was a leader because she risked her own freedom a million times so that others could gain theirs.

DR. JOHNETTA B. COLE
President, Spelman College

Brethren arise, arise! Strike for your lives and liberties. Now is the day and the hour . . . Rather die free men than live to be slaves . . . Let your motto be resistance.

HENRY HIGHLAND GARNETT

Those who profess to favor freedom and yet deprecate agitation are men who want crops without plowing up the ground, they want rain without thunder and lightning. They want the mighty ocean without the roar of its many waters.

FREDERICK DOUGLASS

Snake at your feet—a stick at your hand!

Ethiopian proverb

The White man has given the Negro just about all he intends to give him. From now on, we will win only what we fight for.

ADAM CLAYTON POWELL JR.

I hold that between the white people and the colored there is a community of interest, and the sooner they find it out, the better it will be for both parties; but that community of interest does not consist in increasing the privileges of one class and curtailing the rights of the other.

FRANCES ELLEN WATKINS HARPER

Black women are the backbone of every institution, but sometimes they are not recognized as even being there, even in the civil rights movement.

DOROTHY HEIGHT

One of the biggest myths about slavery is that slave dealers and owners destroyed the spirit of their African captives.

K. MAURICE JONES
Say It Loud

Black people number strong among those who cannot imagine life without books, cherishing them for information and entertainment and inspiration. And then, we who have a mind have a memory of books as verbotens, of reading (like writing) as revolt and resistance.

TONYA BOLDEN, *Literary Critic*

Amiri Baraka, Sonia Sanchez and Nikki Giovanni are still involved and are living institutions—walking, talking, breathing, living institutions.

TRACIE MORRIS, *Poet*

Our sense of self as Black people is always under attack in this society, but it's reaffirmed and enhanced at the moment you take a stance.

DERRICK BELL

A white dog does not bite another white dog.

Kenyan proverb

Too many people are going for self and not trying to help their communities.

KEVIN POWELL, *Writer*

If something is yours by right, then you fight for it or shut up. If you can't fight for it, then forget it.

MALCOLM X

For the rest of my life I am committed to taking part in the black struggle that's going on in this country.

JIM BROWN

I saw their noses being broken and blood flowing from their wounds; and I saw them continue and not retaliate, not one of them, with violence.

> DR. MARTIN LUTHER KING
> *marvelling over the impressive discipline*
> *of gang members who often served as march*
> *marshals during the Chicago Freedom Movement*

I want to live in a black neighborhood, and if banks would give us money to fix up the houses we live in, nobody would have to move.

> A CHICAGO ALDERMAN

The Chicago Freedom Movement was the most publicized effort in the nation's history to spotlight the curse of housing barriers.

> JAMES R. RALPH JR.
> Northern Protest: Martin Luther King Jr.,
> Chicago, and the Civil Rights Movement

Frankly, I have never seen as much hatred and hostility on the part of so many people. To my mind those people represent the most tragic expression of man's inhumanity to man.

> DR. MARTIN LUTHER KING
> *after being felled by a rock*
> *on Chicago's south side*
> *during his Chicago Freedom Movement*

We march, we return home emotionally drained, from some inner reservoirs we replenish our strength and go back.

> A CHICAGO ACTIVIST,
> *about the Chicago Freedom Movement*

[The Chicago Freedom Movement did prove that] large numbers of people in a Northern city can be mobilized for nonviolent direct action in the face of mass violence.

BERNARD LAFAYETTE
Organizer, Chicago Freedom Movement, 1966

I helped to build a union which enables sailors to marry and have children and a home just like other workers, instead of being kicked around like bums.

FERDINAND C. SMITH
*denouncing ship owners of the 1930s
for using racial prejudice
to divide black and white union members*

The labor movement traditionally has been the only haven for the disposed, the despised, the neglected, the downtrodden and the poor.

A. PHILLIP RANDOLPH

[T]he stormy night of reaction will pass and the American people will return their government to the hands of the masses to whom it belongs.

FERDINAND C. SMITH
*a founder of the National Maritime Union,
about his impending deportation to
Jamaica, a victim of McCarthyism*

I represent more groups who have been victims of second-class citizenship than any other delegate; however, I am a proud member of all these groups, and in my small way I have tried to make my contribution to the cause of dignified humanity.

DOLLIE LOWTHER
*Activist and Union Organizer whose duties included
investigating the conditions of migrant workers,
about her position as delegate to the
1967 New York State Constitutional Convention*

Do you want work?
Do you want equal rights?
Do you want justice?
Then prepare to fight for it!

A. PHILLIP RANDOLPH

Down here we hear relaxed, matter-of-fact conversations center-ing around how best to kill all the nation's niggers and in what order. It's not the fact that they consider killing me that upsets. They've been "killing the niggers" for nearly half a millennium now, but I am still alive. I might be the most resilient dead man in the universe. The upsetting thing is that they never take into consideration the fact that I am going to resist.

GEORGE JACKSON

Look upon your mother, wife, and children, and answer God almighty; and believe this, that it is no more harm for you to kill a man who is trying to kill you than it is for you to take a drink of water when thirsty.

DAVID WALKER

I know one thing we did right, was the day we started to fight. Keep your eyes on the prize. Hold on, hold on.

Civil Rights Anthem

I was so consumed with being a medical student—and it was very hard to be—that I didn't have time for a social conscience. I'd like to say I was more noble than that, but I wasn't. *All* I thought about was getting myself through. I didn't worry that I couldn't eat in the dining room with the white students. I didn't worry that there were places that white students could go to for graduation parties that I couldn't. I didn't worry that people who came to the hospital made comments to me that amounted to "What are you doing here?" Once, I had a professor say to me, "You know you have as much education as a lot of white people." Doctor, I have *more* education than most white people.

DR. JOYCELYN ELDERS

Blacks will simply never gain full equality in this country. Rather than eliminate racial discrimination, civil rights laws have only driven it underground, where it flourishes even more effectively.

DERRICK BELL

My bones are tired. Not tired of struggling, but tired of oppression.

QUEEN MOTHER MOORE
Community Organizer

The race is divided between those who think that white folks should think for us and those who think we should think for ourselves. That was the struggle yesterday, that is the struggle today.

ALTON MADDOX

Toussaint (L'Ouverture) had the advantage of liberty and equality, the slogans of the revolution, they were great weapons in an age of slaves, but weapons must be used and he used them with a fencer's finesse and skill.

C. L. R. JAMES

I do not carry innocence to the point of believing that appeals to reason or to respect for human dignity can alter reality. For the Negro who works on a sugar plantation, there is only one solution: to fight. He will embark on this struggle, and he will pursue it, not as the result of a Marxist or idealistic analysis

but quite simply because he cannot conceive of life otherwise
than in the form of a battle against exploitation, misery, and
hunger.

FRANTZ FANON

When it comes to blacks, whites have no conscience. Whites
don't bend unless forced to bend. They don't give one inch if
they don't have to.

NATHAN McCALL
Makes Me Wanna Holler: A Young Black Man in America

Brother, nobody can protect you from a Muslim but a Muslim—
or someone trained in Muslim tactics. I know; I invented many
of those tactics.

MALCOLM X

Even when the battle is long and the path is steep, a true warrior does not give up. If each one of us does not step forward
to claim our rights, we are doomed to an eternal wait in hopes
those who would usurp them will become benevolent. The Bible
says, WATCH, FIGHT, AND PRAY.

INDIA ANETTE PEYTON
Grandmother of Melba Patillo Beals,
in Warriors Don't Cry

While many White Americans have considered (and fretted
over) the Black preacher-as-slave-revolt leader and conspirator
(e.g. Nat Turner) as an oxymoron, Black Christians never did
and don't.

TONYA BOLDEN, *Writer*

COURAGE

Even over cold pudding, the coward says, "It will burn my mouth."

Ethiopian proverb

I have come to believe over and over again that what is most important to me must be spoken, made verbal and shared, even at the risk of having it bruised or misunderstood.

SUSAN L. TAYLOR

But what people don't realize is that ultimately the sacrifice that they are making by not speaking up is too high, because what they are giving up is their integrity and their sense of purpose and their sense of what they are.

LANI GUINIER

A coward sweats in water.

Ethiopian proverb

My road to the top occurred because I stood up and was heard.

MARY HATWOOD FUTRELL
President, International Teachers Union

Now it looks finished. I'm through—at least for a while. After all this is over, maybe I'll go to Europe, perhaps Paris, and try to start all over. Sure, I know about Gene Krupa—but don't forget he's white and I'm a Negro. I've got two strikes against me and don't you forget it.

I'm proud of those two strikes. I'm as good as a lot of people of all kinds—I'm proud I'm a Negro. And you know the funniest thing: the people that are going to be hardest on me will be my own race.

BILLIE HOLIDAY
following her arrest on a drug charge

If Billie Holiday had never existed, I probably wouldn't have either.

CARMEN MCRAE

The pain is in the book now.

MELBA PATILLO BEALS
speaking about Warriors Don't Cry

That night a rock was thrown through my window. Instinctively, I threw myself to the floor. I was covered with shattered glass . . . I reached for the rock lying in the middle of the floor. A note was tied to it. I broke the string and unfolded a soiled piece of paper. Scrawled in bold print were the words: "Stone this time. Dynamite next."

DAISY BATES, *NAACP Organizer*

I am a radical and I am going to stay one until my people get free to walk the earth.

PAUL ROBESON

I'm not going to be kicked by no donkey, but neither am I going to be stomped by no elephant.

THE REVEREND AL SHARPTON

I am a living symbol of the white man's fear.

> WINNIE MANDELA
> Part of My Soul Went with Him

The women of this family don't break down in the face of trouble. We act with courage, and with God's help, we ship trouble right on out.

> INDIA ANETTE PEYTON
> *Grandmother of Melba Patillo Beals,*
> *in* Warriors Don't Cry

Do not confuse being alert with being fearful.

> *Ugandan proverb*

We both knew the end was near. You don't challenge the system like that without knowing the price to be paid. We lived with threats on a daily basis, and both of us knew in the last three weeks that it wasn't going to be long.

> MYRLIE EVERS-WILLIAMS

One must stretch beyond self for greatness.

> RALPH WILEY

When a needle falls into a deep well, many people will look into the well, but few will be ready to go down after it.

> *Guinean proverb*

Your daring has to be backed up with a willingness to lose that point. To make a bigger point, you might have to lose.

> KATHERINE DUNHAM

Negroes have straightened their backs in Albany and once a man straightens his back you can't ride him anymore.

MARTIN LUTHER KING JR.

I used to ask Medgar: "How could you say you love this state when all these horrible things are happening?" but he always said it was his home and he wanted to make it a better place. I always had difficulty understanding the depth of his feeling for his native state, but over the years I've come to understand it a little more.

MYRLIE EVERS-WILLIAMS

I come here to make a speech, to tell you the truth. If the truth is anti-American, then blame the truth, don't blame me.

MALCOLM X

Those wanting to truly honor Malcolm X should emulate his resolve. He declared, "Anyone who wants to follow me and my movement has got to be ready to go to jail, to the hospital and to the cemetery before he can truly be free."

GEORGE E. CURRY, *Journalist*

I grew up like a neglected weed—ignorant of liberty, having no experience of it. Now that I've been free, I know what a dreadful condition slavery is.

HARRIET TUBMAN

I dared to speak when I should have been silent.

LANI GUINIER

I had much rather starve in England, a free woman, than to be a slave for the best man that ever breathed upon the American continent.

ELLEN CRAFT
Escaped from a Georgia plantation

The cost of liberty is less than the price of repression.

W. E. B. DU BOIS

What is at the summit of courage, I think, is freedom.

PAULA GIDDINGS

I want people to understand the enormity of what it means to mistreat another human being; to know that it is wrong.

MELBA PATILLO BEALS
Warriors Don't Cry

Responsible civil and human rights leaders have a moral imperative to struggle for a national-change agenda. The task is enormous and the challenge truly historic. It requires a bold, courageous, independent and uncompromising leadership with a radically altered perspective; a new perspective that emphasizes more systemic and macroeconomic analysis, a more long-range strategic thinking, planning and coordination and less knee-jerk, ad hoc reacting; more collective initiative and less individualism.

DON ROJAS, *Activist, Journalist*

If they take my life, it won't stop the revolution.

NIKKI GIOVANNI

Liberation theology teaches you to fight for what is right, to fight on principle not on profit.

THE REVEREND AL SHARPTON

Black women whose ancestors were brought to the United States beginning in 1619 have lived through conditions of cruelties so horrible, so bizarre, the women had to re-invent themselves.

MAYA ANGELOU

The American Negro must remake his past in order to make his future.

ARTHUR SCHOMBURG

Jesus, Jesus will go with you.
He will lead you to his throne;
He who died has gone before you,
Trod the wine-press all alone.

HARRIET TUBMAN's *call to freedom*

The legacy of courage left by heroic black women was amassed, deed by deed, day by day, without praise or encouragement.

JOHNETTA B. COLE

I'm a fighter; nobody has ever bought me or bossed me.

SHIRLEY CHISHOLM

Ordinary women of grace are, in a sense, my real role models.

MARIAN WRIGHT EDELMAN

The only road was survival. The only guide was the improvisational genius of Harriet Tubman.

LERONE BENNETT JR., Historian

> *Glory to God and Jesus too,*
> *One more soul is safe!*
> *Oh, go and carry the news,*
> *One more soul got safe!*

HARRIET TUBMAN'S anthem
as she carried another group of bondsmen and
bondswomen across the Canadian border

In the winter of 1966 at the Peg Leg Bates staff meeting in upstate New York, a motion was passed late one night stating that the Student Nonviolent Coordinating Committee should be an all-black organization. Along with others, I voted against this motion, stressing that a viable organization did not expel people from its ranks based on their skin color.

JAMES FORMAN
Black Power Activist

We took on the powers that said that the members of the mob that killed Michael Griffin should be charged with reckless endangerment. We knew that allowing this lightweight charge in a brutal killing would pose a threat to an endangered species: black boys!

THE REVEREND AL SHARPTON

What is said over the dead lion's body could not be said to him alive.

Congolese proverb

You have to understand that people have to pay the price for peace.

FRED HAMPTON, *Black Panther*

Throughout this struggle for racial justice I have constantly asked God to remove all bitterness from my heart and to give me the strength and courage to face any disaster that came my way.

THE REVEREND MARTIN LUTHER KING JR.

He who fears is literally delivered to destruction.

HOWARD THURMAN

All people of goodwill are moved by truth when it is honestly and sincerely told. . . . So your first concern must be to tell the truth without rancor or bitterness.

THE REVEREND MARTIN LUTHER KING JR.

We are not born revolutionary. Revolutionaries are forged through constant struggle and the study of revolutionary ideas and experiences.

JAMES FORMAN
Black Power Activist

Look for me in the whirlwind.

MARCUS GARVEY

We prefer death to slavery.

A GROUP OF AFRICAN WARRIORS *in revolt against their captors*

THE MANY FACES
OF SUCCESS

Success is a journey, not a destination.

Traditional

Black people have to stop apologizing for success. Success is a journey, not a destination. You're always going to reach for it. My earnings will allow my homies to sit up in a nice hotel, or fly around the world five times.

ICE T

Money is sharper than a sword.

Ashanti proverb

My father taught me that the two most important things in life are—you have to pay the rent, and second you have to do what you love. And that is really the way I look at things. You can get confused when your sense of responsibility to the world isn't necessarily doing what you love. You don't realize that the real success in your life is based upon doing what you love to do.

WALTER MOSLEY

The thing that makes me happiest, that's what I do for a living. And when you have that, there's really nothing you can complain about.

SPIKE LEE

I love what I'm doing.

BETTY CARTER, *Jazz Singer*

I'm still the person I was when I was nine. I just love singing. I was always taught to accept success humbly and thank God for my success and know that He is the only reason I received it. That's what my mother taught us.

TEVIN CAMPBELL
Singer, on his eighteenth birthday

Society can place judgments, pressures and expectations on a public figure. Fortunately, I learned from my father to follow my heart and only answer to God. It frees you from a lot of pain and heartache.

ARSENIO HALL

By the time I was twenty I'd experienced things people well into their thirties haven't gotten to yet. I had my own house, I'd made and lost my first million. I'd won a Grammy, traveled the world.

WILL SMITH

The success of the race depends on science and religion.

MARCUS GARVEY

I prayed and I worked hard for success.

BRANDY NORWOOD, *Singer*

I worked hard.

REGGIE MILLER, *NBA Superstar*

My mother taught me that nothing worthwhile is gained without hardships or determination, and I attribute whatever success I may have had to her. I call her every day.

DOROTHY DANDRIDGE

[Don't] set your goals to be a star. Set your goals to be the best that you can be and go from there.

DOMINIQUE DAWES
Olympic Gymnast

Failure is a word I don't accept.

JOHN JOHNSON
CEO, Johnson Publishing Co.

The greatest inventions in the world had hundreds of failures before the answers were found . . . I can't accept failure. Everyone fails at something. But I can't accept not trying.

MICHAEL JORDAN

By trying often, the monkey learns to jump from the tree.

African folk saying

You don't know what you can do until you try.

African-American folk saying

Success is within your grasp. If you believe it is possible, you can make it happen. If you decide to become negative and believe that things will never be right, you will also have those results. So, be very careful what thoughts you put in your mind. For good or bad, they will boomerang right back to you.

BEATRYCE NIVENS
Beating the Odds: Success Strategies
for African Americans

Opportunities are like doors that swing both open and closed. Once the door of opportunity closes, it may never open again.

Traditional

Successful people know how to seize opportunity—not tomorrow, not later on today, but right now!

LES BROWN
Live Your Dreams

Opportunity is not a lengthy visitor.

West Indian folk saying

Seize the day. Seize every moment of the day. Why wait when you can do it right now?

ROLANDA WATTS, *Talk Show Host*

A man can do as much as he wants, but not as long as he likes.

West Indian folk saying

If we are to succeed we must communicate.

BOB JOHNSON
CEO, Black Entertainment Television

Motown is still very much a part of me. It's my legacy.

BERRY GORDY

When I was at Motown we made movies, we did TV shows, we made records, we made deals.

SUZANNE DE PASSE

I never made a point of defending anything. I was too busy moving forward.

BERRY GORDY

... That's when I suddenly saw Berry Gordy, one of my main idols, sitting at a desk with five stacks of money. He sat there and paid off person after person, and you know what, after he paid off all of those people, he still had five stacks of money left! I said right then and there, that is the business I want to be in.

CHARLES UNDERWOOD
Independent music mogul

The reason I became a ballerina of the Metropolitan Opera was because I couldn't be topped. You don't get there *because,* you get there *in spite of.*

JANET COLLINS

[S]ome of us get successful, and we start thinking that white folks are loving us. But sooner or later they remind you that you're still a nigger in their eyes.

SPIKE LEE

One of the real hurtful things that's happened since we got married is that I've taken a lot of criticisms for marrying a light-skinned man. I fell in love with a black man. He's [David Justice] very light, but he's still black. He's discriminated against every day—in baseball and in life. A few months ago in a restaurant in Atlanta, a lady just told us we were "nuttin' but niggas."

HALLE BERRY, *Actress*

A key criterion for success is how you use your pennies, not just how you manage your dollars.

HAKI MADHUBUTI
Founder, Third World Press

By concentrating on what resources we have, rather than on those that we lack, we have something to build upon.

GEORGE C. FRASER

I think it takes a certain masochism to stay in this industry, having to put on a ton of makeup and eyelashes and these big clothes and go out there and say "Yessir, yessir, yessir." Despite the glamour and fun, actors are really low men on the totem pole and aren't really treated all that wonderfully well. So my advice to any young people who ask me is to be producers, directors, writers, not performers.

LONETTE MCKEE, *Actress*

I don't know the key to success, but the key to failure is trying to please everyone else. Do what you want to do.

ARSENIO HALL

I'm extremely ambitious. I don't know why people are afraid to say that. I won't sell my soul to the devil, but I do want success and I don't think that's bad.

JADA PINKETT, *Actress*

The best role models are those who tell you of their failures and how they turned them into successes.

JOHN LUCAS, *NBA Coach*

If we as a people all around the world looked at and paid heed to the teaching, philosophy and wisdom of our ancestors such as Marcus Garvey we would have the keys to success.

ALTON MADDOX

Lower your head modestly while passing, and you will harvest bananas.

Congolese proverb

We are prone to judge success by the index of our salaries or the size of our automobiles, rather than by the quality of our service and relationship to humanity.

THE REVEREND MARTIN LUTHER KING JR.

Those of us who do "succeed" must remember that the freedoms and protections that enable us to study, work and achieve are the fruits of the labor of so many other folks. If you get there—to success that is—you will not have gotten there on your own.

DR. JOHNETTA B. COLE
President, Spelman College

Always leave the door open for a lost dog.

Traditional wisdom

Celebrity is people pointing you out in drugstores and shopping malls.

HAKI MADHUBUTI
Founder, Third World Press

Richard [Pryor] will say that, but that's like the teacher who taught Einstein. I was the first black comedian that stood up and was able to do comedy in white clubs. Before that, it didn't happen. But if there's anybody who should get credit for protecting First Amendment rights, it's Richard.

DICK GREGORY
responding to a question suggesting that
he paved the way for Richard Pryor

Work! There ain't no shortcuts!

JOHN CHANEY
Basketball Coach, Temple University

Sports: Stars and Superstars

We were like the New York Yankees. We had that winning tradition, and we were *proud*. We had a strict dress code—coat and tie, no baseball jackets. We stayed in the best hotels in the world. They just *happened* to be owned by black people. We ate in the best restaurants in the world. They just *happened* to be run by blacks. And when we were in Kansas City, well, 18th and Vine was the center of the universe. We'd come to breakfast at Street's Hotel, and there might be Count Basie or Joe Louis or Billie Holiday or Lionel Hampton.

BUCK O'NEIL
Kansas City Monarchs, Negro Leagues

Integration came because of economics. The major league teams drew small crowds during the war and they panicked. Those owners saw us play in their own stadiums and pull 35,000 the day after their teams drew 6,000. They thought black players would pull black crowds and help them out at the box office. They were right.

GENE BENSON
Philadelphia Stars, Negro Leagues

Well, I got on the horn and said, "Now hear this! Now hear this! The Dodgers have signed Jackie Robinson." You should

170

have heard the celebration. Halfway around the world from Brooklyn, we were hollering and firing our guns into the air.

BUCK O'NEIL
Kansas City Monarchs, Negro Leagues

I used to have talks with Jackie Robinson not long before he died, and he impressed upon me that I should never allow myself to be satisfied with the way things are. I can't let Jackie down. The day I become content is the day I cease to be anything more than a man who hit home runs.

HANK AARON

In every sport we enter in large numbers we change how it's played and coached.

ARTHUR ASHE

We weren't a minstrel show. We didn't just pile into a Cadillac and pick up a game here and there. We had a schedule. We had spring training. We had an all-star game. Most years, we had a World Series. We were professional ballplayers.

BUCK O'NEIL
Kansas City Monarchs, Negro Leagues

I knew I could be a big man in baseball, a little man in basketball and a broken man in football. I made the right choice.

DAVE WINFIELD

Everybody got dressed to the nines to go to the ball game, not like today, when people dress like they're going to rake leaves. Negro leaguers, especially the big ones, were the event of the week.

CHARLIE BIOT
New York Black Yankees

Baseball filled me like music. I played most of my life and I loved it. Waste no tears on me. I wasn't born too early. I was right on time.

BUCK O'NEIL
Kansas City Monarchs, Negro Leagues

Negro League hitters were smart. They would deliberately hit to the opposite field, bunt, fake bunts, and swing. They always had the hit and run on. Major league hitters were not smart. They'd bunt with a fast man on first, but never again. When I came up to the Dodgers, I found pitching against the major leaguers a breeze. It was much harder getting Negro Leaguers out. After my first year on the Dodgers, I made a list in my hotel room of Negro leaguers who were better than the Major Leaguers I pitched against. I had thirty-five names on the list.

JOE BLACK
Baltimore Elites, Negro Leagues
Brooklyn Dodgers, Major Leagues

Sometimes, I think the Lord has kept me on this earth so long as He has so I can bear witness to the Negro leagues.

BUCK O'NEIL
Kansas City Monarchs, Negro Leagues

The house seemed big when we first got it, but then the boys grew so big and my mom lived with us, too. She died last fall. We always made room for each other.

There were some days I would be behind with bills and the money needed for the boys just wasn't' there. And I would be back in that bedroom on my knees in prayer and crying. I would pray, "Lord, help me to raise my kids." I know sometimes they would hear me. But I tried never to let the kids see me upset. I would tell them, "I can't buy you all of the name-brand clothes or what some of the other kids have." They were close to the same size then, so they could share their clothes. We shared nearly everything.

LUCILLE McNAIR
Mother of Alcorn State's football star, Steve McNair

What's mine is also my family's. Always has been that way. Always will be.

STEVE McNAIR
*commenting on his multimillion-dollar
pro football contract*

When the moon is not full, the stars shine more brightly.

African folk saying

When I started raising my kids, I looked around and saw how children were getting out from under their roofs and running away from everything they had been taught at home. I wanted my kids to have the same upbringing I had been taught at home. The kids loved to play football but they knew that work came first. And when they forgot that, they were punished, but I always let them back out to play football afterward. I wanted my kids to be raised to be respectful, and around here, that's the only way you are raised. So, this was good for them. They always listened. I am fortunate to have had that.

LUCILLE McNAIR

If you're black, you have to walk on water or be gone.

DOUG WILLIAMS
NFL Quarterback

I told him it was fine to shoot to be better than Fred but to not think of his brother as competition. Blood is thicker than water.

I told him Fred was a good influence on him. Learn from him, but don't make him the enemy.

> LUCILLE MCNAIR TO STEVE MCNAIR
> *about his teenage desire to beat his older brother's*
> *sparkling athletic and scholastic reputation*

When I was growing up there were no black players in the NBA; if you had some talent the most you could hope for was a spot on the Harlem Globetrotters.

> DR. DICK BARNETT
> *New York Knicks*

I'd like to see a black manager get a quality ball club for once. It would be nice to see a black not get the worse team.

> HAROLD MCRAE

Nothing is going to be handed to you. You have to make things happen.

> FLORENCE GRIFFITH JOYNER

When I was running, I had the sense of freedom, of running in the wind. I never forgot all the years when I was a little girl and not able to be involved. When I ran, I felt like a butterfly.

> WILMA RUDOLPH

There's nothing greater for a human being than to get his body to react to all the things one does on a ball field. It's as good as sex; it's as good as music. It fills you up.

> BUCK O'NEIL
> *First Baseman, Kansas City*
> *Monarchs, Negro Leagues*

Records are made to be broken.

JIM BROWN

Here's what sprinting is all about. It's Evelyn Ashford chasing records set by Marita Koch and Marlies Gohr. It's Heike Drechsler chasing the records set by Ashford. It's me chasing records set by Drechsler. It's the wanting and the hard work that go into the chase.

FLORENCE GRIFFITH JOYNER

The common denominator among [jump] shooters is that we all worked hard to develop our shot. I don't think kids do that today. These days you don't go to the playground to shoot your J. You got to try to dunk on someone's head. I did that, too, but I always brought my jump shot with me.

REGGIE MILLER, *NBA Star*

There are a million excuses for not paying the price.

MICHAEL JORDAN

Shooting is concentration and rhythm, and sometimes it is pure confidence.

REGGIE MILLER, *NBA Star*

In a sense, we were all probably better back then because the game didn't come all that easily to us. The players today probably have more natural talent and get less out of it than we did fifteen and twenty years ago.

WALT FRAZIER, *NBA Star*

I was not going to let anyone hurt me or make me feel anxious. I'd learned something by then. If I could control myself, I could make *them* feel anxious.

LENNY WILKENS, *NBA Coach*

A little rain each day will fill the rivers to overflowing.

Liberian proverb

As a player, you don't go out to be liked. You earn that respect.

SCOTTIE PIPPEN, *NBA Star*

Our great defensive tackle [was] Big Daddy Lipscomb. He adopted me, took me under his wing. He said, "I'm going to make you the best tackle in the game."

In the off-season he'd be at my house every morning at 5:30. We'd go out to the park at Sparrow's Point and work on technique. He'd pull out this big sheet and say, "O.K., here are the defensive ends you're going to be playing against in this league." He taught me which ones go inside, which go outside, which ones like to take that half a step cheat-step to the right; he taught me about the speed rushers and bull rushers, how to set up and keep my back straight against the guys who try to bowl you over.

Big Daddy was what I call a football fanatic, because he knew every aspect of the game. He would have made a great coach.

JIM PARKER
NFL Hall of Famer

Move your neck according to the music.

Ethiopian proverb

I made sure I never set the same way twice, never gave a guy the same look. I watch guys now, and they'll get beat, and instead of figuring, O.K., I've got to give him a different look, now a different technique, they'll do the exact same thing and get beaten exactly the same way.

JIM PARKER
NFL Hall of Famer

The opportunity that God sends does not wake up him who is asleep.

Senegalese proverb

You don't have to be seen to be heard.

Traditional wisdom

Black male college basketball players continue to be bounced through the educational system, leaving scores of them without degrees and with uncertain futures after helping to raise millions of dollars for their respective universities.

BETSY M. PEOPLES AND ALVIN A. REID
Journalists

The colleges have helped reinforce the very strong perception that one will have a very good chance in life if you pursue a career in sports. But it's just not so for most people.

ARTHUR ASHE

That's [academic success] what the word "student-athlete" is all about. The first word is "student" and you shouldn't forget that. The phrase is not "athlete-student," so that should be indicative of what an athlete's priorities should be.

DR. GREGOR K. P. SMITH
Athletic Director

It's always exciting to sit in the stands and cheer for my favorite players and teams. However, it's disheartening to find out that most of the Black student-athletes get slam dunked when it comes to graduating.

BETSY M. PEOPLES, *Journalist*

Imagine the impact it would have if the top athletic prospects began to decline offers because the university generally doesn't do well by African-Americans and is not taking any steps to correct the problem.

> CHARLES S. FARRELL
> *National Director, Rainbow*
> *Commission for Fairness in Athletics*

Do not let the ball play you, you play the ball.

> LAFAYETTE STRIBLING, *Coach*

I make no claims to perfection. I stumbled like everyone else. But I managed to get my degree and accomplish a few things.

> KAREEM ABDUL-JABBAR

I want a Chief. I want all my players to be like Robert Parish. One face.

> JOHN CHANEY
> *Coach, Temple University*

He equips you more for manhood than for the NBA. On most NBA teams it's all free-flow. Temple players aren't used to that. They're used to structure. It becomes a habit to do what you've been told rather than to improvise. But out in society every one of them is making a positive impact. I love the man ...

> MICHAEL HARDEN
> *about John Chaney, his basketball*
> *coach at Temple University*

Prayer is as important as road work.

> JOE FRAZIER

I gave up a lot of things and accepted Jesus Christ into my life.

CRIS CARTER, *NFL Star*

If you want to run like a man, you have to train like a man and [lifting] weights are the main factor.

FLORENCE GRIFFITH JOYNER

... when I participated in the world of sports . . . We stuck with the basics: determination, inspiration and hard work.

WILMA RUDOLPH

Most people used to look at what I *couldn't* do, but when I got involved in sports, they began to look at what I could do.

JENNIFER JOHNSON
World-Class Wheelchair Athlete

Let the legend grow.

EARL WOODS
Father of Golfer Tiger Woods

You ever go up to a tee and say, "Don't hit it left, don't hit it right?" That's your conscious mind. My body knows how to play golf. I've trained it to do that. It's just a matter of keeping my conscious mind out of it.

TIGER WOODS

I'm not a political scientist; I'm just a sports fan who also reads. But I can count. And what I see on TV each weekend tells me that if black folk can influence anything, it ought to be sports. How about a game where the price of admission is a bag of groceries for the needy, or a student report card with no D's, or U's or Fails? Even having a say in where new stadiums are built would have an impact on the communities that produce these athletes in the first place. Besides producing team captains we need to produce corporate captains.

TONY COX, *Writer*

EMPLOYEE OR
ENTREPRENEUR:
THE WORLD OF WORK

Be the best! Be the best!

DR. RONALD MCNAIR

If you want to be the best, baby, you've got to work harder
than anybody else.

SAMMY DAVIS JR.

It is easy to excel at what you are good at. So, work hard and
explore your talents.

TONYA BOLDEN, *Author*

Last hired, first fired.

Traditional wisdom

You were looking for a job when you found the one you just
lost. You'll be looking for a job when you find the next one.

Traditional wisdom

We must not only be able to black boots, but to make them.

FREDERICK DOUGLASS

It is no shame at all to work for money.

Ashanti proverb

Without question my work ethic comes, in large part, from my father. He had his faults—and I know I have mine—but one thing that he always taught us was that, irrespective of the situation, a man works. Right now I work five jobs.

HARRY EDWARDS

I believe in universality, in working all over the place. We have to know and be there in every field if we're going to survive.

GORDON PARKS

When I was a girl, I had my fantasies, but one fantasy I never had was that one day my prince would come, and I'd be spared the need to work. . . . I believe my parents did absolutely the right thing in preparing me to work and take care of myself. So, I'm a working woman and proud of it.

BETTY WINSTON BAYE
Journalist, Activist

Cultural diversity in the work place is no longer a moral objective; it's a business necessity.

PRISCILLA LISTER

It does no good to have a diverse workforce if you don't listen to their opinions and thoughts.

DEBORAH S. KENT
Plant Manager, Ford Motor Company

The first impression of your aspirations you give a potential employer in an interview is in your attire.

SHARWYN DYSON, *Educator*

Today's competitive job market is another good reason to consider career planning. In the current market, job slots are at a premium and only well prepared, astute applicants land jobs. You can no longer approach job hunting casually.

BEATRYCE NIVENS
The Black Woman's Career Guide

The only choice permitted us is either to be servants for $7.00 a week or portray them for $700.00 a week. It is much better to play a maid than be one.

HATTIE MCDANIEL, *Actress*

My advice is to stay out of journalism schools that don't stress a strong liberal arts background. The who, what, when, where, how and why formula in journalism will serve you well so long as you have an understanding or a foundation that is rooted in an understanding of the economic, political and social issues and problems of the world.

CHARLAYNE HUNTER-GAULT

I hope we can pay teachers the salaries that they deserve. It is absolutely [horrifying] that we have given such a poor status level to the most important shapers of human character and development we have in this country.

JEWEL PLUMMER COBB

There are a lot of stories that turn me on. Why shouldn't I be as free as any of the white producers who produce black films and black television.

SUZANNE DE PASSE

I have to be a mind reader and a poet. I translate emotions into flowers.

SANDRA PARKS
Founder, the Daily Blossom

The depression came and most black people could not tell the difference.

Traditional wisdom

In corporate America, you have to work just as hard—if not more so—to gain the approval of others as you do to put out quality work. And when you do put out work of exceptional quality, your rewards are relatively minuscule—unless you're the CEO of something. Maybe you'll get a 2 percent raise for all your efforts. But by putting that same effort and care into your own business, you can perhaps double, even triple your income—and eliminate the organizational politics to boot.

MARSHALL BROWN, *Entrepreneur*

I am not bragging, but at this stage in my career, I could easily run a major division. No question about that. However, I do not like beating someone else's drum, so it would have to be one heck of an offer.

CHARLES UNDERWOOD
Independent music mogul

I've always felt that if we try hard enough, we can do a lot of things.

JAMES M. WOODS SR., *Entrepreneur*

Set your goals. Make the commitments, and stick with them until they become a reality.

SANDRA BATES, *Entrepreneur*

Find a need and fill it. . . . A young man on his way up should keep his eyes open. He should study the people around him. How do they live? What makes them tick? What do they want? Out of these questions, out of a real need, came the first substantial Gaston Business.

ARTHUR GEORGE GASTON
Entrepreneur, Millionaire

Stop talking and do something. . . . You have to do something to make your dream real.

. . . You have to do your homework. And there is no excuse for not doing the necessary research.

MARSHALL BROWNE, *Entrepreneur*

Make the most of the resources that are already at your immediate disposal.

The Network Journal

I opened my doors with no clients and my mother as the receptionist.

ROBERT H. ALEXANDER JR.
Attorney-at-Law

Black entrepreneurs have to recognize that there is lots of money to be made outside of the U.S. and that we have to get away from traditional [business] ways. As technology expands and offers more opportunity, we've got to be able to link on to different ways of doing business, diversify, if we're going to be a player.

LORRIE GRANT, *Journalist*

There can be only a single dominant force within a business.

BERT MITCHELL, *CEO*

My slogan is if it don't fit don't force it. In other words, if you can't make it, don't fake it. Let somebody else take it.

MOMS MABLEY

Being independent is where it's at for many reasons. One, you are working for yourself and not just making someone else rich. Second, as an independent you have your ears closer to the ground and can spot the latest trends new ideas, and not be hampered by bureaucrats and accountants. We independents allow the majors to stay in their ivory towers, because we are the ones who discover the new stuff. Rap, alternative, punk, you name it, the independents were there first. We independents just need to stick together a bit more so that the majors don't come in and eat us alive with their big bucks.

CHARLES UNDERWOOD,
Independent music mogul

In my career as an artist-businessperson, I've found it necessary to maintain a hands-on attitude regarding all my activities. That's the only way to insure things go your way.

QUEEN LATIFAH

Regardless of what show business seems to be from afar, it's hard work, and what separates the women from the girls is one's willingness to strike a balance between show and business.

BETTY WINSTON BAYE
Activist, Journalist

There are four main principles for a successful business. Choose your clients very selectively; hire only high-quality people; always do what's best for the firm and its clients; and develop a strategic plan that identifies the markets you want to target.

BERT MITCHELL
Accountant, CEO

Employment is the big issue the government needs to be dealing with.

DELLA SIMMONS, *Detroiter*

Just look around and you see the systematic disemployment of black men that white America imposes on blacks.

DERRICK BELL

The struggle is much more difficult now because racism is more entrenched and complicated.

ANGELA DAVIS
Political Activist, Professor

It is a waste of words to talk of ever enjoying citizenship in this country.

JOHN B. RUSSWURM

The way it normally works is that an editor will take a young reporter under his or her wing and pass the craft along, give him good stories, show him what mistakes he made. But the craft was not taught to black people—so I stole it.

LES PAYNE, *Journalist*

Black professionals must focus on crashing the glass ceiling, while upholding their integrity.

CARRIE B. ROBINSON, *Writer*

Being a black man in American is like having another job.

ARTHUR ASHE

Trying to land one's first job is the most formative experience of [black] youth.

NELSON PEERY

[N]o race can occupy a soil unless that race can get as much out of that soil as any other race gets out of it.

BOOKER T. WASHINGTON

It is imperative that Black women in corporate settings make efforts to befriend and support one another.

C. R. SALTPAW, *Computer Programmer*

While specific success rates may vary across networks, one thing is clear: Black women, having finally begun to move into positions of power and influence in both the public and private sectors, are uniting to open up opportunities for other black women.

CAROLYN ODOM STEELE

Ensuring the progression of younger generations in publishing requires that the all too few of us who have long experience in the business share our knowledge and resources with them. To do this calls for sacrifice and integrity.

MARIE DUTTON BROWN

Ensuring the intergenerational progression of black women in corporations requires that women support each other's efforts, share their resources, and lend advice and counsel.

CAROLYN ODOM STEELE

We must successfully transfer to the next generation of leadership the business principles that enable us to survive and thrive.

BERT N. MITCHELL, *CEO*

It's not about teaching. It's about doing and being allowed to do. What I can give them or say to them is, "You've got to *work* to get better." What I've been able to offer them are *jobs*. And, in the meantime, I put in a dose of skill. I can talk about what I've gone through, why this works and that doesn't. They're eager and really listen. They're in a hurry to cram it all in a short space of time, and that's okay because things these days are in a hurry.

> BETTY CARTER, *Jazz Singer,*
> *about the generations of young*
> *musicians she has employed*

Miles [Davis] was always moving forward and developing his music. It never ceased during his life, and I think Betty [Carter] is the same way. She's not happy to just settle back and do the set routine. Many vocalists find something that's comfortable and stick with it, but Betty is constantly looking for the next movement *forward*, for something that gives a piece a little something extra special.

> DAVE HOLLAND, *Bassist*

Once you know the ultimate goal is to succeed then you are selective about the cases you agree to take. You have to be selective to succeed.

> ALTON MADDOX, *Activist, Attorney-at-Law*

To negate our hard-won achievements and carefully developed skills (as classically trained musicians) by suggesting that we should now be hired by color is to render meaningless an entire life's work.

> MICHAEL MORGAN, *Conductor*

It is currently so fashionable to speak of self-help and personal responsibility that little attention is paid to institutional barriers to black economic development.

> JULIANNE MALVEAUX
> *Economist, Activist*

When you are rich, you are hated; when you are poor, you are despised.

Ashanti proverb

I learned a lot from my papa about coping with institutionalized racism. The way to succeed was simple: You had to be better at what you did than any of your white competition. That was the main thing. But you couldn't be too smug about it, or white folks would feel threatened.

Sadie Delany
Having Our Say: The Delany
Sisters' First 100 Years

To survive in today's marketplace, we must be smarter, faster and more determined to win.

Andrea Davis Pinkney
Editor, Business Analyst

Wanting the American Dream is not enough; you must be armed with an approach that works. Sure, succeeding involves learning the rules and playing by them even before you land your first job, but it comes down to being prepared! Before writing your résumé and beginning your job search, do your homework.

The Minority Career Guide

If you are committed to pursuing your dreams, you too must expect that you will run against those who feel you can't do the job.

Mary Hatwood Futrell
President, International Teachers Union

Little things are man's work. Nothin' we can do about big things, about God's work. But little things infuriate me, because there's no excuse not to manage them.

John Chaney
Basketball Coach, Temple University

Racism exists in some form or other everywhere. The key to succeeding in a workplace where you are the only Black person is to hold strong to your *internal* power. Remember, you define how good you are at what you do. Don't blame outside forces for your failures or credit them for your successes. One of the stumbling blocks many African-Americans face is that we become emotionally crippled by workplace racism. Take the emotion out of work. From nine to five, lead with your head, not your heart. Find mentors you trust and who support you emotionally. Call on them when you want to vent your frustrations, after hours.

ANDREA DAVIS PINKNEY
Editor, Business Analyst

Once you understand what your work is and you do not try to avert your eyes from it, but attempt to invest energy in getting that work done, the universe will send you what you need. You simply have to know how to be still and receive it.

TONI CADE BAMBARA
Novelist, Lecturer, Activist

The best thing that ever happened to this industry was competition. We can't ever again become complacent about any indicators, not quality, not costs, not our customers.

DEBORAH S. KENT
*Plant Manager, Ford Motor Company,
who manages a complex assembly
line that stretches 19.5 miles*

*Hey Mr. Foreman, slow down this assembly line,
I don't mind workin, but I do mind dyin.*

BLACK AUTOWORKERS' LAMENT

PLANNING'S POWERFUL FRUIT

If you don't know where you are going, any road will take you there.

African proverb

Before the Negro race can successfully combat with all the hinderances which are now appearing, it must equip itself with nerve, ability, aggressiveness, and all the intellectual powers that can be attained. To accomplish anything along these lines, one must sacrifice time, money and pleasure. Spending all of your time in saloons will not make you a Booker T. Washington; standing on the street corners will not give you the inspiration to be a Dunbar; the pool room will not make of you the great benefactor to yourself or race as was Fred'k [*sic*] Douglass. If you would have the oratorical powers of an M. S. B. Mason, a close study of good books, a careful literary training and an exhibition of will-power and a determined ambition would be an important factor in qualifying you for that line of work.

W. A. LEWIS
Writer, Activist, 1907

See today, but remember tomorrow's coming.

Haitian proverb

Set your goals, but learning to do the steps in between is the surest way to get there.

MILDRED GREENE
Armchair Philosopher

Intelligence is based on anticipation and planning.

ALTON MADDOX, *Esquire*

You cannot build a house for last year's summer.

Ethiopian proverb

I set goals and go after them.

JERRY RICE

For couples, financial planning must be a family affair. Aside from individual resolutions, you must think about how your decisions will affect your significant other, which may help or hinder your quest to make your goals a reality.

GRACIAN MACK

He who does not mend his clothes will soon have none.

Nigerian proverb

The Holy Bible is a source of help and inspiration on a range of financial matters, including lack, abundance, greed, debt, stewardship, and sharing.

TONYA BOLDEN, *Author*

Ideally in a marriage where both partners are contributing financially, I think that living expenses should be split so that a certain percentage of the income can be used just for investments.

THERESA GARDNER, *Entrepreneur*

Prioritizing your goals is an essential in financial planning.

GRACIAN MACK

A little rain each day will fill the rivers to overflowing.

Kenyan proverb

I try to save a quarter out of every dollar I earn.

DRIEK FARRINGTON, *Entrepreneur*

One cannot both feast and become rich.

Ashanti proverb

Being well dressed does not prevent one from being poor.

Congolese folk saying

He who wears too fine clothes shall go about in rags.

Mauritanian proverb

Even though the old man is strong and hearty, he will not live forever.

Ashanti proverb

There comes a time, though, when you realize you're not invulnerable, that you have to set up things that are relatively guaranteed.

DAVID GREENWOOD

Death does not sound a trumpet.

Congolese folk saying

A pretty basket does not prevent worries.

Congolese proverb

At first financial planning may seem a bit overwhelming, but if you think of it as a guide to a better life you may just find yourself creating your own financial treasure map.

GRACIAN MACK

He who has means does not suffer.

Haitian proverb

Most black companies fold because they've taken on too much debt.

KASSAHUN CHECOLE, *CEO*

A business ventured without clear business plans is a business strategy without a prayer.

ANONYMOUS

Different strokes for different folks.

African-American folk saying

What is bad luck for one man is good luck for another.

Ashanti proverb

The day on which one starts out is not the time to start one's preparations.

Nigerian proverb

Plan today or pay tomorrow.

Axiom

It is best to bind up the finger before it is cut.

African folk saying

He who hunts two rats, catches none.

African folk saying

Step by step. I can't see any other way of accomplishing things.

Michael Jordan

Drop by drop the ocean is filled.

Swahili proverb

The moon moves slowly, but it crosses the town.

Ashanti proverb

Little by little grow the bananas.

Congolese proverb

Piece by piece a bundle is made.

Ugandan proverb

She who goes slowly, goes far.

Ugandan proverb

... You have to perfect the first step and then move on ...

MICHAEL JORDAN

It's your job to create a financial plan that ensures that your nonworking years are indeed golden and not blue.

CAROLYN M. BROWN, *Writer*

To make preparations does not spoil the trip.

Guinean proverb

The earlier you begin to save, the better off you'll be when those retirement years roll around.

CAROLYN M. BROWN, *Writer*

No matter how full the river, it still wants to grow.

Congolese proverb

He who waits for chance may wait a year.

African proverb

Three kinds of people die poor: those who divorce, those who incur debts, and those who move around too much.

Senegalese proverb

Despite such monetary constraints, baby boomers continue to give substantial amounts of money to their adult children and grandchildren, as well as to frail and aging parents. The upshot of this family generosity is that many of them may have to work well beyond age sixty-five.

CAROLYN M. BROWN, *Writer*

If you want to accomplish the goals of your life, you have to begin with the spirit.

OPRAH WINFREY

If you are on the road to nowhere find another road.

Ashanti proverb

ENVIRONMENTAL RESPONSIBILITY: A BLACK THING, TOO

We have not inherited the Earth from our fathers—we are borrowing it from our children.

ANONYMOUS

The fact of killing animals is not as frightening as our human tendency to justify it—to kill and not even be aware that we are taking life. It is sobering to realize that when you misuse one of the least of Nature's creatures, like the chicken, you are sowing the seed for misusing the highest of Nature's creatures, man.

DICK GREGORY

One does not slaughter a calf before its mother's eyes.

Kenyan proverb

Animals and humans suffer and die alike. If you had to kill your own hog before you ate it, most likely you would not be able to do it. To hear the hog scream, to see the blood spill, to see the baby being taken away from its momma, and to see the look of death in the animal's eye would turn your stomach.

199

In like manner, if the wealthy aristocrats who are perpetrating conditions in the ghetto actually heard the screams of ghetto suffering, or saw the slow death of hungry little kids, or witnessed the strangulation of manhood and dignity, they could not continue the killing.

DICK GREGORY

The egg-eater does not know the pain of the mother hen.

Haitian proverb

The stone in the water does not know how hot the hill is, parched by the sun.

Nigerian proverb

Receiving a new bracelet is not sufficient reason to throw away the old one.

African proverb

Health, Food, Habit, and Discipline: An Amazing Relationship

Inside every African-American churns a cultural and physiological stewpot. On the one hand, we bring our heritage and a great many genes from Africa, a continent whose people have for generations been blessed with normal blood pressure, good cardiovascular fitness and relatively little obesity. On the other, colonialism and slavery have immersed us in a Western culture where plentiful food, sluggish lifestyles, disproportionate poverty and deep-seated racism all contribute to heavy hearts and round middles.

KIRK A. JOHNSON, *Writer*

At the root of every black woman's illness is disappointment and sorrow.

ANONYMOUS

The mind is like the body. If you don't work actively to protect its health, you can lose it, especially if you're a black man, nineteen years old and wondering, as I was, if you were born into the wrong world.

NATHAN MCCALL
Makes Me Wanna Holler:
A Young Black Man in America

Within white-supremacist capitalist patriarchal culture, black people are not supposed to be "well." This culture makes wellness a white luxury. To choose against that culture, to choose wellness, we must be dedicated to truth.

BELL HOOKS
Sisters of the Yam:
Black Women and Self-Recovery

The average child receives four times more exposure than an adult to at least eight widely used cancer-causing pesticides in food. The food choices you make now will influence your child's health in the future.

AFRIKAN WORLD COMMISSION
ALL NATURAL FOOD CO-OP

Somewhere between selfish and selfless is self-care.

JULIA BOYD
The Company of My Sisters

When you work you need time to slow down in. It's like the ebb and flow of the ocean. You can't flow all of the time; there are times when you must ebb.

THELMA DINWIDDIE

Forgiving and thanksgiving are the keys to spiritual preparation for healing.

QUEEN AFUA
Heal Thyself

The most important thing to remember is to treat your voice like an instrument. Certainly don't take it for granted. We all know that smoking is bad and pollution, but some things can't be avoided. Things you can do are deal with nutrition and health.

ROBERTA FLACK

Black people who fall under tobacco's spell die at much higher rates than Whites.

HARRIET A. WASHINGTON

To me, cigarettes snuffed out a face's innocence, drawing the features into one big squint, transforming people into unadorable, fuming dragons.

JANET SINGLETON,
*Writer remembering how
cigarette smokers appeared
to her as a small child*

When the cock is drunk, he forgets about the hawk.

Ashanti proverb

The key word, though, is *planning*; good health doesn't just happen. You have to make it happen. Believe me, I know.

VICTORIA JOHNSON, *Author*

Ideally, all of us [physicians] would like to see a pregnancy planned, because planned pregnancies tend to have less complications.

FRED L. DANIELS, M.D.

As soon as I notice that I have gained a few pounds, I take a tall stem glass, fill it with one-third sugar, one-third lemon juice, and one-third water. Mix them together and drink it down. The sugar feeds the body, the lemon juice squeezes everything, and the water washes it away.

JOSEPHINE BAKER

I have realized that keeping my weight under control is a life-long process.

CHRISTINA E. SHARPE, *Writer*

You can't eat everything you see.

BESSIE DELANY

If young people eat better and exercise more, it reduces the chances of developing hypertension, diabetes, heart disease and cancer. I believe that and practice it every day with my kids. I want them to be happy and just enjoy themselves and laugh at themselves. I allow them to be silly so that they will worry less.

ALMENIA FREEMAN WILLIAMS
Physical Education Teacher

Don't take another mouthful before you have swallowed what is in your mouth.

Madagascan proverb

It is not in the tradition of our ancestors to want a small and boyish woman.

LUCILLE CLIFTON

Food has always been a good friend. But now I find I have to give up—or cut down—on things that aren't good for my voice. I love chocolate. But it's very bad for your voice—it just rests there on your vocal chords, and of course, it goes on your hips too. It's the milk involved. It has a tendency to cling to the vocal chords, and causes a lot of phlegm and mucus.

ROBERTA FLACK

The food we eat can be either our poison or our medicine.

QUEEN AFUA
Heal Thyself

Some of my most profound moments and experiences have occurred during periods when I have observed a strict vegetarian diet.

CHARLES JOHNSON
The Electrifying Mojo

Disease is too often a matter of habit.

MILDRED GREENE

A proper diet is a must in managing stress, which can manifest as diabetes, hypocalcemia, high blood pressure, stress, heart disease, obesity and any number of physical ailments.

HARRY X. DAVIDSON, PH.D.

There is no one who became rich because he broke a holiday, and not one who became fat because he broke a fast.

Ethiopian proverb

Take a stand! Aim to be healthy and increase your longevity.

VICTORIA JOHNSON, *Author*

The two strongest tools we have in medicine are diet and exercise.

LINDA VILLAROSA, *Author*

I work out every day. I've been doing that for thirty years. And I'm a vegetarian.

CICELY TYSON

A lot of what we attribute to aging is simply poor nutrition and lack of exercise. The woman who maintains a combination of healthy diet and consistent exercise may notice fewer age-related changes.

ROBERT N. BUTLER, M.D.

If you're eating a nutritiously balanced diet, you'll get all the essential vitamins necessary to sustain not only pregnancy but normal health as well.

FRED L. DANIELS, M.D.

If you smoke and drink and have high blood pressure, you will eventually have complications. You can't do everything to yourself. Chronic abuse of your body takes a toll. So you can't be surprised that taking some medication will not solve the problem.

DR. J. R. TODD

There are some rigid physicians like myself who feel that all drugs should be excluded from pregnancy. And since alcohol is a drug, that should be excluded, too.

FRED L. DANIELS, M.D.

It's never too early to begin raising a healthy child.

MURIEL L. WHITSTONE, *Writer*

We must treat bad habits like enemies; fight them off until they are at bay. And, always be looking for where they might seek an opening for a sneak attack so that you can keep them at bay.

MILDRED GREENE
Armchair Philosopher

You can't expect roots to grow if you don't plant the seed.

GARY BYRD
Radio Talk Show Host

I *do* know my nonsmoking, seldom-drinking, seat belt-wearing ways will not change the fact that life is temporary.

JANET SINGLETON, *Writer*

Your food ought to be able to do your body some good.

DR. J. R. TODD

Before healing others, heal thyself.

Nigerian proverb

A year prior to my going to OA [Overeaters Anonymous], I had turned my life over to the Lord. He had helped me clean up some other areas in my life, but this food issue needed a different approach. I had been sitting there waiting for God to remove my weight problem from me. But not until I humbled myself—and acknowledged that I had a problem that I really could not deal with on my own—did the healing finally begin. I've learned that you *have* to play an active part in your healing.

TRACY REDDICK, *Marketing Analyst*

I drink as much water as I can, because it is still one of the best agents for flushing out the body.

AUDREY EDWARDS
Author, Editor

Avoid fried meats, which angry up the blood. If your stomach disputes you, lie down and pacify it with cool thoughts. Keep the juices flowing by jangling around gently as you move. Go very light on the vices, such as carrying on in society—the social ramble ain't restful. Avoid running at all times. And don't look back; something might be gaining on you.

SATCHEL PAIGE's *rules for longevity*

If you asked me the secret to longevity, I would tell you that you have to work at taking care of your health. But a lot of it is attitude.

SADIE DELANY, *at age 103*

One thing Sadie and I do is stay away from doctors as much as possible. And we avoid hospitals because, honey, they'll kill you there. They overtreat you.

BESSIE DELANY, *at age 101*

Take care of your feet!

TONYA BOLDEN, *Author*

... good health is not something you stumble upon; it's something you really have to plan.

FRED L. DANIELS, M.D.

LANGUAGE

The patterns of what's called "speaking black" have been preserved in the black church, where great preachers shift in and out of vernacular and Standard English. That's part of the magic of African-American oral tradition.

GENEVA SMITHERMAN
Professor, Linguist

All languages to some degree are bastards, created by both rulers and the ruled, kings and proletariat, masters and slaves, citizens and visitors.

HAKI MADHUBUTI

Words mean not only what you want them to mean. Words mean what they mean to the people who understand them.

ANONYMOUS

Black people need to work on their speaking and writing skills to avoid the pitfalls of exploitation, exclusion, and economic illiteracy. Knowing the language of power and finance is gaining clout, not selling out.

GERRARD McCLENDON, *English Teacher*
The African American Guide to Better English

Be skilled in speech so that you will succeed.
Sacred wisdom of ancient Egypt

Language used correctly . . . expands the brain, increases one's knowledge bank, enlarges the world, and challenges the vision of those who may not have a vision.

HAKI MADHUBUTI

I think all the artists who use the black vernacular in this society understand that, to white minds, the black vernacular has always been associated with the idea of being stupid. I guess I feel like part of my mission as an artist—this is what binds me culturally to an Ice Cube and even a Snoop Doggy Dogg—is understanding the beauty and aesthetic complexity in the vernacular.

BELL HOOKS

No word spoken is ever lost. It remains and it vibrates; and it vibrates according to the spirit put into it.

ANONYMOUS

One of the most effective ways to keep a people enslaved, in a scientific and technological state which is dependent upon a relatively high rate of literacy, is to create in that people a disrespect and fear of the written and spoken word.

HAKI MADHUBUTI

People must learn all forms of language, and they must value them.

GENEVA SMITHERMAN
Professor, Linguist

Great events may stem from words of no importance.

Congolese proverb

We have kids in the inner cities who are verbal geniuses, but we call them deficient in school and attempt to eradicate a part of their identity. But by teaching them the rules of language appropriateness, by showing them the similarities between the way they speak and Standard English, you can encourage them without disrespecting them.

GENEVA SMITHERMAN, *Linguist*

Bad language brings bad problems.

Ugandan proverb

We must understand that we will be charged heavily in the work place if we don't have a grasp of Standard English. We should not delude young people into thinking they don't have to learn Standard English.

HILDA VEST

I grew up in Chicago, where all the kids played the dozens, but I never played. The words were too real. You've got to be careful when playing the dozens because someone can get hurt—like yourself.

ROBERT TOWNSEND

Young people need to understand that it's a tool. They also need to be able to use Standard English, or what I call the language of wider communication. But we all need to respect all forms of language. They're all useful and they're all good.

DR. GENEVA SMITHERMAN

I've struggled so hard, you know? It took me five years, I guess, to quit saying ladies and gennerman . . .

SAMMY DAVIS JR.

Therefore, it is a political act to keep people ignorant. We can see that it is not by accident that Black people in the United States watch more television than any other ethnic group and that more of our own children can be seen carrying radios and cassettes to school than books. The point is that it is just about impossible to make a positive contribution to the world if one cannot read, write, compute, think, and articulate one's thoughts. The major instrument for bringing out the genius of any people is the productive, creative, and stimulating use and creation of language.

HAKI MADHUBUTI

In this language we have what we call a civil war.

GIL SCOTT HERON

Language . . . can powerfully evoke and enforce hidden signs of racial superiority, cultural hegemony, and dismissive "othering" of people.

TONI MORRISON
Playing in the Dark:
Whiteness and the Literary Imagination

JUSTICE

Let us realize that the arc of the moral universe is long but it bends toward justice.

THE REVEREND MARTIN LUTHER KING JR.

> *And, your sin-cursed, guilty Union,*
> *Shall be shaken to its base,*
> *Till ye learn that simple justice,*
> *Is the right of every race.*

FRANCES ELLEN WATKINS HARPER, *Poet*

No Justice! No Peace!

AL SHARPTON

How can we have justice on stolen land?

KRS 1

O God is there no redress, no peace, no justice in this land for us?

IDA B. WELLS

And how can I get justice from a judge who honestly does not know that he is prejudiced?

DICK GREGORY

A rising tide will lift all ships.

Axiom

Following the acquittal of the officers in the Simi Valley trial, the King case might have quietly receded into the shadows of history. But the fires of Los Angeles and national outrage over the verdict created the "compelling federal interest" that forced Bush and Barr to heed the advice of black leaders and bring federal charges against the officers.

EARL OFARI HUTCHINSON

Someday there will be a Great Trial. . . . At that Great Trial, I want to be able to plead "not guilty" to obeying laws [set] against humanity.

DICK GREGORY

In the final analysis, the vindication that is promised the oppressed will come not only because it is just, and right and overdue—it will come because it is mandated by Divine Will.

DR. AUDREY T. McCLUSKEY
Professor of English

Right now our societal intent is clear. In Brownsville, the city is at work on a $30 million youth detention center so young people don't ever have to leave the neighborhood, even to go to jail.

GREG DONALDSON

All cornered animals bite.

Haitian proverb

Once you censor Snoop, why not Public Enemy? Censorship is merely putting a band-aid on cancer. What we should be doing is addressing the deterioration of the community that this music stems from.

THE X-MAN
Washington, D.C. Disc Jockey

We are experiencing a hardening of racial attitudes, a rising desperation among the black poor, a coarsening of the quality of urban life, a growing willingness to disregard the Bill of Rights when dealing with certain criminal defendants and an inability to debate our social ills honestly.

ROGER WILKINS

You go down there lookin' for justice, and that's what you find, Just-Us.

RICHARD PRYOR

When you are poor, everything can be blamed on you.

Haitian proverb

Don't fight in the streets; do your fighting in the courtroom.

JOHNNIE COCHRAN JR.
about police brutality

The black men of American have a duty to perform, a duty stern and delicate—afterward movement to oppose a part of the work of their greatest leader. So far as Mr. [Booker T.] Washington preaches Thrift, Patience, and Industrial Training for the masses, we must hold up his hands and strive with him, rejoicing in his honors and glorying in the strength of this Joshua called of God and of man to lead the headless host. But so far as Mr. Washington apologizes for injustice, North or South, does not rightly value the privilege and duty of voting, belittles this emasculating effects of caste distinctions, and op-

poses the higher training and ambition of our brighter minds—
so far as he, the South, or the Nation does this, we must unceas-
ingly and firmly oppose them.

W. E. B. Du Bois

... I think on a practical level, race plays a part in just about
every aspect of America.

Johnnie L. Cochran Jr., *Esquire*

The Sixth Amendment requires that a defendant receive a fair
trial by "an impartial jury." Through much of American history
juries have been neither fair nor impartial toward blacks ...
Prosecutors in nearly every jurisdiction in the country have exploited the hidden racial and personal biases of jurors.

Dr. Earl Ofari Hutchinson

In a court of fowls, the cockroach never wins his case.

Burundian proverb

Injustice anywhere is a threat to justice everywhere.

Dr. Martin Luther King Jr.

In terms of Mike Tyson and Desiree Washington, I refuse to be
put in the position where I have to choose one or the other.
Both of them are part of my family. Part of what happens when
you grow up in a racist society is that you're taught to dichoto-
mize all the time, to make choices that are fundamentally
unhealthy.

June Jordan, *Poet*

The Queen of Sheba was Ethiopian, yet this is the first time a
person of color has ever played the lead in a major biblical

production. The way I see it, when Gina Lollobrigida did the movie the first time, it was an injustice.

HALLE BERRY, *Actress*
about her role in Solomon and Sheba

Where are the women in Black Studies? And, where are the blacks in Women's Studies?

JOHNETTA B. COLE

The fact is, the moment black people give up on our sexism and take advantage of the incredible leadership potential in black women, we can go forward and have a renewed black liberation struggle.

BELL HOOKS

I wonder what would happen if we refused to appear half-naked in videos, stopped tolerating verbal and physical abuse, and refused to let men touch us until they treated us like equals. No, ingrained sexist attitudes would not cease immediately. But brothers would *definitely* stop and think about their actions.

LICHELLI LAZAR-LEA, *Filmmaker*

There is a great stir about colored men getting their rights, but not a word about the colored women.

SOJOURNER TRUTH

We will not be satisfied until justice rolls down like waters and righteousness like a mighty stream.

DR. MARTIN LUTHER KING JR.

There is a subtext to the O. J. Simpson case that is troubling to Afro-Americans: the demonization of black males as violent sexual predators. There is a long history of this and it has often supplied the rationale for the oppression of black men in America, especially the odious practice of lynching. When I was growing up in the south, if white men wanted to eliminate black men as competitors in politics, economics, or the sexual favors of white females they resorted to the ritualized murder of lynching. That's the real reason why most black Americans believe that O.J. may have been framed by jealous white men; it's a function of racial memory.

PLAYTHELL BENJAMIN, *Columnist*

Politics

My grandmother told me about heathens when I was little, but I didn't know they were running the world.

Amiri Baraka

[T]he government they devised was defective from the start, requiring several amendments, a civil war, and momentous social transformation to attain the system of constitutional government, and its respect for individual freedoms and human rights that we hold as fundamental today.

Thurgood Marshall

Structuring decision making to allow the minority "a turn" may be needed to restore the reciprocity ideal when a fixed majority refuses to cooperate with the minority. If the fixed majority loses the incentive to follow the Golden Rule principle of shifting majorities, the minority never gets to take a turn. Giving the minority a turn does not mean the minority gets to rule; what it does mean is that the minority gets to influence decision making and the majority rules more legitimately.

Lani Guinier
The Tyranny of the Majority:
Fundamental Fairness in Representative Democracy

A democratic way of life occurs when we are every day reaffirming the rights of ordinary, everyday people.

Cornel West

I love America more than any other country in the world, and exactly for this reason, I insist on the right to criticize her perpetually.

JAMES BALDWIN
Notes of a Native Son

I take hold of this constitution. It looks mighty big, and I feel for my rights, but there ain't any there. Then I say, "God what ails this constitution?" He says to me, "Sojourner, there is a little weasel [weevil] in it."

SOJOURNER TRUTH

Privilege is anathema to democracy.

NIKKI GIOVANNI

Democratic anything presupposes equal membership in the body politic. But we will never even approximate the equality a democratic state depends upon, we will never even understand the equality each American one of us requires for our rightful self-respect, as along as we will deny all that we feel and need in common.

JUNE JORDAN, *Poet*

At the moment when a people begin to realize a meaning in their suffering, the civilization that engenders that suffering is doomed.

RICHARD WRIGHT

Americans had better watch out, for the political philosophers have warned us that a people will eventually get the kind of government they deserve.

PLAYTHELL BENJAMIN, *Columnist*

I don't believe you can have a peaceful, multiracial society when people are parceled or separated out, ghettoized, Balkanized or however you want to say it. I think people have to learn to live together at a very early age. Because we made mistakes at the first stab at it, at desegregation—I wouldn't call it integration—doesn't mean we shouldn't keep trying to do it, because that seems to me in the long run the only way you can bring about any kind of peaceful, diverse society.

JOHN HOPE FRANKLIN

It is useful here to dispose of one common but rather silly affirmative action bromide: the old question, "Do you really want to be treated by a doctor who got into medical school because of skin color?" The answer is, or ought to be, that the patient doesn't particularly care how the doctor got *into* school; what matters is how the doctor got *out*. The right question, the sensible question, is not "What medical school performance did your grades and test scores predict?" but "What was your medical school performance?"

STEPHEN L. CARTER
Reflections of an Affirmative Action Baby

People have been sitting on my neck or my head for a century, and when I get a piece of my neck out, they start this reverse discrimination cry.

JOHN HOPE FRANKLIN

When we get into medical school we just try like hell and high water to keep from being put out.

RAMONA TASCOE

Sure, graduation rates will rise under Proposition 48—what else are they going to do after you *top off* the bottom? Do you only perpetuate yourself? Is that the only goal of higher education?

To educate the educated? I wouldn't have passed that SAT test coming out of high school. Where would I be? Can an SAT measure heart? If a kid can't read in twelfth grade, it's because he didn't learn in *first* grade! That's where our society needs to start! But we gotta keep the window to heaven open for poor kids! We *gotta* keep the hole open in the sky!

JOHN CHANEY
Executive Committee member
of the Black Coaches Association

. . . Judge Thomas was a man who had used the system to get where he wanted to be, but then felt that everyone else should pull themselves up by their own bootstraps.

DR. JOYCELYN ELDERS

There's no way for the back wheels of the car to catch up with the front wheels if both are moving at the same rate.

WHITNEY YOUNG JR.
on Affirmative Action

Crime and violence starts at the top and trickles down.

BROTHER PROPHET
Sixteen-Year-Old Political Activist

Violence is as American as cherry pie.

H. RAP BROWN

You can give a man some food and he'll eat it. Then he'll be hungry again. But give a man some ground and he'll never be hungry no more.

FANNIE LOU HAMER

It doesn't mean we're [Congressional Black Caucus] going to always be right. But we are going to be principled and let history judge us as it should and as it must.

KWEISI MFUME

Like most black institutions limited by an exhausted liberal vocabulary, the NAACP had little energy or inclination to defend people whose experiences was [sic] alien to its core constituency. For many poor and young blacks, it has become a relic, an ethnosaur.

MICHAEL ERIC DYSON, *Professor*
on the firing of Ben Chavis
as Executive Director and CEO of the NAACP

Negro creative intellectuals must not become political leaders or mere civil rights spokesmen in the traditional sense. To do so means that intellectuals who are creative will be forced to subordinate their potential to the narrow demands of nationalism and civil rights.

The only real politics for the creative intellectual is the politics of culture.

HAROLD CRUSE
The Crisis of the Negro Intellectual

Our cultural and political hearts beat in Africa.

JOHN HENRIK CLARK
Historian Emeritus

I can be critical of the National Book Award or the Pulitzer Prize or the Nobel Prize, but until we as an alternative kind of ideological force in society—not only among black people but throughout the multinational class society that America is—till we have an alternative network of journals, magazines and newspapers and publishing companies, then the views of one particular sector of society will dominate.

AMIRI BARAKA

The number of female-headed households continues to grow among black families. Let it be known that the problem with such households is not that a woman is in charge. The problem is that they are poor households.

JOHNETTA B. COLE

[R]emember that a policy of neglect and containment will lead to more misery and killing.

GREG DONALDSON

The humble pay for the mistakes of their betters.

Bagurimi proverb

I am profoundly frightened by a society where there are people who know so much but do so little for others.

DR. JOHNETTA B. COLE

What we presently need from civil rights organizations is a truly new agenda: Independent monitoring of social programs and public services, favoring neither Republicans nor Democrats. Accurate assessments of the successes and failures of public education, law enforcement, programs to reduce teenage pregnancy, etc. Yearly reports, region by region, major city by major city, of how well our taxes are being used . . . Quite soon, these reports would influence elections, allocations and programs and inspire innovative policies, allowing us to attack the corrupt and the ineffectual elements that undermine the handling of our national problems.

STANLEY CROUCH
Essayist, Critic

Bill Clinton didn't pick me to be a rubber stamp on him. If that was all he wanted, he would have left me in Arkansas.

DR. JOYCELYN ELDERS

Cultural needs and ideals change with the momentum of time; the need to redefine our laws in keeping with the spirit of cultural flux is what keeps a society alive and humane.

PATRICIA WILLIAMS

It's funny how young Black men seem to be the catalytic agent for so much behavior. They even shape the protocol of White baseball executives. And let a young Black woman not be able to find a husband, or a young White man not be able to find a job, or a young Polynesian not be able to resist taking steroids to look good at the beach, and they will tell you it is not their fault, but the residual effect of a young Black man somewhere. I had no idea young Black men were so influential in everyday American life.

RALPH WILEY
What Black People Should Do Now

As a Christian, as an individual, as a doctor, I am absolutely opposed to the death penalty.

DR. JOYCELYN ELDERS

I have consistently maintained that all citizens have the right to go to any country that will admit them, and that newsmen in particular should not be prohibited by the U.S. government from traveling wherever news is breaking.

WILLIAM WORTHY

What the world needs is more love and less paperwork.

PEARL BAILEY

You watch your back. You don't take things for granted. You work real hard and you fight for what you believe in.

KWEISI MFUME
*comparing life in Congress
with life on the streets*

It is amazing that black people still think that people who are not in the social registry can make major decisions. Giuliani [Mayor of New York City] is following orders.

ALTON MADDOX, *Esquire*

Giuliani has been unremittingly insensitive and hostile to blacks by cutting affirmative action programs and other programs that serve them. But the really frightening thing is that he seems to have such overwhelming support. I think his policies will get short-term applause, but in the long run they are going to do a lot of harm.... I told David [Dinkins] that he had better keep his hat and windbreaker handy, because when the riots break out, he is the man they're going to call to calm things down.

DERRICK BELL

And the social security system that all of us count on to support us in our old age will depend on the contributions of fewer children—children we are failing today.... America cannot afford to waste a single child. With unprecedented economic competition from abroad and changing patterns of production at home that demand higher basic educational skills, America cannot wait another minute to do whatever is needed to ensure that today's and tomorrow's workers are well prepared rather than useless and alienated—whatever their color.

MARIAN WRIGHT EDELMAN

The government tends to be more a part of the problem than part of the solution.

RONALD MYERS, M.D.

Racial scapegoating allows white America to hide its problems behind a black face.

LEE A. DANIELS
Editor, Scholar

For many politicians and policy makers, the remedy for racism is simply to stop talking about race.

LANI GUINIER
The Tyranny of the Majority:
Fundamental Fairness in Representative Democracy

Americans have a crisis mentality. We have a riot, and then we rush around trying to talk about race. We should be having an ongoing discussion about how we can heal ourselves.

GWENDOLYN GOLDSBY GRANT
Mental Health Educator

Race has become metaphorical, a way of referring to and disguising forces, events, classes, and expressions of social decay and economic division far more threatening to the body politic than biological "race" ever was ... It seems that it has a utility far beyond economy, beyond the sequestering of classes from one another, and has assumed a metaphorical life so completely

embedded in daily discourse that it is perhaps more necessary
and more on display than ever before.

Toni Morrison
Playing in the Dark:
Whiteness and the Literary Imagination

Indeed, the media's coverage of the recent racially tinged cases
proves, once again, that Black America remains the "mirror"
most white Americans don't want to look into: They don't want
to acknowledge that, because we really are one nation indivisi-
ble, there is no "Negro problem." There is only, as author Gun-
nar Myrdal pointed out fifty years ago, an American Dilemma
which encompasses a wide variety of profound problems. Black
America's burden, unfortunately, is that resolving the dilemma
is what frightens White America most of all.

Lee A. Daniels, *Editor*, Emerge *magazine*
"The American Way: Blame a Black Man"

The function of education in the United States is to develop
citizens who are fully oriented to cultural diversity—and are
not hung up on race.

Albert Murray

If America is to become the country called for in the Declaration
of Independence, then the cosmology of every group must be
treasured.

Johnetta B. Cole

The social problems of urban life in the United States are, in
large measure, the problems of racial inequality.

William Wilson, *Sociologist*

... [I]ntelligence scores by themselves mean almost nothing.
They don't predict who will end up in the boardroom versus

who will end up in the mail room. As we all know, most of that is determined by politics.

BRENT STAPLES, PH.D., *Author*

In the ruling circles of America—on Capitol Hill, Wall Street and corporate boardrooms—the vast economic inequalities between blacks and whites are casually accepted as inevitable. The prevailing attitude is one of callous indifference. But there is nothing inevitable about either poverty or unemployment. They can be eradicated, indeed eliminated with the right mix of government and private initiatives spurred on by activist-oriented civil and human rights movements.

DON ROJAS
Activist, Journalist

There is enough money to solve any problem. It is just a question of where you want to place it.

NORMAN ADLER
Political Consultant

The Negro troops got a taste of racial equality in foreign lands. As they came home, that had to be beaten and lynched and terrorized out of them before they would go back to building levees and picking cotton.

NELSON PEERY
Black Fire:
The Making of a Revolutionary

Aristide and Mandela must not forget that it was the government that gave them a problem.

THE REVEREND AL SHARPTON

The people's pencil has no eraser.

Haitian proverb

God's pencil has no eraser.

Haitian proverb

The rampant corruption, warfare, overpopulation, authoritarian rule and political mismanagement are only symptoms of Africa's morass. The real cause is the colonial legacy.

EARL OFARI HUTCHINSON

There is not a single African nation in Africa. They are all imitation European nations.

JOHN HENRIK CLARK, *Historian*

No matter how long the night, the day is sure to come.

Congolese proverb

The dialectic is a theory of knowledge, but precisely for this reason, it is the theory of the nature of man. Hegel and Marx did not first arrive at a theory of knowledge which they applied to nature and society. They arrived at a theory of knowledge from their examination of men in society. Their first question was: What is man? What is the *truth* about him? Where has he come from and where is he going? They answered that question first because they knew that without any answer to the general question, they could not think about particular questions.

C. L. R. JAMES

Whether one likes it or not, the bourgeoisie, as a class, is condemned to take responsibility for all the barbarism of history, the tortures of the Middle Ages and Inquisition, warmongering and the appeal to the *raison d'Etat*, racism and slavery, in short everything which it protested in unforgettable terms at the time when, as the attacking class, it was the incarnation of human progress.

AIME CEASAIRE

Everyone in American wants to be bourgeois. Face it, most people do. But my parents worked really hard for what they have. My father was born in northeast D.C. to uneducated parents. And he became a dentist and he made money and became successful and instilled his children with a sense of collective.... We're the only people I've ever seen who sort of methodically go about hating their middle class.

JILL NELSON

But if Black Power was condemned with a near unanimity in the white community, it found no early welcome in the black community either. Goaded by the plantation mentality of white editorials and the "we-wuz-robbed" charging of white liberals, the negro Establishment picked up its water buckets of accommodation and threw soothing words of denunciation on the fire of Black Power, precisely as they had been ordered to do by the white contributors controlling their organizations.

CHUCK STONE

Just as it takes the black and white keys of a piano to play "The Star-Spangled Banner" it takes blacks and whites and people of all races to make this city great.

FREEMAN R. BOSLEY JR.
First Black Mayor of St. Louis, Missouri

... But every war, it seems, is ruled by a chap. I wondered if a woman foreign minister was strategizing, talking to another woman foreign minister ... I just think there would be a very different outcome.

JOAN ARMATRADING, *Singer*

The struggle in the 1960s was to get blacks into the political system. The challenge of the '90s is to get the right blacks elected to office. It is not that the political system does not work, we just have not tried it.

THE REVEREND AL SHARPTON

A [black] woman who has already done a lot of things and proven herself is often put in an even higher category than a man.

YVONNE BRATHWAITE BURKE, *Politician*

The government to which we pay our tax monies will be against everything we need and want and will attempt to keep us from making any progress. The way my mother puts it, "It is like Reagan wants to take us all the way back to slavery.

DR. MARY FRANCIS BERRY
Author, Professor of History and Law

Given the disproportionate influence of big money over the electoral political process, elections are a charade [that] masks the real power, privileges, and control of the corporate elite.

RON DANIELS, *Political Activist*

Lord, ain't it good to be an *American*.

ANNIE ELIZABETH DELANY
Having Our Say: The Delany Sisters' First 100 Years

There were some of us who sincerely never saw the sixties as a fashion. It was a newfound understanding, a newfound spirit. A spirit that was to be worn proudly. Black spirit. Beautiful

Black spirit. You see, there were those of us who would continue to deal with the world politically. Nothing would change that.

TONI CADE BAMBARA
Writer, Professor

We formed our own party because the whites would not let us register.

FANNIE LOU HAMER

Reading is a political act.

JANE TILLMAN IRVING, *Journalist*

Our people are just waiting to read words written about them by their own authors. They want to hear these words read. They want to talk about these words. It's affirmation and discovery.

LANA TURNER
Founder, New York Literary Society

The work of the political activist inevitably involves a certain tension between the requirement that positions be taken on current issues as they arise and the desire that one's contribution will somehow survive the ravages of time. In this sense the most difficult challenge facing the activist is to respond fully to the needs of the moment and to do so in such a way that the light one attempts to shine on the present will simultaneously illuminate the future.

ANGELA DAVIS

Media Madness

The fool speaks, the wise man listens.

Ethiopian proverb

There is no greater impact made on our present society than the images seen, the sounds heard, and the drama brought daily by the media.

HARRY BELAFONTE

... the rush for ratings overcame the standards of journalism.

JANINE JACKSON, *TV Journalist*
about the coverage of the O.J. Simpson case

We don't have the luxury that White people have of not identifying with people who are in the news, positive or negative, in a very personal, visceral way, because of our history in this nation.

DONNA BRITT, *Columnist*

He who has done evil, expects evil.

Guinean proverb

Considering how many African-American men are not Bigger Thomas, walking around with a gun, but instead living quiet lives of dignity and responsibility, one often wonders who writes for them.

E. ETHELBERT MILLER, *Anthologist*

It is assumed that all non-Anglo-Saxons are uncomplicated stereotypes . . .

ZORA NEALE HURSTON

We have a right to a diversity of voices. We are diverse. We don't have to all agree on anything.

JILL NELSON

You can have a Top 10 record, and if you're black, they're gonna ask you, "So whatta you think about AIDS?" People who aren't really qualified to speak on stuff are given mikes and a forum. Just because you can dance or shoot a basketball doesn't mean you're an authority on subject matters not in your arena. It's been a drag, because anytime something happens in America or the world to black people, my phone rings off the hook.

SPIKE LEE

When you see black people on television brushing their teeth . . . like everybody else, that says much more than any civil rights activist or orator.

CONSTANCE BAKER MOTLEY, *Federal Judge*

When the NAACP and other black bourgeois organizations succeeded in driving the television version of *Amos 'n' Andy* off the air in 1953 it was both a victory for those stressing the necessity of positive middle-class media images for blacks and a setback in terms of the presentation of genuine black humor in mass media.

MEL WATKINS

People know who Martin Luther King was, but they don't recognize the name Medgar Evers. It appears as though the media allows us to have only one hero at a time.

Medgar was a pioneer. He helped to pave the way for Dr. King.

MYRLIE EVERS-WILLIAMS

They're blowing the whole black-Jewish thing up. There is no conspiracy among African-Americans against Jewish people. I'm sorry. I mean, the average black person doesn't know who's Jewish. It's just another white person.

SPIKE LEE *on the media*

One falsehood spoils a thousand truths.

Ashanti proverb

For various reasons, the average, struggling, nonmorbid Negro is the best-kept secret in America.

ZORA NEALE HURSTON

When it comes to the African American male and the media, materials are slanted and distorted through omission and commission.

EARL OFARI HUTCHINSON

What I've taken away from the coverage of the O.J. Simpson case in general is just how much the corporate goal of media as a profit-making business is in conflict with the goals of journalism to serve the public interest.

JANINE JACKSON, *TV Journalist*

When Blacks do something wrong, the coverage goes no farther than the individual. I think the White media needs to be responsible. And of course, Black people and other people of color have to not let themselves be targets. There's responsibility on both sides.

LEE A. DANIELS, *Scholar*

It is horrendous what they are doing to us on television. They are increasing the numbers of negative images about African Americans. Every time we see anything relative to a lower-income black community, they show criminals, drugs and low-life sex—those kinds of things. Programs like *Roc* and *Frank's Place* don't last long.

CAMILLE COSBY

True culture is built upon a certain measure of restraint, that is, a cultured man remembers that others have feelings like himself.

J. A. ROGERS

There are zillions of wonderful stories to tell, but they—meaning television's controlling, hegemonic strata—won't deal with those stories. They only want to perpetuate what they have always perpetuated: that we are buffoons and mammies and lazy. If you turn on the television today, you will see that; and if you look at old movies that were made in the 1920s, '30s and '40s, you will see the same images.

CAMILLE COSBY

FOR THE LOVE OF MONEY

Virtue is better than wealth.

KENYAN PROVERB

... the by-product ... of capitalism happens to be racism ...
capitalism comes first and next is racism.... When they brought
slaves over here, it was to make money. So first the idea came
... to make money, then the slaves came in order to make that
money. That means that racism had to come from capitalism.
It had to be capitalism first and racism was a by-product of that.

FRED HAMPTON, *Black Panther*

Atlanta must not lead the South to dream of material prosperity
as the touchstone of all success; already the fatal might of this
idea is beginning to spread; it is replacing the finer type of
Southerner with vulgar money-getters; it is burying the sweeter
beauties of Southern life beneath pretence [sic] and ostentation.
For every social ill the panacea of wealth has been urged—
wealth to overthrow the remains of the slave feudalism; wealth
to raise the "cracker" Third Estate; wealth to employ the black
serfs, and the prospect of wealth to keep them working; wealth
as the end and aim of politics, and as the legal tender for law
and order; and, finally instead of Truth, Beauty, and Goodness,
wealth as the ideal of the Public School.

... [The] habit is forming of interpreting the world in dollars
... What if the Negro people be wooed from a strife for righ-

238

teousness, from a love of knowing, to regard dollars as the be-all and end-all of life?

> W. E. B. Du Bois

The worship of money is so intense that kids nickname themselves "money," talk incessantly about "loot" and refer to stealing as "getting paid."

> GREG DONALDSON
> *about teenage life in the*
> *Brownsville section of Brooklyn*

We need to stress the difference between substance and style. The man who drives a Mercedes down the street is not necessarily the man to be respected.

> THADDEUS GARRETT JR.
> *Political Consultant*

Hell yeah, I did it for the money! Ain't nothing wrong with that. Brothers need to do more productive, legal things for the money.

> ICE T

... if there were not a direct relationship between history and money, a direct relationship between history and power, history and rulership, history and domination, then why is it that the European rewrote history?

> AMOS N. WILSON
> The Falsification of Afrikan Consciousness

A man with too much ambition cannot sleep in peace.

> *Bagurimi proverb*

The English economist, J. E. Carines, stated that the state of Virginia alone bred and exported to other states no less than 100,000 slaves in the short span of 10 years (between 1840 and 1850), and each slave was sold for about $500 totaling the huge sum of $50 million. Even George Washington—the first president of the United States of America—sold a slave to the West Indies for one hogshead of "best rum" and molasses and sweetmeats.

LOUISE SPENCER-STRACHAN

When I was a child, my owner saw what he considered to be a good business deal and immediately accepted it. He traded me off for a horse.

DR. GEORGE WASHINGTON CARVER

A man's wealth may be superior to him.

African folk saying

Don't tell your plans to those waiting men who receive presents of old coats from their masters. They will surely betray you.

PETER POYAS

Morally and practically, the Freedmen's Bank was part of the Freedmen's Bureau, although it had no legal connection with it. With the prestige of the government back of it, and a directing board of unusual respectability and national reputation, this banking institution had made a remarkable start in the development of the thrift among black folk which slavery had kept them from knowing. Then in one sad day came the crash—all the hard-earned dollars of the freedmen disappeared; but that was the least of the loss—all the faith in saving went too, and much of the faith in men; and that was a loss that a Nation which today sneers at Negro shiftlessness has never yet made good. Not even ten additional years of slavery could have done so much to throttle the thrift of the freedmen as the mismanagement and bankruptcy of the series of savings banks chartered by the Nation for their especial aid.

W. E. B. Du Bois

Chrysler and Lee Iacocca didn't do it alone. Defense contractors don't do it alone. Welfare queens can't hold a candle to corporate kings in raiding the public purse.

MARIAN WRIGHT EDELMAN

He who loves money must labor.

Mauritanian proverb

. . . The lure of free money is the opening to every sucker game.

NELSON PEERY
Black Fire: The Making of a Revolutionary

It is a spiritually impoverished nation that permits infants and children to be the poorest Americans.

MARIAN WRIGHT EDELMAN
Is the Child Safe?

Marian Wright Edelman isn't a leader because she cares about and works in defense of her own children. Marian Wright Edelman is a leader because she fights for the rights of all children.

JOHNETTA B. COLE
President, Spelman College

The incredible burst of prison construction, the harshness of welfare reform proposals and the unwillingness to put black economic distress on the national agenda are all evidence of the strength and pervasiveness of racism.

ROGER WILKINS, *Journalist*

You are beautiful because of your possessions.

Bagurimi proverb

There exists the idea that there is only so much of the good things in our land—and so each time one group dips in and receives a dipper of goodies, there is that much less for another group. Now this idea is being promoted in the richest and most technologically advanced country in the world.

JOHNETTA B. COLE

The eighties caught us in a peculiar dilemma ... There was a belief that if we could only achieve economic power, then we would be all right. Those views, of course, fly in the face of history that teaches us that in America, even Black men and women with money get lynched, get beaten ... To young people who tell me that they want to be rich and famous, I say, "You'd better have a militia."

TONI CADE BAMBARA
Novelist, Professor

ʃ EX

Sexual chaos was always the possibility of slavery, not always realized but always possible: polygamy through the concubinage of black women to white men; polyandry between black women and selected men on the plantations in order to improve the human stock of strong and able workers.

W. E. B. DU BOIS

White men raped black women for centuries without any conscience of wrongdoing. Sadly, enslaved African American women, being powerless, were beaten savagely by the same demonic hand that caressed and impregnated them.

THE REVEREND ANDREW BOONE

Due to the excess [of] slaves in Jamaica, the planters worked them to death, ignoring all physical and human needs. Like the United States, slaves on the island were not allowed to marry. They had no rights to their persons and, because of the disproportionate number of white males to white females, African females unwillingly became concubines or surrogate wives to their oppressors.

LOUISE SPENCER-STRACHAN
Color Crisis

It seems less degrading to give one's self, than to submit to compulsion. There is something akin to freedom in having a lover who has no control over you, except that which he gains by kindness and attachment ... There may be sophistry in all this; but the condition of a slave confuses all principles of morality, and, in fact, renders the practice impossible.

HARRIET JACOBS
Incidents in the Life of a Slave Girl

But as early sex became the norm for young couples in the late eighties, so did a growing sense of frustration and anger. The door for gentleness quietly closed in all interactions. You couldn't just bump into a brother on the street without fearing he might shoot you. Or look at a sister too hard without fearing she'd straight up cut you.

TARA ROBERTS, *Writer*

... [S]he tried to make me see that sex could be no more than a metaphor for violence if there was no love.

WILLIAM BANKS, *Novelist*

[A]ny passing of money in matters of sex taints the character of him doing the passing.

EWIN JAMES, *Writer*

Pornography emphasizes sensation without feeling.

AUDRE LORDE, *Poet*
Wild Women Don't Wear No Blues

I prayed hard before I began to speak. And when I finished, these kids stood up and applauded. It wasn't because of me, it was because the words I spoke were from truth and love. I wasn't telling them my opinion: that used to be my life. I've been there and it's not about partying, boogie, videos showing girls grinding on the floor. Our kids need to know that today they may look like a prince and princess because they're young.

But at the pace most of these kids are going, they'll look and feel like a dog at an early age. So go slowly and as for sex, stop it now!

LOLA FALANA

It is easy to become a monk in one's old age.

Ethiopian proverb

I'm celibate. And I've been celibate for fifteen years. I just don't see that in my future.

LOLA FALANA

The black men who cheer-led Mike Tyson badly missed the point. Sexual victimization of black women is a serious issue that can't be ignored or lightly dismissed.

EARL OFARI HUTCHINSON, PH.D.

A ladies' club had provided me with an office and a secretary to administer this particular strike, and since it happened that the secretary was single and quite companionable, the two of us disappeared into the city for the weekend. When I surfaced again on Monday, one of the old union hands, Pete Perry, informed me that the strike had been broken while I was off satisfying my urges. "Son," he said, "the human race is perpetually involved in two separate struggles—the class struggle and the ass struggle. If you want to make a difference in this world, it's important not to get your struggles mixed up."

COLEMAN YOUNG
Union Organizer and first
African-American Mayor of Detroit, Michigan

You should never have sex with a man you really don't know anything about. Casual sex and one-night stands can be dangerous to the soul and the body.

The Editors, Essence *magazine*

Don't go to bed with a woman you're not willing to marry in the morning.

NELSON PEERY'S FATHER

If you can't feed them, don't breed them.

Traditional wisdom

To truly make love is to cherish all parts of our partner and ourselves—body, mind, spirit.

The Editors, Essence *magazine*

Men and women should approach sex very slowly from a strong base of friendship.

GWENDOLYN GOLDSBY GRANT
The Best Kind of Loving

Men are pushed into activity so quickly that penetration, not communication, is about the only thing some know.

The Editors, Essence *magazine*

Youth who are not corrupted by base desires are not blamed, and those who control their sexual appetite, their name does not send forth an unpleasant odor.

Sacred wisdom of ancient Egypt

Kwanzaa and Christmas

Kwanzaa was created essentially to reaffirm the common destiny of African American people, to strengthen their common bonds, and to give black Americans another holiday in which to honor their heroes and heroines. From a philosophical point, Kwanzaa was an opportunity to introduce and reinforce the *Nguzo Saba* (the Seven Principles).

RON KARENGA

He who receives a gift does not measure.

Kenyan proverb

This year-end period became the choice for the time of celebrating Kwanzaa for several reasons. First, it would answer the concern for cultural authenticity in terms of time correspondence between Continental celebration and Kwanzaa. Secondly, this time celebration of Kwanzaa fits into the existing pattern of year-end celebrations in the U.S.

RON KARENGA

With the Kwanzaa celebration coming at both the end and at the beginning of the year it gives you time to evaluate the past year and to rededicate yourself to the coming year. In this way it is like Sankofa in the Akan culture of Africa—you look back at the past to get a better idea about what's ahead. It is clearly a holiday about family and peoplehood, and a link to the motherland and the unity of African people.

MALIK CHAKA
Activist, Writer

Kwanzaa is not an alternative to one's religion or faith, but a common ground of African culture which [we] can share and cherish. It is this common ground of culture on which [we] all meet, find ancient and enduring meaning, and by which [we] are thus reaffirmed and reinforced.

RON KARENGA

We often invite our neighbors to participate in the holiday with us. It's all about sharing as we become more aware of our common heritage and the need to build a stronger more reliant community. There is something inspiring and affirming about the spirit of Kwanzaa and we hope it continues to grow each year.

MALIK CHAKA
Activist, Writer

African-Americans have a wonderful opportunity to extend the joy of the season beyond the single twenty-four-hour confines of Christmas in our celebration of Kwanzaa as a harvest of goodwill and renewal. We might even extend the spirit of peace to our national observance of Dr. King's birthday. As a modern-day Christian disciple of peace, the birth of the Prince of Peace could certainly find an appropriate echo in that observance . . . As an African-American, I marvel at the creative possibilities that are present to help our community savor the wonder of the birth of Christ in the happy moments that reflect our own heritage as people of color.

THE MOST REVEREND WILTON D. GREGORY
Roman Catholic Bishop

When I reflect upon Christmas as the celebration of the birth of Jesus the Christ, I am struck by the degree to which the major characters in the birth narratives were willing to make their lives fully available to God. It was clear that once they said yes to God their lives would never be the same. Mary and Joseph planned a marriage, not a life parenting the child of God and Savior for the world. Even Mary's cousin Elizabeth, mother of John the Baptist, rejoiced at the news that she would become a childbearing, child-rearing senior citizen. Life for each of these ordinary people was forever changed by their availability.

My prayer for the Christmas season is that more of us will be inspired to make our lives available to God for the Divine mission of justice and peace on the earth. Indeed our lives would be forever changed, but so would our world. We would be agents of God who put Mary's song into action. We would continually "lift the lowly and fill the hungry with good things." We would do this good work, not for the holiday, but for life. We would put the spirit back into Christmas because the spirit would be active in our lives.

THE REVEREND PRATHIA HALL WYNN, *Pastor*

Jesus is alive today, born of a woman and God is his father.

THE REVEREND GEORGE FOREMAN
Heavyweight Champion of the World

... It is a message of joy and happiness as the whole Christian world celebrates the birth of our savior, Jesus Christ.

We celebrate the day when the Son of God became the Son of Man. We celebrate the day when the Son of the Highest stooped to the lowest, a day when the King of Glory shed his splendor and became poor that we through his poverty might be rich.

... Christmas is and should be, the happiest, most joyful time of the year.

THE REVEREND ARTHUR M. BRAZIER, *Pastor*

It is difficult for many to remember that Christmas is religious in character because of this commercialization.

DR. KENNETH B. SMITH, *Theologian*

Most people don't plan. They think happy holidays are just supposed to happen, like when they were kids.

DR. JOYCE HAMILTON BERRY, *Psychologist*

If you recognize what you have, then what you don't have will become less significant, or at least it will be put in perspective.

LAURENCE COLEMAN, *Futures Trader*

Single people should not sit around talking about "I ain't got no man or woman." That's not how to spend the holidays. You should be counting your blessings and thinking about how you don't have anyone worrying you or pulling you down. Everything that we need for happiness, we have already been given.

ELAINE R. FERGUSON, M.D.

Family, faith and friends are the three things that really make the holidays happy for me. Those are things that money can't buy.

KONRAD L. DAWSON, M.D.

Christmas is the gift of God's love. Let us be inspired to give a little of our own.

DR. KENNETH B. SMITH, *Theologian*

We can put the spirit back into Christmas by not only remembering the birth of the Christ child, but also by working to save the lives of all children.

THE REVEREND SUSAN D. NEWMAN, *Pastor*

To put the Spirit back into *CHRISTMAS* is to make further identification between the *CHRIST* of *CHRIST MASS* and the sheep of his pasture—the Black sheep, that is. Jesus was a home-body, descended through "Black and comely" Solomon; as a baby, taken down into Black Egypt to hide him from the wrath of Herod, demonstrating the efficacy of hiding chocolate among chocolate, not vanilla.

THE REVEREND CECIL I. MURRAY, *Minister*

You can't hide no blond, blue-eyed child in Harlem. . . . It was government that sanctioned the death of young black men after Jesus's birth. Here we are two thousand years later and it is the government that sanctions the killing of young black men today. The wicked won't change their tactics.

THE REVEREND AL SHARPTON

The true meaning of Christmas has become obscured, if not obliterated, by our genuflection before the golden calf of materialism.

PLAYTHELL BENJAMIN
Essayist, Novelist

Too many of us are celebrating Christmas and looking at figures that don't look nothing like Christ . . . They have made Santa Claus the figure of Christmas. They use this image, this distortion to pimp children on what should be a Holy day. To do this is blasphemous, ungodly.

THE REVEREND AL SHARPTON

Truth is, no matter how fat your bank account, there are just some things that money can't buy, things like friends and family and love and laughter, as you will find out the first time you wrap yourself in shoulder-to-hem mink, slide behind the wheel of a shiny new Benz and drive to the most exquisite restaurant in town to eat Christmas dinner or ring in the New Year—alone.

LAURA B. RANDOLPH, *Columnist*

How do you celebrate somebody's birthday by giving yourself a gift? You celebrate Jesus by doing what he preached.

THE REVEREND AL SHARPTON

The greatest gift of all was born in a barn.

THE REVEREND GEORGE FORMAN
Heavyweight Champion of the World

Christmas is giving thanks—to God, to family, to friends. Crassness is giving things—to impress, to placate, to influence. Christmas is opening a mind. Crassness is opening a charge account. Christmas is showing kindness. Crassness is showing off ... Crassness is about worshipping the almighty dollar. Christmas is about worshipping the Almighty.

LAURA B. RANDOLPH, *Columnist*

Let's put Christ back into Christmas. O, come let us adore Him—not each other.

TONYA BOLDEN, *Writer*

LET'S STAY TOGETHER

Hold a true friend with both thy hands.

Kanuri proverb

Loneliness thrives on unforgiving and hardness of heart.

THE REVEREND GARDNER C. TAYLOR
Pastor Emeritus

A good friendship makes you feel at ease.

Ugandan proverb

In terms of our relationships, it is time for Black Americans to sound a wake-up call. It is time to reexamine how we talk to each other, how we view each other. We need to pull back on that and see that too often these are very destructive and self-destructive things.

EARL OFARI HUTCHINSON

Mutual gifts cement friendship.

Ivory Coast proverb

There is a great stir about colored men getting their rights, but not a word about the colored women; and if colored men get their rights, and not colored women theirs, you see the colored men will be masters over the women, and it will be just as bad as it was before. So I am for keeping the thing going while things are stirring; because if we wait till it is still, it will take a great while to get it going again. I want women to have their rights.

SOJOURNER TRUTH

The notion of limited good—that every advance by a black woman is at the expense of a black man—and therefore should not be—ultimately leads to the notion that you can buy one group's freedom off of another's slavery.

DR. JOHNETTA B. COLE

If two horses are fighting, the grass underneath their hoofs will suffer.

Nigerois proverb

Black men and women have far more to gain by finding common ground than by allowing resentments or outmoded ideas about gender-defined roles to separate them.

DRS. DEREK S. AND DARLENE POWELL HOPSON
Authors

Living life as art requires a readiness to forgive.

MAYA ANGELOU
Wouldn't Take Nothing for My Journey Now

No problem in a relationship is ever so black and white that one person is solely to blame.

DRS. DEREK S. AND DARLENE POWELL HOPSON
Authors

Take your chances and don't pity your circumstances. Taking your chances makes you a free agent; feeling pity turns you into a victim.

GWENDOLYN GOLDSBY GRANT, *Advice Columnist*

Beauty with no brains and no morals is a complete turnoff to me.

MATTHEW LAWSON

It is not a person's physical appearance that matters.

Ugandan proverb

We black men need to feel in control at home, because we can't get it anywhere else. Almost all black men work for somebody. We don't have no control in the workplace. A woman can get anything she wants out of a man if he loves her, and if she pretends to let him be in control.

ICE T

There are two types of people in your life. Those who nourish you, and those who drain you. Those who help you grow and those who are *toxic* to your growth.

LES BROWN

A close friend can become a close enemy.

Ethiopian proverb

Beautiful teeth do not necessarily mean he's your friend.

Haitian proverb

You gotta be careful who you let close. They're the only ones who can hurt you.

JOHN CHANEY

No person is your friend who demands your silence, or denies your right to grow.

ALICE WALKER

Do not leave your friends alone at the dinner table or your enemies will multiply.

SAM CHEKWAS, *Author*

An old man can't do nothin' for me but bring me a message from a young man.

MOMS MABLEY

Men will cheat on a woman, give the other woman his home phone number, not tell her that he has a girl, and then come home all late smelling like sex.

ICE T

Two flavors confuse the palate.

Ivory Coast proverb

If you do not step on the dog's tail, he will not bite you.

African folk saying

Men chase, women choose.

ROBERT VAN LIEROP, *Esquire*

Being an old man's darling is better than being a young man's fool.

Traditional wisdom

It's important to have role models who challenge you, who are willing to say they don't agree with you.

EVELYN MOORE

Don't ever talk down to somebody by talking less than you are able.

BRYANT GUMBEL'S FATHER *to his son*
about the use of coarse language

He had a great sense of perspective. He knew the importance of family, of education, of occupation, of religion.

BRYANT GUMBEL *about his father*

In all my years of involvement with girls, I had always been loved by the parents and dumped by the daughters.

BILL COSBY

When I got into my addiction, people I thought were really my friends weren't.

JOHN LUCAS, *NBA Coach*

Every shut eye ain't sleep. Every good-bye ain't gone.

Traditional wisdom

We must learn to deal with people positively and on an individual basis.

MARY MCLEOD BETHUNE

In order to have a healthy and happy relationship, both parties must have some of their expectations met. But, both parties must also be willing to put aside self and meet the other partner's expectations. One of the biggest problems in relationships is that couples have not learned how to be friends.

PASTOR THEODORE JOHNSON
Marriage Counselor

Romantic relationships should be entered into with an attitude of negotiation and the knowledge that relationships are not always fifty-fifty. There may be times when there will not be an even compromise.

MONIFA HAKIM, *Writer*

Bryant's taught me not to be so afraid. When I was growing up in Detroit, I was always so terrified. Every time my father left to go to Ford's, I was afraid we were going to find him lynched because he had married a white woman and had these mixed kids. I still have the same fear for Bryant, who is the sweetest, gentlest, most spiritual man I've every met, that he'll get shot because his skin is black and he has dreads. But since he's come into my life, the world isn't half as terrifying.

LONETTE MCKEE, *Actress*

Despite all the talk about a shortage of Black men, here's a fact: It may be true that there are not enough doctors, lawyers, MBAs and professional sports figures to satisfy every sister; however, there are plenty of good, kind, sincere, decent, loving men.

GWENDOLYN GOLDSBY GRANT
The Best Kind of Loving:
A Black Woman's Guide to Finding Intimacy

Defying a history of horror and a nowness of brutality, Black men glisten with strength; sparkle with wit and glow with love.

MAYA ANGELOU

I love Black men for the incredible strength in the face of the rage, the racism and the rancor they must face on a daily basis. Movie and media images of Black men in trouble and in crisis permeate our lives while every day, all across the country, millions of Black men go out and do what they do like nobody else on the planet: raise their children, serve their communities, love their women. Like millions of Black women, I know the special joy of marriage to a strong Black man with whom you share the same struggle. Only a Black man can truly understand the fight and the plight of our people. For me, that fight is made infinitely easier because of David [Justice]. When I see him across the room, or wake up and see his face, I'm always renewed because I never have to explain myself or feelings to him. He understands my pain because it is his pain; he understands my struggle because it is his struggle. What bond can be more powerful? What love can be more profound?

HALLE BERRY, *Actress*

I love Black men because when I put my hands on my hips and say, "You better go away from me," they just look at me and say, "Come on here baby" and you come on. I don't think any other man in the world could talk to me like that but a Black man and make me feel good.

JACKIE HARRY, *Actress*

Black men are like precious minerals. They allow negative experiences and pressures to work for them and we see those results all around us . . . *diamonds*.

CHANTE MOORE, *Singer*

I've never been afraid or alone in my life.

BESSIE DELANY
Having Our Say:
The Delaney Sisters' First 100 Years

It takes two to make a quarrel.

Ivory Coast proverb

If you tell people to live together, you tell them to quarrel.

Congolese proverb

Life is a balancing act of meeting your needs and the needs of those around you.

LAVERNE MARKS, *Social Worker*

People do not want to be treated as if they are invisible.

LES BROWN

Just because a man breaks up with his wife he's not going to jump into the arms of the first woman he sees.

THE REVEREND AL SHARPTON

The monkey knows which tree to climb.

West Indian saying

You never miss the water until the well runs dry.

Axiom

Don't drink the bush [herbs] for another man's fever.

West Indian saying

Nobody is going to choose who I relate to; just like who I relate to is not going to choose what I do.

THE REVEREND AL SHARPTON

The spine of my life, intellectual and otherwise, has essentially been Ruby.

OSSIE DAVIS

The ant travels while spreading its teeth.

Ugandan proverb

Widen your options and start noticing men you may not have noticed before.

GWENDOLYN GOLDSBY GRANT
Advice Columnist

What I didn't foresee was how much their lives would spill over into mine; how they would shape the choices I made. I was too young to know that in many ways you become who you love, but one day I would wake up and find that instead of simply sleeping with trouble, I was engulfed by it.

PATRICE GAINES
Author, Journalist,
Wild Women Don't Wear No Blues

There are those of us who reside in a universe of perfected equilibrium. Others are caught in an uncontrollable lurch whose unwieldy motion began generations ago. Still others are the wild flowers who survived; or the lonely whose abandonment began in centuries past.

PAULA GIDDINGS
Professor of Women's Studies

Find yourself before you look for a man.

GWENDOLYN GOLDSBY GRANT
The Best Kind of Loving:
A Black Woman's Guide
to Finding Intimacy

The major thing Black women can take from *The Assassination of the Black Male Image* is the determination to not stereotype, categorize or typecast Black men. There is diversity among African American men just like there is diversity among white men, among Asian men and among Latin men.

EARL OFARI HUTCHINSON

It is the calm and silent water that drowns a man.

Ashanti proverb

One who runs alone cannot be outrun by another.

Ethiopian proverb

From Genesis to Revelation God is telling us how we may have a positive relationship with Him.

THE REVEREND GARDNER C. TAYLOR
Pastor Emeritus

LOVE

Agape is understanding creative redemptive goodwill toward all men. Agape is an overflowing love which seeks nothing in return. Theologians would say that it is love of God operating in the human heart. When you rise to love on this level you love all men not because you like them, not because their ways appeal to you, but you love them because God loves them.

MARTIN LUTHER KING JR.

The Bible tells us that "Love never quits. It is not possible to stop love." Today we have weakened the meaning of love. We have reduced it to a sentimental feeling.

THE REVEREND LUCIUS WALKER JR.

Love is like a baby: it needs to be treated tenderly.

Congolese proverb

Part of my soul went with him.

WINNIE MANDELA

Life is a short walk from the cradle to the grave—and it sure behooves us to be kind to one another along the way.

ALICE CHILDRESS
A Short Walk

Imagine a society in which every woman *and* man is a nurturer!

DR. JOHNETTA B. COLE

To love someone who does not love you is like shaking a tree to make the dew drops fall.

Congolese proverb

I was madly in love with him at that stage, and so was he with me in his own way. It was such a mutual feeling and understanding that we didn't have to talk about it.

WINNIE MANDELA
Part of My Soul Went with Him

Baby, any and every burden . . . God cares.

TONYA BOLDEN
Just Family

God loves you, child; no matter what, he sees you as his precious idea.

INDIA ANETTE PEYTON
Melba Patillo Beals'
grandmother in Warriors Don't Cry

We didn't look at it as being poor because you don't know you're poor until you actually get out into the world. The love and the family support overshadow that in my life.

WILMA RUDOLPH

Self-denial is not a very popular word in our English vocabulary and yet the only way to live out the spirit of love which

Paul and Jesus taught us is to know that we must, in practicing love, step outside of our own comfort zone.

THE REVEREND LUCIUS WALKER JR.

Following and doing for the Lord made me more peaceful and love-oriented.

MELBA MOORE

The teeth are smiling, but is the heart?

Congolese proverb

If the heart is sad, tears will flow.

Ethiopian proverb

It seems as if a large percentage of talented Black people, men and women, end up marrying people other than Black people after they get pseudo-rich and semifamous. I hate to see the talent and the wealth dispersed, but on the other hand, what fool would try to legislate against the power of love? ... When people are in love, there's no reasoning with them, anyway.

RALPH WILEY
What Black People Should Do Now

When one is in love, a cliff becomes a meadow.

Ethiopian proverb

Don't be so much in love that you can't tell when the rain comes.

Madagascan proverb

Love is like a magnet that draws us to the highway of life.

THE REVEREND LUCIUS WALKER JR.

Hearts do not meet one another like roads.

Kenyan proverb

God is longing to love you.

Tonya Bolden
Just Family

Mutual affection gives each his share.

Ivory Coast proverb

I had so little time to love him, and that love has survived all these years of separation. I'm not trying to suggest that he is an angel. Perhaps if I'd had time to know him better I might have found a hell of a lot of faults, but I only had time to love him and to long for him all the time.

Winnie Mandela
Part of My Soul Went with Him

Thought breaks the heart.

African proverb

She had to love and not be scared, and show the cat that it did not need to growl to protect itself.

Rita Dove
Poet Laureate of the United States
through the ivory gate, *a novel*

When the heart overflows, it comes out through the mouth.

Ethiopian proverb

Dine with a stranger but save your love for your family.

Ethiopian proverb

Talking with one another is loving one another.

Kenyan proverb

[O]ne cannot have both compassion and innocence.

EUGENIA COLLIER
Breeder and Other Stories

Life is the first gift, love is the second and understanding is the third.

ANONYMOUS

Psychologically, you cannot save yourself until you love yourself.

JOHN HENRIK CLARK

If we love ourselves, we love Africa and the Caribbean. We are indissolubly joined.

RANDALL ROBINSON

I collect black memorabilia and I love Aunt Jemima. I do. No matter how they try to depict her as being fat, black and ugly . . . she symbolizes for me what has held us in good stead all of these years.

MAXINE WATERS

Absence makes the heart forget.

Kenyan proverb

... a vocabulary grounded in forgiveness ... is the real foundation of love.

MARITA GOLDEN
Wild Women Don't Wear No Blues

Sorrow is like a precious treasure, shown only to friends.

Madagascan proverb

The best and most beautiful things cannot be seen or touched. They must be felt with the heart.

ANONYMOUS

Love is like young rice: transplanted, still it grows.

Madagascan proverb

Let your love be like the misty rain, coming softly, but flooding the river.

Madagascan proverb

[Mother] believed in bonding, believed in love. "Love is the only thing we have that never runs out. You can't empty a cup of love. The more other people drink from it, the fuller it is."

GLORIA WADE-GAYLES
Professor of English

The heart is not a knee that can be bent.

Senegalese proverb

Parents render lessons about love in subversive, ironic ways.

MARITA GOLDEN
Wild Women Don't Wear No Blues

He may say that he loves you. Wait and see what he does for you!

Senegalese proverb

Men fall in love with what they see. Women fall in love with what they hear.

ROBERT VAN LIEROP, *Esquire*

... he had the irresistible beauty of someone who had found his place.

RITA DOVE
Poet Laureate of the United States
through the ivory gate, *a novel*

You don't have to have a college degree to serve. You don't have to make your subject and verb agree to serve. You don't have to know about Plato and Aristotle to serve. You don't have to know Einstein's theory of relativity to serve. You don't have to know the second theory of thermodynamics in physics to serve. You only need a heart full of grace; a soul generated by love.

JOHNETTA B. COLE

It's up to black men to provide more than love at this point in history. It's up to the black man to provide a presence, a buttress. We have to get busy working business plans. Love has to wait, not according to me, but according to the way America has treated black men and women so far, which is to say, to try to get rid of us. Sometimes work comes before love. We do love you sisters, we love you because you brought us here, every ... one of us ... Hang in, hold on ... For as Sterling Brown once revealed, "strong men keep coming."

RALPH WILEY
What Black People Should Do Now

You catch more flies with sugar than vinegar.

Traditional wisdom

Don't try to make someone hate the person he loves, for he will still go on loving, but he will hate you.

Senegalese proverb

Now, when I close my eyes and images of uncles and widowed aunts flicker before me—men who died and women who cared for them—I understand the meaning of love and the profound connection between life and death.

MIRIAM DeCOSTA-WILLIS
Wild Women Don't Wear No Blues

. . . and almost everyone, as I hope we all know, loves a man who loves to listen.

JAMES BALDWIN

The time that we spend in friendship is a practical investment in our lives: One of the fringe benefits from this investment is love.

MILDRED GREENE
Armchair Philosopher

If you can't hold them in your arms, hold them in your heart.

CLARA "MOTHER" HALE

I leave you love. Love builds. It is positive and helpful. It is more beneficial than hate. Injuries quickly forgotten quickly pass away. Personally and racially, our enemies must be forgiven. Our aim must be to create a world of fellowship and justice where no man's skin, color, or religion is held against him. "Love they neighbor" is a precept which could transform the world if it were universally practiced. It connotes brotherhood and to me, brotherhood of man is the noblest concept in all human relations. Loving your neighbor means being interracial, interreligious, and international.

MARY MCLEOD BETHUNE

I run on faith and love.

JUNE JORDAN

Who knows at what point of discouragement and despair the simplest act of love may reach a soul and turn it again to the light? This simple act of love taught me that my family of origin might never be there for me, but in the providence of God many others have been sent to reach out and to touch my life with love, concern, compassion, and care.

LINDA M. HOLLIES
Doublestitch:
Black Women Write About
Mothers and Daughters

Being judgmental prevents us from loving.

SUSAN L. TAYLOR

I love [my mother] totally without wanting her to change anything, not even the things about her that I cannot stand.

BELL HOOKS

MARRIAGE

We are looking for a real righteous brother. An all grown up, ain't scared of nuthin', and knows it's time to save the race righteous brother. A good father/good husband/good lover/ good worker/good warrior/serious revolutionary righteous brother ... We are looking for a real good brother. We are looking for a brother who will turn the ships around.

PEARL CLEAGE
Deals with the Devil

When we first started dating we would talk on the phone for hours. We'd just tell stories about growing up, our families, and all kinds of stuff. I think that's what really created our bond.

TRACEY EDMONDS
Wife of Kenny "Babyface" Edmonds

When I married Tracey, she became my partner for life and I became hers.

KENNY "BABYFACE" EDMONDS

Now I just can't think about me ... Now I have to consider how decisions I make will affect David, and he has to do the same with me. Now I have to check with my partner. It's a challenge.

HALLE BERRY, *Actress*

One must talk little and listen much.

Mauritanian proverb

The one who gives the blow forgets. The one who gets hurt remembers.

Haitian proverb

Woman without man is like a field without seed.

Ethiopian proverb

If a friend hurts you, run to your wife.

Ethiopian proverb

Since I've been married I've learned to be more giving. I know that every decision I make in my life affects Kenny . . .

TRACEY EDMONDS

Marriage is about building a family. I'm very committed to the idea of being married and to the idea of creating a family, and to keeping it together [despite] whatever we may go through.

KENNY "BABYFACE" EDMONDS

A home without a woman is like a barn without cattle.

Ethiopian proverb

A woman who stands behind her man will not be able to see where *she* is going! But when one person stands alongside another, there is an increased strength and 1+1=11!

JOHNETTA B. COLE

Marriage is not a fast knot, but a slip knot.

Madagascan proverb

One of the best ways a young couple can make a marriage work out is by communicating openly and honestly and then being through with it. Don't harbor little, old feelings.

LILY JEAN RUSSELL
married forty-two years

Every day I discover that being supportive of a high-profile woman beats competing with her.

ARTHUR J. ROBINSON JR.
married to Johnetta Cole

Do not order your wife about in her house when you know she keeps it in excellent order. Do not ask her "Where is it?" or say to her "Bring it to us" when she has put it in the proper place. Watch her carefully and keep silent and you will see how well she manages. How happy is your house when you support her.

There are many men who do not know this. But if a man refrains from provoking strife at home, he will not see its inception. Thus, every man who wishes to master his house, must first master his emotions.

Sacred wisdom of ancient Egypt

In Africa, where the families and community are actively involved in helping to select mates and sustain marriages, the divorce rate is about five percent.

JAWANZA KUNJUFU
Educator, Writer

There was an urgency in almost everything [Medgar] did. He was never mine, totally. He belonged to his people, the struggle, and his country.

MYRLIE EVERS-WILLIAMS

He who marries a beauty marries trouble.

Nigerois proverb

If slavery had been abolished, I also could have married the man of my choice; I could have had a home shielded by the laws ... all my prospects had been blighted by slavery. I wanted to keep myself pure; and under the most adverse circumstances I tried hard to preserve my self-respect; but I was struggling alone in the powerful grasp of the demon slavery.

HARRIET JACOBS

It's [marriage] an everyday job. I've learned if you want it to work, you have to respect it. And that means it has to come first, before everything else in your life.

HALLE BERRY, *Actress*

But wishing each other well is something that you have to practice doing—wishing each other well and believing that your light will shine also.

RUBY DEE

Home is where I know true peace and love.

ANITA BAKER

Well, I made up my mind that, given infidelity, I would have to do battle. Because I'm not willing to let this man go for any such reason. I want him. So if you want something, you put your weight on it. You just get in there and fight for it.

RUBY DEE

Marriage was invented so children would have a chance to grow.

OSSIE DAVIS

Someone once asked me my marital status, and I said, "happy woman," that's all I can tell you.

NTOZAKE SHANGE

Belonging is one of their [Ruby Dee and Ossie Davis] favorite themes, and they firmly believe that belonging to Black people, to marches and pickets and kids, is one of the greatest things in the world for a marriage; that the life and health of the family is, in fact, inextricably tied to the life and health of the community.

KHEPHRA BURNS

A good marriage belongs to the vital statistics of any people. It is a credit to the group they belong to.

OSSIE DAVIS

I have had seven marriages, all with the same man. The phases of our marriage have been so distinct that each has seemed like a separate entity. Not all of them were happy, but they were all healthy in that they served the purposes of our family in productive ways. This year (1996) we celebrate our thirty-first wedding anniversary. Our success can be attributed to a recognition on both of our parts that as we changed many of the assumptions of our relationship also changed. The only constant is love.

DR. BESSIE W. BLAKE, *Dean*
College of New Rochelle,
School of New Resources

I'd rather pay a young man's way from here to California than to tell an old man the distance.

MOMS MABLEY

My marriage to Medgar was probably the most significant thing to happen in my life.

MYRLIE EVERS-WILLIAMS

A solid monogamous union can, in the right hands, be a tool for sculpting the most exciting treasures from the material of the known, the established, the safe and secure.

TINA MCELROY ANSA
Novelist, Wild Women Don't Wear No Blues

People jump into marriage without realizing it takes work and time.

T. C. CARSON, *Actor*

If you can find your soul mate, marriage is a wonderful, wonderful union!

KIM COLES, *Actress*

I believe in marriage. That's why I haven't jumped into it. When I go there, I want it to be for real.

ERIKA ALEXANDER, *Actress*

For those couples fortunate enough to be in longtime unions, the keys to longevity lie in commitment, trust, friendship and love.

LYNN NORMENT
Writer, Editor

There has to be a commitment to the marriage. You have to be there for the long haul, through the good and the indifferent. Most people have the perception that marriage is always a honeymoon trip. And that's not real. You have to be committed to the partnership so it will last.

DR. SHARON AMES-DENNARD
Clinical Psychologist

Couples have to talk about what they expect from each other.

BILLY DAVIS, *Singer*

There is no secret to a long marriage—it's hard work ... It's serious business, and certainly not for cowards.

OSSIE DAVIS

Don't look where you fell, but look where you slipped.

Liberian proverb

My husband and I function as partners, not only in marriage, but in terms of business. It should be that way. There are a lot of discussions, and there is a lot of respect for each other as well. We are a team.

CAMILLE COSBY

Marriage is a beautiful institution.

WHITNEY HOUSTON

Any woman who has a husband who does what I do for a living and gives birth to two human beings and nurtures them to splendidly promising adulthood is the honoree.

BERNARD SHAW
accepting the Sol Taishoff Award for
Excellence in Broadcast Journalism

DEDICATION, DISCIPLINE, AND MOTIVATION

Be diligent as long as you live, always doing more than is commanded of you.

Sacred wisdom of ancient Egypt

You should concentrate on the heights which you are determined to reach, not look back into the depths to which you once fell.

MARTIN LUTHER KING JR.

He who starts behind in the great race of life must forever remain behind or run faster than the man in front.

BENJAMIN E. MAYS

Blacks must earn their way to higher achievement.

THURGOOD MARSHALL

A man who will not labor to gain his rights is a man who would not if he had them prize and defend them.

FREDERICK DOUGLASS

Black is dutiful.

RICHARD BARTEE

First forget *inspiration*. Habit is more dependable. Habit will sustain you whether you're inspired or not. . . . Habit is persistence in practice.

OCTAVIA E. BUTLER
Bloodchild and Other Stories

Christ was a revolutionary person, out there where it was happening. That's what God is all about, and that's where I get my strength.

FANNIE LOU HAMER
*a founder of the Mississippi
Freedom Democratic Party*

What motivates me is a sense of accountability to people who are important in my life. There are a lot of people I can't let down.

RICHARD D. PARSONS
CEO, Dime Savings Bank

My family is my life.

ANITA BAKER

Take responsibility for every area of your life.

Axiom

It doesn't matter what you are trying to accomplish. It's all a matter of discipline.

WILMA RUDOLPH

The summer after I graduated, I was at Columbia Pictures for an eight-week internship. I saw a dearth of faces of color. I just knew that if I wanted to get through, I would have to go the independent route.

SPIKE LEE

The role of the genuine scholar is not only to understand the world, but to help to change it.

JOHNETTA B. COLE

The right mental attitude is more important than knowledge.

DENNIS KIMBRO
Think and Grow Rich: A Black Choice

In the scale of life, what's important? My belief in God. My family. And being accountable for who I am. If these three things are in place, all other things are attainable.

LENNY WILKENS, *NBA Coach*

There is one helluva difference in fighting in the ring and fighting in Vietnam.

MUHAMMAD ALI

My career change was just a moral and ethical thing.

DICK GREGORY

And I just really asked God, because I believe in God, I asked God to give me a chance to just let me do something about what was going on in Mississippi.

FANNIE LOU HAMER

Everybody on the bus was shaking with fear . . . [but] then this voice singing church songs just came out of the crowd and began to calm everybody. . . . It was then that I learned that Fannie Lou Hamer was on the bus. Somebody said, "That's Fannie Lou, she know how to sing."

CHARLES MCCLAURIN, *Freedom Rider*

The pleasure you get from your life is equal to the attitude you put into it.

ANONYMOUS

So I set a goal of becoming a starter on the varsity. That's what I focused on all summer. When I worked on my game, that's what I thought about. When it happened, I set another goal, a reasonable, manageable goal that I could realistically achieve if I worked hard enough.

MICHAEL JORDAN

The tragedy in life doesn't lie in not reaching your goal. The tragedy lies in having no goal to reach. It isn't a calamity to die with dreams unfulfilled, but it is certainly a calamity not to dream. It is not a disaster to be unable to capture your ideal, but it is a disaster to have no ideal to capture.

BENJAMIN E. MAYS

People who expect to achieve their goals don't stand around talking about them.

LES BROWN

Life is not easy. If you want to have it together you've got to work hard.

EMANUEL FRANCOIS, *Tailor*

People have to go after their dreams and goals. Be true to yourself, because if you're not, it will show.

QUEEN LATIFAH

The man on his feet carries off the share of the man sitting down.

Guinean proverb

Sleep is the cousin of death.

Congolese folk saying

Sitting is being crippled.

Ethiopian proverb

I have never ever set out to be a role model. I set out to be the best actress I could be.

CICELY TYSON

Employ your spare time.

JAMES WELDON JOHNSON

Time is a thief ... and the things we wanted to say must be waiting somewhere like the things we wanted to do and never did.

KIM MARIA JONES-BROWN

When I decided to make the transition and become a pop performer, I had to sit down and learn pop music with the same discipline and approach that I learned classical pieces.

ROBERTA FLACK

One must stretch beyond self for greatness.

RALPH WILEY

Your world is as big as you make it.

GEORGIA DOUGLASS JOHNSON

Go after whatever you want. But, don't step on anybody to get it. Just step over them.

VICKIE WARD'S FATHER

When everyone around you is trying to fill you with their dreams, you must stop and fill yourself with your own dreams.

A MOTHER *to her college bound son*

All during my college course I had dreamed of the day when I could promote the welfare of my race.

MARY CHURCH TERRELL

In my music, my plays, my films I want to carry this central idea: to be African. Multitudes of men have died for less worthy ideals; it is even more eminently worth living for.

PAUL ROBESON

Medgar died for the NAACP. I am living for it.

MYRLIE EVERS-WILLIAMS

I must attribute my motivation and my desire to be an artist to the people of the black community.

JACOB LAWRENCE, *Painter*

Without the church experience, I don't know that I would have been able to sing in front of the public.

LEONA MITCHELL

It's the work that should keep you going rather than the acknowledgment.

JUNE JORDAN

Up you mighty race, you can accomplish what you will.

MARCUS GARVEY

The outside world told black kids when I was growing up that we weren't worth anything. It told us we were second class, that poor kids weren't valued. But our parents said it wasn't so and our churches and our schoolteachers said it wasn't so. They believed in us and we, therefore, believed in ourselves.

MARIAN WRIGHT EDELMAN
I Dream A World

Your world is as big as you make it.

GEORGIA DOUGLASS JOHNSON

Aim for things that might not be achievable. You may come real close.

ANONYMOUS

If you are interested in acting or whatever, just do it. Don't let anyone say you can't.

JAMES EARL JONES

Strive to make something of yourself; then strive to make the most of yourself.

ALEXANDER CRUMMELL, *Clergyman*

Anticipate the good so that you may enjoy it.

Ethiopian proverb

I come from a line of industrious people. I don't mind hard work, for you see I believe it develops character and one of its more sterling traits: dignity.

MONIFA HAKIM, *Writer*

You can do whatever you want to do. All it requires is hard work.

CONSUELO B. MARSHALL, *Federal Judge*

In everything I do, I want to be challenged.

QUEEN LATIFAH

Young musicians inspire me.

BETTY CARTER, *Singer*

The knowledge that you had a dream but did not pursue it is killing knowledge.

LES BROWN

Most people think I am a dreamer. Through dreams many things come true.

MARY MCLEOD BETHUNE
Voices of Triumph

From 1863, when slavery was abolished in this country, down to the present time (1907) history reveals to us the fact that the Negro race, though spurned on every hand, has made the most rapid progress, under the most trying circumstances, of any race on the globe.

W. A. LEWIS

If you want that hill, you got to bleed for it.

NELSON PEERY
Black Fire: The Making of A Revolutionary

Greatness is not measured by what a man or woman accomplishes, but by the opposition he or she has to overcome to reach his or her goals.

DOROTHY HEIGHT

I am not an American hero. I'm a person who loves children.

CLARA "MOTHER" HALE

I care about all people, especially those most vulnerable in our society, like children, and seniors, and the disabled.

DAVID DINKINS

It doesn't work in practice. You can't give something to somebody to have. Then they don't value it. Value is associated with hard work.

RICHARD D. PARSONS
CEO, Dime Savings Bank

No race can prosper till it learns that there is as much dignity in tilling a field as in writing a poem.

BOOKER T. WASHINGTON

When I tried to sell my company, I realized then what Motown meant. Before that, I was busy building and moving and having fun.

BERRY GORDY

When you know that you don't know, you've got to read.

S. B. FULLER, *Entrepreneur*

Complacency is the enemy of achievement.

DENNIS KIMBRO

To achieve your goals, you must be crystal-clear about what you want and why you want it.

VICTORIA JOHNSON, *Author*

Maybe I was rude to people and had very little to say to anybody. The reason is that I was focused mentally on that coming game. I was concentrating, visualizing things that I knew could happen and what I would do if it went this way or that way. I knew I had it working right when I started seeing plays in my mind almost like I was watching television. I'd see my own line in front of me, the guards, the halfbacks, the quarterback, and the other team over there . . .

JIM BROWN

These experiences solidify my belief that I can do anything I set my mind to do. The possibilities are boundless.

NATHAN MCCALL
Makes Me Wanna Holler:
A Young Black Man in America

Useful was always the word, useful to yourself, useful to life.

ANNA ARNOLD HEDGEMAN

When rungs were missing, I learned to jump.

WILLIAM WARFIELD

We hear bout Molly Pitcher ... about Betsy Ross. ... The Negro woman has never been included in American history.

JACOB LAWRENCE, *Painter*
about the Harriet Tubman *series*

When my parents were away, I would take the braces off and try to walk without them. I have to attribute that motivation to my mother. She was instrumental in making me believe that you can accomplish anything if you believe in it. ... I also come from a Southern Baptist background and God has always been in my life.

WILMA RUDOLPH

I came from a people who viewed the world as attainable.

FAYE WATTLETON

What could be greater than being part of such a cause no matter how infinitesimal our contribution is?

WINNIE MANDELA
Part of My Soul Went with Him

I have a legacy to leave my people; it is my philosophy of living and serving.

MARY MCLEOD BETHUNE

Mary McLeod Bethune wasn't a leader because she sacrificed and struggled for her own education. Mary McLeod Bethune was a leader because she dreamed and planned and worked for the education of others.

JOHNETTA B. COLE
President, Spelman College

We've got some difficult days ahead, but it doesn't matter with me now, because I've been to the mountaintop.

MARTIN LUTHER KING JR.

FAITH

Every Blessing you get from God is by faith.

AMANDA SMITH
Nineteenth-century Evangelist

If you offend, ask for pardon; if offended, forgive.

Ethiopian proverb

Keep the faith!

ADAM CLAYTON POWELL JR.

[I]t is so liberating to believe in something that is larger than a job for you.

LANI GUINIER

Saying racism is permanent is no different from saying poverty is permanent or evil is permanent. It is the challenge to use one's life in a way that responds to evils in your midst. That is what we all must do.

DERRICK BELL

There is no medicine to cure hatred.

Ashanti proverb

It evokes for me the necessity for humility, the sense that it is only when we bow down in a religious sense, when we humble ourselves, that we can be more open.

BELL HOOKS
about the church song "When I Fall on My Knees"
Breaking Bread: Insurgent Black Intellectual Life

The fish in the river dart before thy face,
and thy rays are in the midst of the great green sea . . .
and none knows thee as does thy son, Akhenaton,
Whom thou has made wise with thy designs
and thy strength.

A Hymn of AKHENATON
Egyptian Pharaoh

If all the oceans on earth were ink and all the trees pens, they couldn't write the knowledge that God has.

MUHAMMAD ALI

He asked if she knew where a clear river ran, for tomorrow he was going to tell it through colored land that Sunday was singing and shouting day. Let the burdened bring their weary loads to the riverside and comfort the fevers and frets of their souls with the blessed balm of being baptized.

DOROTHY WEST
The Wedding

With this faith we will be able to transform the jangling discords of our nation into a beautiful symphony of brotherhood.

THE REVEREND MARTIN LUTHER KING JR.

You can find victory in Christ, and you don't have to pay for it.

THE REVEREND BERNICE A. KING

I am a prisoner of hope.

CORNEL WEST

How do you spell relief? Praise the Lord.

THE REVEREND BERNICE A. KING

The opportunity that God sends does not wake up him who is asleep.

Senegalese proverb

Praxis is a specific kind of obedience that organizes itself around a social theory of reality in order to implement in the society the freedom, inherent in faith. If faith is the belief that God created all for freedom, then praxis is the social theory used to analyze what must be done for the historical realization of freedom. To sing about freedom and to pray for its coming is not enough. Freedom must be actualized in history by oppressed peoples who accept the intellectual challenge to analyze the world for the purpose of changing it.

We need national forums to reflect, discuss, and plan how best to respond. It is neither a matter of a new Messiah figure emerging, nor of another organization appearing on the scene. Rather, it is a matter of grasping the structural and institutional processes that have disfigured, deformed, and devastated Black America such that the resources for collective and critical consciousness, moral commitment and courageous engagement are vastly underdeveloped. We need serious strategic and tactical thinking about how to create new models of leadership and forge the kind of persons to actualize these models. These models must not only question our silent assumptions about Black leadership such as the notion that Black leaders are always middle class but also force us to interrogate iconic figures of the past. This includes questioning King's sexism and homophobia and the relatively undemocratic character of his organization, and Malcolm's silence in the vicious role of priestly versions of Islam in the modern world.

CORNEL WEST
Breaking Bread: Insurgent Black Intellectual Life

Ain't ya'll heard? Pharaoh got drowned.

JESSE JACKSON

Everything that has happened to me seemed as though it were being coordinated by divine intelligence. I have only to be sensitive and obedient, to avoid being overly anxious, and to do the best I can with today, and He will guide me tomorrow.

THE REVEREND ANDREW YOUNG

Faith is the first factor in a life devoted to service. Without faith, nothing is possible. With it nothing is impossible.

MARY MCLEOD BETHUNE

I recognize that it's not always about me; it's about service. Sometimes my going to a meeting [Overeaters Anonymous] can help someone else. I also know that the Lord didn't bring me here just so I can wear a size 6 and be decoration. He helped me do what I did for a purpose.

TRACY REDDICK, *Marketing Analyst*

The joy of loving God is found in the understanding that I should be thankful for anything that I do.

MILDRED GREENE

Simply trusting every day is my key to happiness and fulfillment. To the extent that I am able to trust completely God's promise that He will work all things together for my good because I am called according to His purpose, I receive and accept strength for the day.

CAROLYN TONGE

As a Christian I look at the world from the point of view of the Cross.

CORNEL WEST

The [multiple sclerosis] gradually took its toll over a six- to seven-year period. It was disintegration of my strength and whatever control I had of my muscles. Little by little, the entire left side of my body, from head to toe, was paralyzed. My left shoulder and hip fell out of their sockets, my left jaw dropped, and my tongue was paralyzed, as were my left-side facial muscles. I was totally helpless. If there was no one to help me, I had to crawl on my stomach in order to get around my house.

I had three, sometimes four, doctors and they all told me there was nothing in this world that could help. There's no cure for MS and that I would only get worse because the disease is degenerative and this is my life's sentence. After hearing that, I knew it was my cue to let "the world" go. I saw a vision of the Virgin Mary. I knew that I would be healed. I'm Catholic and all of my life I had believed in God, said my prayers, etc. God allowed me to have MS in order for me to be remade over again and totally submit myself and my life to his will.

It took about a year and a half, with some relapses here and there. You see, I had to work on my faith. I knew if I had the faith of a mustard seed—that was pure faith—then I would be totally healed. I was so well prepared in faith, that God gave me a complete miracle healing ... That person who used to be concerned with the vanity of my career, my wealth, my fame is now gone forever.

LOLA FALANA

No matter how long the winter, spring is sure to follow.

Guinean proverb

I'm lucky to be alive ... and that's a tribute to God and the wonderful doctors who treated me.

BEN VEREEN

I'm indebted to my Heavenly Father, who looks beyond my faults and sees my needs.

NATALIE COLE

As I read the Bible, the excitement to me is not just the fact that it is the inspired Word of God; that should be enough. But what really turns me on is that I am in touch with God—speaking through real human beings with real life struggles and real life agonies and real imperfections. That's what gives me hope.

BISHOP STITH

My people are destroyed by their lack of knowledge. I need not your thoughts; I need the thoughts of God.

ANONYMOUS

Singing "Halleluia" everywhere does not prove piety.

Ethiopian proverb

I have prayed for him often. But Richard has to begin praying for himself. He cannot serve two masters. He still has one foot here and one foot there.

LOLA FALANA
about her close friend
Richard Pryor and his multiple sclerosis

Come day,
Go day,
God send Sunday!

Slave prayer

Christianity is a system claiming God for its author, and the welfare of man for its object. It is a system so uniform, exalted and pure, that the loftiest intellects have acknowledged its influence, and acquiesced in the justness of its claims. Genius has bent from his erratic course to gather firm from her altars, and pathos from the agony of Gethsemane and the sufferings of Calvary. Philosophy and science have paused amid their speculative researches and wondrous revelations to gain wisdom from her teachings and knowledge from her precepts.

FRANCIS WATKINS HARPER
Abolitionist, Poet

It was a special transcending moment when the early church discovers the impact of faith transcending cultures.

BISHOP STITH

Then that little man in black there, he says women can't have as much rights as men, because Christ wasn't a woman! Where did your Christ come from? Where did your Christ come from? From God and a woman! Man had nothing to do with him . . .

SOJOURNER TRUTH

Everyday I preach with my life.

MATTHEW JEREMIAH

What one hopes for is always better than what one has.

Ethiopian proverb

I have always felt that a word was being spoken through me. Three-fourths of the time, I didn't get it right.

HOWARD THURMAN

At the root of our existence is God.

> BROTHER PROPHET
> *Sixteen-year old Political Activist*

I believe my success has been in my faith. The day I chose to have God in my life made all the difference.

> HORACE GRANT, *NBA Star*

I am a living example of someone whose life has been changed from cold and callous to a disciplined person because of my belief in the Christian Gospel.

> CORNEL WEST

So our Lord eats and drinks with bad sinners. He sits and talks with prostitutes. He heals a Roman soldier's child. He declares that neighbor even extends to the Samaritans, a culture historically rejected. He changes values by declaring the lost coin more important, the prodigal son a priority, and the lost and rejected those he came to save.

> BISHOP STITH

Death holds no fear for folks who are Christians.

> MICHAEL WEAVER
> *Poet, about his grandfather's death*

Some fear being a Christian. I fear not being one.

> BRENDA PRICE

When an insurance company pulls the plug, you need all the faith in the world that the Lord will take care of things.

> PATRICIA LEWIS

They can laugh, but they can't deny us. They can curse and kill us, but they can't destroy us all. This land is ours because we come out of it, we bled in it, our tears watered it, we fertilized it with our dead. So the more of us they destroy the more it becomes filled with the spirit of our redemption.

RALPH ELLISON
Juneteenth

Faith is stepping out on nothing and landing on something. As some one who got fifteen months behind in [his] mortgage, someone who lost [his] house, someone who went through nineteen months of litigations ... the only thing that got me through was my faith.

WALLY "FAMOUS" AMOS

I am that I am, a shining being and a dweller in light who has been created from the limbs of the divine.

Ancient Egyptian incantation

... Today we must upturn the world. I listened to God this morning and the thought came to me, "any idea that keeps anybody out is too small for this age ..."

MARY MCLEOD BETHUNE
Her Own Words of Inspiration

Blessed art Thou
Oh Eternal, our God,
King of the Universe

Ethiopian Hebrew prayer

Prayers, more than any other aspect of religion, contains the most intense expression of African traditional spirituality.

JOHN S. MBITI

Make it a habit to begin each day affirming that God is great and that life is a blessing.

SUSAN L. TAYLOR

The joy of the Lord is our strength and there's a simple confidence and contentment in being in the will of God.

BILLY GAINES
Gospel Singer

I knew that there was purpose and design in creation and that my life was somehow part of that grand scheme.

NATHAN MCCALL
Makes Me Wanna Holler:
A Young Black Man in America

If I gave [my mother] an irreverent shrug, her caveat would put my college degrees in proper perspective: "I don't care how much education you get, if you lock out the Spirit, you're empty. Being connected is a blessing, but it can be taken from you."

GLORIA WADE-GAYLES
Scholar, Poet

Take your head, collect your bones, gather your limbs, shake the earth from your flesh! . . . The gatekeeper comes out to you, he grasps your hand, takes you into heaven.

Old Kingdom Egyptian pyramid text

We were good Christians, and God never let us down.

ANNIE ELIZABETH DELANY, *D.D.S.*
Having Our Say: The Delany Sisters' First 100 Years

I realized . . . that I didn't belong to my parents, nor did I belong to myself. I belonged to something or someone beyond me—the Creator . . .

ANDREW YOUNG

If you're going to preach about the cross and resurrection, you ought to believe that God will take care of your family.

JEAN YOUNG
Wife of Andrew Young

I decided that purpose, meaning, and order in nature emanated from God and that the same must be true for me.

ANDREW YOUNG

Life with hope is a much better life, no matter how short, than one with despair.

JEAN YOUNG
Wife of Andrew Young

Yes, sir, the heavyweight champion of the world was in church this morning and who was he talking about? Jesus Christ. I will never cease to praise Jesus Christ.

GEORGE FOREMAN

Our crown has been bought and paid for. All we must do is put it on our heads.

JAMES BALDWIN

I saw how difficult it was for a soul to be lost, and how easy it was to be deceived by believing in universal salvation without repentance.

AMANDA SMITH
Nineteenth-century Evangelist

When God has put a dream in your heart, He means to help you fulfill it. To gain His help you must ask for it ... and this asking is prayer.

WILLIAM TUBMAN

Church is the life's blood of our folks; community.

INDIA ANETTE PEYTON
Grandmother of Melba Patillo
Beals in Warriors Don't Cry

O silent God, Thou whose voice afar in mist and mystery hath left
  our ears a-hungered in these fearful days—
    Hear us, good Lord!
Listen to us, Thy children; our faces dark with doubt, are made a
  mockery in Thy sanctuary. With uplifted hands we front Thy
  Heaven, O God crying:
    We beseech Thee to hear us, good Lord!

W. E. B. DU BOIS
"A Litany of Atlanta"

Come up from the lowlands; there are heights yet to climb. You cannot do healthful thinking in the lowlands. Look to the mountain top for faith.

MARY MCLEOD BETHUNE

FROM SURVIVING TO THRIVING

Go beyond surviving. There is no achievement in surviving. We must prevail!

JOHN HENRIK CLARK
Historian Emeritus

We can overcome the temporary setbacks, like slavery; if in our minds we remain free, all is possible.

DR. AUDREY T. MCCLUSKEY
Professor of English

One thing alone I charge you. As you live, believe in life!

W. E. B. DU BOIS

Life is short and it's your job to make it sweet.

JUANITA BAKER JACKSON MARSHALL
My Aunt

I think everything is possible, especially for the next generation. Just look at what we've overcome.

NIKKI GIOVANNI

I was named appropriately because I am of the earth, and as long as the earth is under my feet I will always be.

EARTHA KITT

To David Duke: This is just to set the record straight. I am a Negro woman. I was brought up in a good family. My papa was a devoted father. I went to college; I paid my own way. I am not stupid. I'm not on welfare. And I'm not scrubbing floors. Especially not yours.

BESSIE DELANY
Having Our Say: The Delany Sisters' First 100 Years

To know the condition of a people, it is only necessary to know the condition of their women.

MARTIN R. DELANY

The founders of Essence understood that by uplifting Black women they would be uplifting Black people.

SUSAN L. TAYLOR

[S]he taught me that my feelings did not matter, that no matter how hurt I was, how ashamed, or how surprised I was, I had to fight back because if I did not, then I would always be somebody's victim.

KESHO YVONNE SCOTT
The Habit of Surviving

Black women have the habit of survival.

LENA HORNE

In the grimmest of days, it is necessary for a woman to look for that thing that lifts her spirit. And if she can see that in

herself, if she can see herself as a phenomenal being, she draws
to herself more pleasant things . . .

MAYA ANGELOU

But what I came to understand on a concrete level through my
mother was the possible necessity of the simultaneous promo-
tion of two contradictory sets of values. *Both* were essential to
the survival—of me as a person in the society in which we
live, and of the African American community as a whole. That
understanding has greatly enhanced my comprehension of political developments in Richmond [VIrginia] and elsewhere.

ELSA BARKLEY BROWN
Doublestitch: Black Women Write
About Mothers and Daughters

The only way black people can protect themselves is by acquiring knowledge. We have to write more books and read more so
that we can be aware of what the hell's going on in the world.

ICE T

For when *we* give our ears, eyes, dollars and whoops to foul-
mouthed songsters, minstrel-men sit-coms, and late-night
clowns . . . when we rah-rah petty fictionists into our pantheon
of great writers . . . well, can we really blame others for trivializ-
ing our culture? . . .

TONYA BOLDEN
Author, Critic

We have survived without outside funding. We have survived
based on putting out good literature and learning from our
mistakes. Our charge now is to move [forward] with hum-
bleness and enthusiasm.

HAKI MADHUBUTI
Founder, Publisher, Third World Press

We fail to understand the difference between movement and progress.

JOHN HENRIK CLARK, *Historian*

She kept nagging about keeping your dress tail down, having your head looking right, and keeping lotion on your legs.

AN AFRICAN-AMERICAN WOMAN
recalling her mother's advice

There's a statement in the Bible which pleases me a great deal. And I try to keep it in front of me, in my mind's front. And that is, a cheerful spirit is good medicine. It is very important for women and young women, to try for cheerfulness. My encouragement is against whining. Whining not only is ugly and uncomfortable and miserable but it also alerts a brute that a victim is in the neighborhood.

MAYA ANGELOU

Got on the train in Tampa, Florida, on the way to New York. Conductor came around, said "Give me your ticket, boy." Gave him my ticket, he punched it and gave it back. Came around again in Richmond, Virginia, said, "Give me your ticket, boy." Gave him my ticket; punched it and gave it back. In the Lincoln Tunnel on the way into New York City, conductor came around and said, "Give me your ticket, boy." Turned around to him and said, "Who the hell you callin' 'boy'?"

African-American folk humor

When you're in front of white people, think before you act, think before you speak. Your way of doing things is alright around our people, but not for *white* people.

RICHARD WRIGHT

Got one mind for white folk to see
'Nother for what I know is me.

African-American folk saying

If you are hiding, don't light a fire.

Ashanti proverb

[Slave deception and trickery] worked against whites acquiring knowledge of slave culture that might have been used to attempt to eradicate that culture.

STERLING STUCKEY

The way you relate to the white man should not be the way you relate to me.

ALTON MADDOX
Activist, Attorney-at-Law

At an early age I learned the game that becomes a serious part of every black person's social personality. We learned roles. One person with our peers, we became a totally different person around whites. It was impossible for them to know us, and this was our defense. I didn't know how our race could stay out of the schizophrenic ward, considering the split personalities they forced upon us.

NELSON PEERY

The thing you have to remember is that white folks don't play fair. They think that when a black person criticizes other black people it has more validity. Then they'll use what you say against the next black they don't want to hire.

DERRICK BELL

I came to the conclusion that whites are strange folk. If the first black they met was a scholar, then all blacks were scholars. If the first was a criminal, then all were criminals. Anyone different from the first was an exception. I began to understand why my parents kept reminding us of the importance of putting "our best foot forward" when dealing with whites. It wasn't, as I assumed, to get along with them, but a good impression made it easier for the next black that came along.

NELSON PEERY

You can handle life better if you make it a policy to learn from your mistakes and keep a record of your blessings.

TONYA BOLDEN

His [drummer Arthur Taylor] was the Harlem upon which the legend . . . was built. The neighborhoods were inhabited by the great men and women of jazz as well as the doctors, the lawyers, the scholars and the workaday people . . .

STANLEY CROUCH

At that time in Harlem, you had buildings with uniformed elevator men—no self-service. We had that life.

ROSA GUY

Rosa Guy is one of those rare humans who emits the initial beauty of a sweet child. She is a soul at peace—a gem from the rain forest on loan to the concrete jungle.

PRIZGAR R. GONZALES
Syndicated Columnist

As we plan where we want to live for the lives of our children at that same time we must think of where we want to live for the comfort of our deaths.

ANONYMOUS

One thing, as much joy as I take in being a writer, I take an equal amount of joy being black. I think being black is really the coolest thing to be in this country. It is certainly bad from a socioeconomic standpoint. Certainly we get the last hired, first fired; and the crap beat out of us all of the time. But really, if you look at this culture, this American culture, it is, I think, essentially black. The whole culture! From rock and roll to language . . . Just look at basketball . . . I think the essence of this culture extends from the contributions of black people. So I think being black is really cool. If we could only recognize that. If we only could see that and draw our strengths from what we've contributed.

EDDY L. HARRIS, *Author*

I pushed 'em out there to find out what they were best in. That's how you learn things, by getting on out there and living. They found their strengths by the best way anybody could: by living them.

TINA MCELROY ANSA
Ugly Ways

Oppressed people have a good sense of humor. Think of the Jews. They know how to laugh, and to laugh at themselves! Well, we colored folks are the same way. We colored folks are survivors.

ANNIE ELIZABETH DELANY, *D.D.S.*
Having Our Say: The Delany Sisters' First 100 Years

If you want to continue living in poverty without clothes and food, then go and drink in the shebeens. But if you want better things, you must work hard. We cannot do it all for you; you must do it yourselves.

NELSON MANDELA
Long Walk to Freedom

UNITY

When spider webs unite, they can tie up a lion.

Ethiopian proverb

Africa for the Africans, at home and abroad!

MARCUS GARVEY

Cross the river in a crowd and the crocodile won't eat you.

Mauritanian proverb

For the whole universe is interconnected; if something is distorted, the other things connected with it suffer.

WALDA HEYWAT
Sixteenth-century Abyssinian Philosopher

Anyone who looks for power bases where there is so much work to be done ... when we have not begun to address the real problems of the poverty of our people is a moron.

WINNIE MANDELA

There are all kinds of investment opportunities in Africa. We expect to make a substantial contribution to the development of Africa.

DR. MACEO K. SLOAN, *Economist*

Come to assist with teaching and training and sharing. I see some people who come here to make a fortune, quick money and get out. Unless we build on the positive and help people, it's going to be difficult for South Africa.

BARBARA LOMAX, *Trade Unionist*

We've got to mobilize black Americans in a new perspective of operational unity. We are under siege in this country. We are threatened at the inner zones of our spirit, and we have a right and a duty to ask every man, woman and child to either lead, teach, preach, follow or get out of the cotton-picking way!

The terrible truth is that if all black Baptists, black Methodists, the black Catholics, the black Episcopalians and the black Muslims . . . if the Kappas, the Alphas, the Omegas, the Deltas, the Sigmas, the AKA's, the Masons, the Elks, and the Odd Fellows . . . if SCLC, PUSH, the NAACP, the Urban League, the black Democrats, the black Republicans, the black Nationalists and the majority of black people . . . who don't belong to anything—could get together tomorrow or next week we could end this thing by January 1st.

LERONE BENNETT JR.
Historian, Author

If we mobilize the masses the classes will have to follow.

AL SHARPTON, *Community Activist*

The idea that black people can have unity is the most dangerous idea we've ever let loose.

BAYARD RUSTIN

Nothing is more terrifying to white supremacy than the prospect that African people might unite and use our enormous resources for our own development.

RON DANIELS, *Political Activist*

In all things that are purely social we can be as separate as the fingers, yet one as the hand in all things essential to mutual progress.

BOOKER T. WASHINGTON

If we have learned anything from the fifties and sixties, it is that we need an organized, collective response to our oppression.

TONI CADE BAMBARA
Author, Lecturer

... we must remain responsible to each other ...

TOM FEELINGS
Artist, My Soul Looks Back in Wonder

We all knew what Jackie Robinson was doing was not just for himself, but for all of us.

HANK AARON

... making millions is never as impressive as knowing what to do when you get them.

CAMILLE COSBY

We must remake the world. The task is nothing less than that. To be part of this great uniting force of our age is the crowning experience of our life.

MARY McLEOD BETHUNE

Black America must never forget the price paid for today's progress and promise.

JOHNETTA B. COLE

When people made up their minds that they wanted to be free and took action, then there was a change. But they cannot rest on just that change. It has to continue.

ROSA PARKS

There was a cohesiveness about poor Black communities before integration that today's middle-class Black communities do not have, or do not need.

GLORIA WADE-GAYLES, *Professor of English*

When you get to be an exceptional black, you don't belong to the white and you don't belong to the black. You are too good for the black and you will always be black to the white.

JANET COLLINS

There is power and unity and strength in networking. I think networking is always relevant. And I think it is particularly relevant for blacks because of our feelings of isolation.

ALVIN POUSSANT

No one does it alone.

OPRAH WINFREY

The friends of our friends are our friends.

Congolese folk saying

I knew that the cohesion of not simply our family but also our race was our only protection.

NELSON PEERY

Pride of Culture is not a fad, but a way of life.

JIMMY SHEPPARD, *Fashion Designer*

Two small antelopes can beat a big one.

Ashanti proverb

The whites, in the military as in civilian life, would ask us to unite with them on issues that concerned them a lot and us a little. They would never unite on issues that concerned us a lot and them a little. More ominous than that, we knew we could expect no more assistance should the military authority move against us than they gave when the Klan moved against us.

NELSON PEERY
Black Fire: The Making of a Revolutionary

Sometimes the devil is in the details.

Saying

A partner in the business will not put an obstacle to it.

Ethiopian proverb

To recognize ourselves as being especially oppressed because we are African Americans does not mean that we cannot also join hands with those from other racial communities, national communities.

ANGELA DAVIS
Political Activist, Professor

A blade won't cut another blade; a cheat won't cheat another cheat.

Ethiopian proverb

The task that remains is to cope with our interdependence—to see ourselves reflected in every other human being and to respect and honor our differences.

MELBA PATILLO BEALS

Let us not respond to our collective painful experiences by withdrawing into ourselves. Rather, let us, together, seek ways to do better.

AMARA ESSY
President, United Nations General Assembly

One finger alone cannot kill even a louse.

Kenyan proverb

The black bourgeoisie has lost much of its feeling of racial solidarity with the Negro masses.

E. FRANKLIN FRAZER

It is only a paycheck or two that separates the "new black bourgeoisie" from their poorer brothers and sisters in the hood.

EARL OFARI HUTCHINSON

The one who is unconcerned never cares.

Ugandan proverb

Black professionals or business owners still tell harrowing tales of being spread-eagle over the hoods of their expensive BMWs or Porsches, while the police ran makes on them and tore their cars apart searching for drugs. In polls taken after the Rodney King beating, blacks were virtually unanimous in saying that they believed any black person could have been on the ground that night being pulverized by the police. These were eternal reminders to members of the "new" black bourgeoisie that they could escape the hood, but many Americans still considered them hoods.

EARL OFARI HUTCHINSON

A strawberry blossom will not sweeten dry bread.

African folk saying

The black poor and the "new" black bourgeoisie are inseparably bound by race, and separably divided by class. The trick is to bridge the class gap and develop a unified program to address the common problems of racism and economic disparity.

EARL OFARI HUTCHINSON

I was, and still am, convinced that the women of the world, united without regard for national or racial dimensions, can become a most powerful force for international peace and brotherhood.

CORETTA SCOTT KING

Despite the strength of a $350 million market, African Americans seem reluctant to show that strength with a well-organized boycott. It is my strong assertion that if African Americans are to be treated as serious economic players in terms of employment, contracts, and business opportunities, we also should consider judicious use of the "stick." I have often said, in slight jest, that we ought to boycott catsup because we overconsume things that are red and sweet. We ought to boycott something, and define a set of requests that [will] trigger the end to a boycott, and they ought to be more than trinkets and meetings. Boycott a hotel chain and end the boycott when 5,000 jobs, 3 board seats, and joint ownership of two hotels is negotiated.

JULIANNE MALVEAUX
Economist, Activist

I don't think we are aware of our power. If African Americans and other people who are being misrepresented would use their dollars to say to television sponsors that we are not going to support you unless you support good programming that represents us fairly, then they would change very quickly. I believe in the old-fashioned boycott.

CAMILLE COSBY

As long as you are a consumer, you are a beggar. You must become a producer. We must learn from the lessons of the Japanese.

HAKI MADHUBUTI

As long as Negroes are hemmed into racial blocks of prejudice and pressure, it will be necessary for them to bank together for economic betterment.

MARY McLEOD BETHUNE
"My Last Will and Testament"

We are going to have to be more self-sufficient, almost the way black communities were when they were segregated. We need to buy the theaters in our communities; we need to buy television stations. We need to have more money in our own banks if we want to purchase and be competitive on that level.

CAMILLE COSBY

Our capital base is very limited. So the cooperative model is key for us. No tooth fairy will save us. We need to start credit unions at churches to finance our own businesses. We need to begin trusting each other with our ideas and dollars.

HAKI MADHUBUTI

They [Asians] are learning how to do our hair and when that happens, the sister will put up a sign that says perm for $25 and the Asian girl will put up an even larger one that says $10 and while the sister goes home to watch "Monday Night Football" with her family, the Asian girl will work all day and all night.

Clarence Ward Sr.

Asians do everything as one . . . The competition is tremendous. Asians don't have overhead, don't have to pay salaries like we do. They bring in relatives and have them living in the business, upstairs or downstairs. They can stay open twenty hours a day. We can't survive with that kind of competition . . . And what happens when they move? And they will move on. They are educating their children. Their children will be doctors and lawyers. They are not going to be in our community selling beauty products. After they have walked all over us and sent their kids to school, what will we have left?

Blacks could achieve if only we'd understand that something as simple as where you buy your hair grease makes a difference.

Esther Peacock
Owner, Peacock Beauty and Barber Supply

It is the fool whose own tomatoes are sold to him.

Traditional wisdom

It is the fools' sheep that breaks loose twice.

Ashanti proverb

We [black beauty suppliers] are in deep trouble. When the smoke clears, none of us may be here.

Esther Peacock
Owner, Peacock Beauty and Barber Supply

I don't think you can bring the races together joking about the difference. I'd rather talk about the similarities, about what's the universal experience.

BILL COSBY

It is time for black people to stop playing the separating game of geography, of where the slave ship put us down. We must concentrate on where the slave ship picked us up.

JOHN HENRIK CLARK, *Historian*

I'm convinced that the black man will only reach his full potential when he learns to draw upon the strengths and insights of the black woman.

MANNING MARABLE, *Professor*
Political Science, Columbia University

OLD WINE, NEW BOTTLES

Be careful what you set your heart upon, for someday it will
be yours.

Traditional wisdom

If you are afraid of falling, don't climb.

JOHN THOMPSON
Georgetown Basketball Coach

... if you don't believe fully in yourself, others sense it, no
matter how much you try to front it off.

NATHAN McCALL
Makes Me Wanna Holler: A Young Black Man in America

New broom sweeps clean.

Axiom

New broom sweeps clean, but old broom knows the corner.

Axiom

To have two eyes is cause for pride, but to have one eye is
better than to have none.

Guinean proverb

Haste makes waste.

Axiom

Where there is a will there is a way.

Axiom

Don't ever let another individual make you act like a dog running and jumping from here to there behind a bone.

MATTHEW JEREMIAH, *Evangelist*

God hates gossips more than he hates fools.

TONYA BOLDEN
Just Family

I guess I never expect anything from a pig but an oink.

JANET SINGLETON, *Writer*

The one you disregard is the one you will meet when you are in need.

Ugandan proverb

Don't burn your bridges behind you.

Axiom

The quarrelsome rarely get help.

Ugandan proverb

Where there is smoke there is fire.

Axiom

Around the flowering tree, one finds many insects.

Guinean proverb

Indecision is like the stepchild: if he doesn't wash his hands, he is called dirty; if he does, he is wasting the water.

Madagascan proverb

Tomorrow is not promised to you ... You've got to live as if it's the last day you have on this earth.

LES BROWN
Live Your Dreams

Life is what you make of it.

Traditional wisdom

Life is a short walk. There is so little time and so much living to achieve.

JOHN OLIVER KILLENS

Whosoever tooteth not his own horn, the same shall not be tooted.

JOHN LEWIS

The end of an ox is beef, and the end of a lie is grief.

Madagascan proverb

What goes around comes around.

African-American folk saying

Clothes put on while running come off while running.

Ethiopian proverb

Easy come, easy go.

Axiom

Soon found soon lost.

Kenyan proverb

You can't yell "Close the gate" when the horse has already escaped.

Haitian proverb

The child of a tiger is a tiger.

Haitian proverb

The fruit does not fall far from the tree.

Traditional wisdom

The Bell Curve by Richard J. Hernstern and Charles Murray continues the tradition of racist theories on race, gender, ethnicity and the self-perpetuating fantasy of white male intellectual superiority.

SHARWYN DYSON, *Educator*

Evil knows where evil sleeps.

Nigerian proverb

It takes one to know one.

Traditional wisdom

You have to be twice as good as white folk.

Traditional wisdom

You have to work twice as hard to get half as much.

Traditional wisdom

Draw on family support wherever you can.

A word to the wise

Do what you love. If that is not possible, do whatever you do with 100 percent of your ability.

A word to the wise

You never know who's watching.

Traditional wisdom

Always put your best foot forward.

Axiom

Since you don't know which opportunity lies just ahead, it pays to always put your best foot forward.

DAVE DINWIDDIE
My Father

When a door slams behind you, look for the one God is opening ahead of you.

Adage

Be polite and helpful to all people.

LILY BAKER
My Grandmother

If you sow falsehood, you will reap deceit.

African proverb

The truth is like gold: keep it locked up and you will find it exactly as you first put it away.

Sengalese proverb

Beware of finding yourself holding on by a raw cotton string.

MINISTER ARLENE CLARK

You don't want to find yourself working overtime to make up for lost time.

Mother wit

Of the dead, say nothing evil.

Traditional wisdom

Mayhem and Madness
or Abuse

"Domestic violence," "spousal abuse," "wife battering," are euphemisms for torture and terrorism perpetuated by some men against women.

CHARLES BAILLOU, *Journalist*

I can understand why women go to jail. I really thought about poisoning my husband. I wanted to stab him in his sleep. I wanted to do anything to get out of the hellish situation. But I didn't have it in me [to commit a violent act].

AMINATA NJERI

You can't let the courts make the decision if you know in your heart you are a good mother.

ASSATI
an abused wife who escaped with her children

You have to become tough. You have to be able to handle it because you are going to be all that the children have to count on for a while.

Upper-middle-class, divorced refugee from wife and child abuse

If I allow [a man] to meet my children and he doesn't treat them with utmost respect, he's history.

Assati

I have never been in trouble before—twenty-seven years to life for protecting myself? The laws don't make sense.

Juanita, *a battered women who killed her husband in self-defense*

Fire and gunpowder do not sleep together.

Ashanti proverb

Leave! Just take whatever you can and go as far away as you can. I wouldn't tell any person to do what I did, because my whole life is gone.

Juanita

When the vine entwines your roof, it is time to cut it down.

African proverb

Don't never let no mens hit you mo than once.

Mother wit

I can't stop wondering what we would do if the [domestic] violence was against black men instead of black women. Would we forgive the perpetrator so quickly and allow him into our private time; our spiritual moments; our sweet surrenders?

Pearl Cleage
Deals with the Devil

If a man hits you once, he'll hit you again. He'll say he's sorry, he didn't mean it. He may even cry. But he'll do it again, and again. Each time with less provocation.

Father wit

It is men and women who suffer the consequences of destruction and disarray. But men and women are also the authors of most of these destructive events and crimes.

AMARA ESSY
Diplomat from Ivory Coast

Any man who will go to bed with his brother's daughter, and then turn around and make five other women pregnant and then accuse all these women of committing adultery is a ruthless man.

MALCOLM X

The die is set, and Malcolm shall not escape, especially after such evil, foolish talk about his benefactor.

LOUIS FARRAKHAN
Muhammad Speaks, *1965*

I believed in Elijah Muhammad stronger than he believed in himself. I believed in his God more than he did and I was not aware of this until I found he was confronted with a crisis in his own personal moral life and he did not stand up as a man. Anybody could make a moral mistake, but when they have to lie about it and be willing to see that murder is committed to cover up their mistake, not only are they not divine, they are not even a man.

MALCOLM X

You Can Say That Again!

There is a struggle underway for the soul of black America. Our future hangs in the balance. We will either be people whose young are strung out on drugs, or a people filled with hope and the promise of the good life.

BENJAMIN HOOKS

A lot of people get turned off from the church early on because churches tend to tell ancient biblical stories that young people can't link up with their present day reality. We have single mothers in church, people with alcohol and drug problems in church. But churches never seem to talk about the real-life problems that its members are obviously having.

SISTER SOULJAH

Little dreams stay home; big dreams go to New York.

DAVID DINKINS
First Black Mayor of New York City

A women who will tell her age will tell anything.

MAYA ANGELOU

You want to live at least as well on vacation as you do at home. Preferably better.

EFFIE BROWN

Reference determines value.

AMIRI BARAKA

It's difficult to lift people up and change them. Some people are like a wet noodle. They just collapse and it's hard to lift them up.

DR. J. R. TODD

He who cannot dance will say: "The drum is bad."

Ashanti proverb

There is a price to pay for wrongdoing.

TONYA BOLDEN
Just Family

Mothers-in-law are hard of hearing.

Congolese folk saying

Too many of the books being published today are no more than a triumph of style over substance, of hype over talent.

MARIE DUTTON BROWN
Literary Agent

Silly things done by really smart people are lots of fun; silly things done by not so smart people are really annoying.

GEORGE C. WOLFE, *Producer*

Never argue with a fool in public cause the folks looking on can't tell who's who.

PLAYTHELL BENJAMIN'S GRANDFATHER

A white man with a million dollars is a millionaire, and a black man with a million dollars is a nigger with a million dollars.

DAVID DINKINS

A lie is a temporary solution to a permanent problem.

TERRY MCMILLAN

Those who are absent are always wrong.

Congolese folk saying

It's easy to get people's attention; what counts is getting their *interest*.

A. PHILLIP RANDOLPH

... by failing to acknowledge racial problems one makes no headway in overcoming them.

NATHAN MCCALL
Makes Me Wanna Holler: A Young Black Man in America

If I had a pet buzzard I'd treat him better than the way some white folks have treated me! There isn't a Negro this side of Glory who doesn't know exactly what I mean.

SADIE DELANY
Having Our Say: The Delany Sisters' First 100 Years

Acts of micro racism occur when the recently immigrated Korean storekeeper shortchanges you. And you know where he learned the operative stereotype in this scenario: Blacks can't count. *Children*, count your change in the store before the cash register, and look him in the eye.

MILDRED GREENE

Man is like palm-wine: when young, sweet but without strength; in old age, strong but harsh.

Congolese folk saying

I don't know what other people should do. It's hard enough for me to figure out what I should do.

JILL NELSON, *Journalist*

... [T]o become and remain a woman commands the existence and employment of genius.

MAYA ANGELOU
Wouldn't Take Nothing for My Journey Now

Some of the rastas are becoming rascals.

JOHN HENRIK CLARK, *Historian*

I'm gonna upset the world!

MUHAMMAD ALI

A woman has to do twice as much good as a man to be considered half as good. Fortunately this isn't difficult.

ANONYMOUS

Memory has a reputation for being compassionately inaccurate.

RITA DOVE
Poet Laureate of the United States
through the ivory gate, *a novel*

I call this the airplane theory: If you're scared to fly, worry about it on the ground while you're standing next to a phone and you can get on a train or bus. Once the plane takes off, relax. There's nothing you can do; it's in God's hands.

WILL SMITH

When I rap, I talk about things that are common sense. I am a "Common Sensitist," which is someone not categorized by color, gender, class or religion. It's just a human thing.

QUEEN LATIFAH

We [blacks] spend a whole lot of time beating in our own bush, while our enemies are all the time gathering strength.

HERB BOYD, *Journalist*

A man that is wrapped up in himself makes a mighty small package.

MARY MCLEOD BETHUNE
Her Own Words of Inspiration

When I did encounter prejudice, I could hear mother's voice in the back of my head saying things like "some people are ignorant and you have to educate them."

DR. BENJAMIN S. CARSON, *Neurosurgeon*

It is the rich and the spoiled and those who have emulated their worst behavior who expect others to suffer for them.

MILDRED GREENE, *Armchair Philosopher*

Support the Black press! In this Age of Information what you don't know can kill you.

GARY BYRD
Radio Talk Show Host

The special plight and the role of Black women is not something that just happened three years ago. We've had a special plight for 350 years.

FANNIE LOU HAMER

It's not true that all barriers to women have come down. We all imagine that some day we will live in a society that does not impede women. But will that happen in my lifetime? I doubt it. And so for now, the best way to deal with it is to separate women so that they can achieve—especially in fields like physics, chemistry and economics.

RUTH SIMMONS, PH.D.
First African-American President of Smith College

She understands the poetry of administration and luxuriates in it.

HENRY LOUIS GATES JR., PH.D.
about the appointment of Dr. Ruth Simmons as the first African-American president of Smith College

She (Dr. Ruth Simmons) believes that you get educated to serve the community. If she can convey that religion, then Smith will run circles around the other Ivy League schools.

FRANK L. MATTHEWS
Publisher, Black Issues in Higher Education

Be wary of the kind of thinking that white American racism has promoted: "If I don't give you credit for what you have done and can do, then I am free to claim what is yours as mine."

MILDRED GREENE
Armchair Philosopher

Black people are already a rainbow coalition, because even if you're Black and Asian, you're Black.

CLARENCE PAGE

Last time I was down South I walked into this restaurant, and this white waitress came up to me and said: "We don't serve colored people here," I said, "That's all right, I don't eat colored people."

DICK GREGORY

An intelligent enemy is better than a stupid friend.

Sengalese proverb

People who are always miserable have invested their time in holding on to their pain.

SUSAN L. TAYLOR

You have got to really think about what you do.

MILDRED GREENE, *Travel Consultant*

What little balance I have emotionally, physically, spiritually, is because I was raised on a farm. It gave me an appreciation for nature, for connecting with the earth.

JAMES EARL JONES

The cricket cries, the year changes.

African folk saying

I guess I've had enough struggles in my life to not take for granted the good times. If you get too big-headed when you're on top, what are you going to do when you hit bottom?

LONETTE MCKEE, *Actress*

From the first gold medal I won in 1939, my mama used to stress being humble. You're no better than anyone else. The people you pass on the ladder will be the same people you'll be with when the ladder comes down.

ALICE COACHMAN
First African-American Woman to win an Olympic Gold Medal

The bird flies high, but always returns to earth.

Nigerian proverb

What goes up must come down.

Traditional wisdom

When you're in a train and it breaks down, well, there you is. But when you're in a plane and it breaks down, there you *ain't*.

Black humor

I have always been insulted when people tell me that my humor has done a lot for race relations. I never thought comedy did anything but make uncomfortable people feel comfortable.

DICK GREGORY

Well, we didn't order any credit cards! We don't spend what we don't have ... Imagine a bank sending credit cards to two ladies over a hundred years old! What are those folks thinking?

ANNIE ELIZABETH DELANY
Having Our Say: The Delany Sisters' First 100 Years

But today the black thinking is: if a white man says something is bad, then it must be very good.

WINNIE MANDELA
Part of My Soul Went with Him

Life is ultimately a challenge and a discipline.

CORNEL WEST

I tell you what, by the white man's own method he's degraded himself because he made himself the weaker one. He said, "If there's one drop of your blood in my veins, then I am what you are."

JOHNNY SHINES

What a country! Where else could I have to ride in the back of the bus, live in the worst neighborhoods, go to the worst schools, eat in the worst restaurants—and average $5,000 a week just talking about it.

DICK GREGORY

Today women show everything. They're crazy. Trust me, you can get in enough trouble just with a little ankle showing.

BESSIE DELANY
Having Our Say: The Delany Sisters' First 100 Years

You can run but you can't hide.

JOE LOUIS

Do women still go every three weeks to get a permanent? It's not permanent, it's temporary!

GIL SCOTT HERON

Never before have so many white Americans paid black Americans that sincerest form of flattery—imitation.

JOHN H. JOHNSON

I do my prayers. But prayer without action is dead.

DELORES BENNETT

PERSEVERANCE: OUR STAPLE

In America the African meets the Absurd.

CORNEL WEST

Beyond mountains, more mountains.

Haitian proverb

Though it is orthodox to think of America as the one country where it is unnecessary to have a past, what is a luxury for the nation as a whole becomes a prime social necessity for the Negro. For him, a group tradition must supply compensation for persecution, and pride of race the antidote for prejudice. History must restore what slavery took away, for it is the social damage of slavery that the present generation must repair and offset.

ARTHUR A. SCHOMBURG

Mistress I shall take what children I've got lef'. If they fine that trunk o' money or silver plate you'll say it's you'n, won't you? Mistress, I can't lie over that. You bo't that silver plate when you sole my three children.

A black slave woman on the eve of emancipation

The fact that another man had the power to tear from our cradle the newborn babe and sell it in the shambels [marketplace] like a brute, and then scourge us if we dare to lift a finger to save it from such a fate, haunted us for years.

WILLIAM CRAFT
Running a Thousand Miles for Freedom

People are always saying that too many Black fathers and mothers have fallen to racism, poverty, and powerlessness, and we know what they mean. But the real miracle, given the three-hundred-year war against the Black family, is not that some Black men and women have fallen but that so many still stand and love and give.

LERONE BENNETT JR.
Historian, Executive Editor of Ebony *magazine*

Given what we've had to struggle against, the wonder is not that so many of us perished, but rather that so many survived.

SUSAN L. TAYLOR
Editor-in-Chief, Essence *magazine*

In discovering the persistence of our culture and the vitality of our spirit, I became filled with esteem.

CHESTER HIGGINS JR

We used to ask Papa, "What do you remember about being a slave?" Well, like a lot of former slaves, he didn't say much about it ... You didn't sit and cry in your soup, honey, you just went on.

BESSIE DELANY
Having Our Say: The Delany Sisters' First 100 Years

You were not expected to aspire to excellence; you were expected to make peace with mediocrity.

JAMES BALDWIN

Has the God who made the white man and the black man any record declaring us a different species? Are we not sustained by the same power, supported by the same food, hurt by the same wrongs, pleased with the same delights, and propagated by the same means? And should we not then enjoy the same liberty, and be protected by the same laws?

JAMES FORTEN

It was at those times that it dawned on me that there was something special and thrilling about my people: our style, our manner and speech. Being among whites made me appreciate black folks that much more.

NATHAN McCALL
Makes Me Wanna Holler: A Young Black Man in America

Today's population of descendants of slaves is testimony to the tenacity, foresight and wisdom of millions of black women.

JOHNETTA B. COLE

I personally believe that if you are able to experience adversity and rise above it, then that in itself builds character.

DEXTER SCOTT KING

The rebby boys don't give colored folks credit for a thing, not a single thing. Why, I think we've done pretty well, considering we were dragged over here in chains from Africa! Why, colored folks *built* this country, and that is the truth. We were the laborers, honey! And even after we were freed, we were the backbone of this country—the maids, cooks, undertakers, barbers, porters, and so on.

SADIE DELANY
Having Our Say: The Delany Sisters' First 100 Years

Ever since I recognized what prejudice is, I've tried to fight it away, and the only weapon I could use was my talent.

SAMMY DAVIS JR.

I am serving the twentieth year of my banning orders! Because they had nothing against me at that time, except that I was Nelson's wife.

WINNIE MANDELA
Part of My Soul Went with Him

... And what needs here to be appreciated—admitted greatly and recognized with gratitude—is the shared sameness in the lives of the descendants of Africa. What needs to be respected is the way those descendants manage to carry on despite it all.

EDDY L. HARRIS, *Author*

The drums of Africa beat in my heart. I cannot rest while there is a single Negro boy or girl lacking a chance to prove their worth.

MARY MCLEOD BETHUNE
Voices of Triumph

I have been to Africa and know that it is not my home. America is; it is my country too, and has been for generations. As I said, I am committed to the search for its true meaning; I hope what I have found is not it. I am forced to hope for it and I have no choice but to meet the challenge of it. Yes, it is true that America has yet to sing its greatest songs, but it had better hurry up and find the key to the tunes.

> JOHN A. WILLIAMS
> This is My Country Too

Don't let anything stop you; there will be times when you'll be disappointed, but you can't stop. Make yourself the best that you can make out of what you are. The very best.

> SADIE TANNER MOSSELL ALEXANDER
> *Economist, Lawyer, Civil Rights Activist*

I remain humble and hungry. And perserverance is a key. I just don't give up.

> AVERY JOHNSON, *San Antonio Spurs*

There's nothing wrong with falling down a few times. You just learn how to get up.

> EMMA J. DOTSON
> *Air Traffic Controller*

Perseverance, because I feel like I just don't give up. I keep pressing on. I can't give up. I've been struggling too long to stop now.

> SYLVIA WOODS, *Restaurateur*

Black people don't buy books. Let's call this a given among White people—the way some of them think Black people use Brazil nuts for toes, or run down property for the hell of it. I wonder why this stereotype has come to be uttered so smugly? . . . I know this: if I had been born one hundred years earlier, a bare sliver of time's difference, I could have been shot or hanged for reading a book . . .

> RALPH WILEY
> What Black People Should Do Now

A boot is a boot. It does not matter who wears the boot if it is pressed down on your neck.

African-American folk saying

I respect people's right to have their opinion, but they got to hear mine!

THE REVEREND AL SHARPTON

At the bottom of education, at the bottom of politics, even at the bottom of religion, there must be for our race economic independence.

BOOKER T. WASHINGTON

Unless the economic basis of racism is relentlessly confronted the victories of the civil and human rights movements will be severely limited and even diminished in the long term. The movement for economic democracy in America must generate the same kind of passionate energy and fighting spirit that the civil rights movement inspired a generation ago.

DON ROJAS
Activist, Journalist

While embracing those aspects of the agenda that have worked in the past, including government programs and lawsuits, bold and independent action is needed to move us past the tortured reality of inequality to challenge institutional economic structures with boycotts, collective development and economic education.

JULIANNE MALVEAUX, *Economist*

If we want to see ourselves in a positive manner, then we must learn to register our votes with our dollars.

CICELY TYSON

Emancipation did not heal the deep and painful scars of slavery.

EARL OFARI HUTCHINSON

The United States will never be able to pay us what they owe us. They don't have the money. But they'll owe it. They've got to do it to save white America, they've got to do it. I'll be able to rest when we get reparations.

QUEEN MOTHER MOORE

We must go from civil rights to silver rights, from aid to trade . . . from the outhouse to the White House.

JESSE JACKSON

Enough is not for people like me. It is a word that has one meaning for us. Trouble. That is the only thing we have enough of. Not wages. Not food. Not money. Not clothes. Not children's books. Not houses. Not marriage. Not doctors. No. Enough is trouble for us.

SINDIWE MAGONA
Living, Loving, and Lying Awake at Night

We have had enough sprinters, we need long distance runners!

JOHN OLIVER KILLENS
Novelist, Playwright

. . . we are engaged in a marathon struggle. We will not sprint to victory. Rather, we are long distance runners in a relay race . . . The baton passed down by our ancestors is in our hands.

SUSAN L. TAYLOR

They came to my house following the demonstration and said, "You under arrest." I said, "All black people under arrest. I ain't even bothered."

JANET DAGGETT
Protester, Teacher

I have seen the faces of young girls fresh from farms, their city day's work done and weary in every bone and muscle, sitting forlorn and already on the verge of hopelessness in their one-room dingy walk-ups. And the men too, I see young men who should be vibrant and enthusiastic and filled with good hopes, and older men who should be serene in accomplishments achieved and satisfactions earned, I see them pouring from factories and construction jobs to trudge on slowing tired legs toward hovels destitute almost of hope.

SEPTIMA CLARK
Educator, Civil Rights Activist

You gotta survive on the *barest* of things! You gotta remember how you were born!

JOHN CHANEY
NCAA Division I Basketball Coach

And like most writers I know, most cultural workers I know, and most especially, most Black women I know, I always have ten or fifteen projects cooking because I never know which one is going to fly first or which one is going to get past the bend in the tunnel where the light is stuck.

TONI CADE BAMBARA
Novelist, Lecturer, Activist

Death neither alarms nor frightens one who has had a long career of fruitful toil. The knowledge that my work has been helpful to many fills me with joy and great satisfaction.

MARY MCLEOD BETHUNE

As South Africa prepares for Black rule, Winnie Mandela still rules the masses and remains a force unbossed and uncowed.

NOKWANDA SITHOLE
South African Journalist

If you asked me whether I would ever live this life of strife again and whether I have any regrets, I will tell you I would live my life exactly the way I have—a hundred times more. If at the end of the day my people will be free, this is my little contribution.

WINNIE MANDELA

He had heard her complain about how hard the white folks worked her; she had told him over and over again that she lived their lives when she was working in their homes, not her own.

RICHARD WRIGHT, Native Son

Too often are the facts of the great sacrifices and heroic efforts of the wives of renowned men overshadowed by the achievements of the men and the wonderful and beautiful part she has played so well is overlooked.

ROSETTA DOUGLASS SPRAGUE
Doublestitch: Black Women Write
About Mothers and Daughters
about her mother, Anna Douglass, wife of Frederick

But we did OK, because my father was very frugal. He had always operated on the theory that you don't buy what you can make, so he had saved money.

VELMA DOLPHIN ASHLEY,
eighty-five-year-old retired schoolteacher
about growing up in Boley, Oklahoma,
an all-black town

You'll have a good life if you remember to always take care of family first. Get your education. Work hard. Save your money, never sell the family land, and don't buy on credit.

DAVE DINWIDDIE, *My Father*

Despite incredible odds, despite suffering numerous casualties, black men have found ways of overcoming the obstacles and making remarkable contributions to ... all of human kind.

HOWARD DODSON

When you're a Black woman, you seldom get to do what you just want to do; you always do what you have to do.

DOROTHY HEIGHT
President, National Council of Negro Women

They came from places called the Carolinas and the Virginias, Georgia, Alabama, Mississippi and Tennessee. They came strong, eager, searching. The city rejected them and they filed and settled along the riverbanks and under bridges in shallow, ramshackle houses made of sticks and tarpaper ...

AUGUST WILSON

I would have turned out another person had I grown up in Birmingham, Alabama, where we had those deafening signs that kept telling you you were not right.

ODETTA

COMING OF AGE, OR FINALLY GROWING UP

But Shelby hadn't had the jolt of seeing her father at fifty in youth's arena. She didn't believe that reflective middle age would allow itself to flirt with irrevocable folly.

DOROTHY WEST
The Wedding

I learned early that loss and pain and death are a part of the fabric of a richly textured life, and that pain can sometimes underscore and intensify a deep and loving relationship.

MIRIAM DeCOSTA-WILLIS
Wild Women Don't Wear No Blues

Up to that stage [Nelson Mandela's imprisonment] I was just his wife. I had no name. Whatever I said was seen as a translation of his ideas, which at that point I was not even sure of. As a result, I had to develop a personality of my own because suddenly I was being pushed around by the police and government. I had a young family to bring up, and I was groping—trying to find my feet politically.

WINNIE MANDELA

Mrs. Mandela is quite radical. She says what she wants to say and how she wants to say it. She is daring, she is glamorous and she is bright. She is really multidimensional. We don't even have an American black woman with this kind of image on film or in a play or anywhere else.

CAMILLE COSBY

I am at a wonderful place in my life. I don't have to rush out and do things anymore.

DELLA REESE

Womanhood has taught me how to discern the changes in the seasons of my life, and to let the seasons be.

RENITA WEEMS

Proverbs are the daughters of experience.

Rwandan proverb

My body has been kind to me, and I have been kind to myself by welcoming what age has brought me.

YVONNE DURANT

A woman is beautiful at any age if she feels good about her self.

ROSE MORGAN
Beauty and Cosmetics Tycoon

I think age is really a plus, because I think I am more mature. I'm a lot calmer, I know myself better and I think my age is actually an advantage. On the other hand, by the time Alexis goes to first grade, I'll be fifty. But I don't think I'll be your typical fifty. I think I'll be sitting at PTA in my tennis skirt just like some of the younger moms.

VALENCIA Y. WHITE

Age is a matter of mind. If you don't mind, it doesn't matter.

ANONYMOUS

I have money. I ain't spending nothing but the evening, and I ain't putting out nothing but the lights.

MAUDE RUSSELL RUTHERFORD
Former Broadway Showgirl at age ninety-eight

You might not be able to kick as high as you used to. But thank the Lord you can still kick.

Traditional wisdom

We never went downtown in our lives without an escort until we were grown women.

SADIE DELANY
Having Our Say: The Delany Sisters' First 100 Years

I love young people. They keep me alive. They will be here even when I'm gone, to remember me.

DOROTHY WEST, *Novelist*

Diana Ross is forty-nine and I'm way younger than she is.

SUZANNE DE PASSE

Part of Jack's ability to hold up in the face of adversity was that slights and attacks didn't chip away at him. He could defend himself by fighting. You didn't empower him—he already felt he belonged in a way that I didn't feel. It took years for me to grow up and feel as strong and as sure of myself as he was.

RACHEL ROBINSON *about her husband,*
baseball great Jackie Robinson

Puberty causes the changing of considerably more than your sheets.

BILL COSBY

Nigel used to say that everything important that ever happened to you happened before you were ten—his explanation for the extraordinary power of puppets to beguile children and adults alike, and why large-as-life puppets were actually larger than life, monstrous, no longer cute but an affront to nature, like dreams and fears blown out of proportion, oversized children almost carnivorous in their demands.

RITA DOVE
through the ivory gate

I get to have later curfews. But I don't stay out all night. My mother trusts me more. When I turned eighteen, it really made my mother proud with graduation coming up. I'm in the class of '95.

TEVIN CAMPBELL, *Singer*

The first thing I would do if I was President would be to say that people over 100 years of age no longer have to pay taxes! Ha ha! Lord knows I've paid my share.

ANNIE ELIZABETH DELANY
Having Our Say: The Delany Sisters' First 100 Years

I can honestly say I'm happy with my life, and there were so many days when I wondered if I'd ever be able to say that.

HALLE BERRY, *Actress*

Sisters and brothers must learn to take responsibility for both their money and their lives.

ANITA BAKER

Before prison, I'd been aware, but not really conscious, that there was a vast psychic difference between men and women. And I'd never really considered what women added to the world. Then I realized that if prison was any indication, a world without women would be crazy, stark raving mad ...

NATHAN MCCALL
Makes Me Wanna Holler: A Young Black Man in America

I refuse to fall into the mind-set of thinking I am right all of the time.

HAKI MADHUBUTI
Claiming Earth: Race, Rage, Rape, Redemption:
Blacks Seeking a Culture of Enlightened Empowerment

On my last trip to South Africa I realized the times things have been most difficult in my life are when I don't let go of something when all the signs are that's what I should do.

PHYLLIS CROCKETT
African-American Broadcast Journalist residing in South Africa

If you allow yourself to get out of the way, grace will come to you.

OPRAH WINFREY

I am my best work—a series of road maps, reports, recipes, doodles and prayers from the front lines.

AUDRE LORDE

The challenge to my generation is to embrace both our traditions and our unique experiences as young African-Americans.

JOAN MORGAN

I've grown as old as I can possibly be; the aging has stopped here, and now I just grow better.

GLORIA NAYLOR

Imagine, forty-six years old and I'm going to be honored in Philadelphia as athlete of the year.

GEORGE FORMAN
Heavyweight Champion of the World

I find myself trying to overcompensate for that. I want to be known as more than a guy who is blessed with the best genes of both his mother and father. But substance is the key. Good looks can work against you when you want to be taken seriously. And I do.

DEXTER SCOTT KING

I don't need anyone to take care of me. I've made that possible myself.

ROSE MORGAN
Beauty and Cosmetics Tycoon

Here is peace. She pulled in her horizon like a giant fishnet. Pulled it around the waist of the world and draped it over her shoulder. So much of her life in its meshes. She called in her soul to come and see!

ZORA NEALE HURSTON
Their Eyes Were Watching God

My mother feels that personal things should remain personal. I explained to her that it is the personal stuff and the secrets that are killing us. And if we don't begin to talk about the stuff that makes us who we are and who we are not, then we are just going to keep repeating the same old things.

SISTER SOULJAH

I am not ashamed of my grandparents for having been slaves. I am only ashamed of myself for having at one time been ashamed.

RALPH ELLISON

When you're a singer, [many think] you're supposed to throw big parties and smoke cocaine, hang out and go to the finest restaurants. That is Hollywood bull. Make your money and take your ass home and share it with somebody. That's always been [my] bottom line.

BARRY WHITE

Boyz II Men is a process, a learning experience. The more you learn, the closer you get to being a man, but you still retain some of that boyishness. The name means learning. And that's what we're doing.

NATHAN MORRIS, *Boyz II Men*

PATIENCE:
A POWERFUL VIRTUE—
TOLERANCE TOO

Handle the delicate with patience.

Ugandan proverb

The calf's process requires patience.

Ugandan proverb

Restless feet may walk into a snake pit.

Ethiopian proverb

Daddy taught me respect. He taught me patience.

HANK AARON

If one is not in a hurry, even an egg will start walking.

Ethiopian proverb

I had much to suffer, in and with my own people—for human nature is the same in black and white folks.

AMANDA SMITH (1837-1915), *Evangelist*

Do not say the first thing that comes to your mind.

Kenyan proverb

One must talk little, and listen much.

Mauritanian proverb

The very thing we fear is what we need more of: solitude.

SUSAN L. TAYLOR

Patience and humility will get you the most in life.

HOWARD CAMPBELL

Humble calf suck the most milk.

Jamaican proverb

Maybe one day we will see that beyond our chaos there could always be a new sunlight, and serenity.

BEN OKRI
Songs of Enchantment

Since time is the one immaterial object which we cannot influence—neither speed up nor slow down, add to nor diminish—it is an imponderably valuable gift.

MAYA ANGELOU
Wouldn't Take Nothing for My Journey Now

It is a work of time, a labor of patience, to become an effective schoolteacher; and it should be a work of love in which they who engage should not abate heart or hope until it is done. And after all, it is one of woman's most sacred rights to have the privilege of forming the symmetry and rightly adjusting the mental balance of an immortal mind.

FRANCIS WATKINS HARPER
Abolitionist, Poet

I pray that in the coming year tolerance will be practiced—as it is in my village—between and within communities, as well as between governments.

AMARA ESSY
President, United Nations General Assembly

Sometimes you have to give a little in order to get a lot.

SHIRLEY CHISHOLM

But discrimination invariably degenerates into gross violations of human rights, even crimes against humanity. Ultimately, discrimination poses a threat to international peace and security. It must be understood: Intolerance is unacceptable.

AMARA ESSY
President, United Nations General Assembly

KNOWLEDGE IS POWER

True knowledge implies morality.

ARLENE CLARK

Woman's sphere is the sphere of knowledge.

MARY McLEOD BETHUNE

A man without the knowledge of where he has been knows not where he is, or where he is going.

DR. YOSEF BEN-JOCHANNAN

The human being is transformed by where his mind goes, not where his body goes.

NA'IM AKBAR

Knowledge is like a garden: if it is not cultivated, it cannot be harvested.

Guinean proverb

Be committed to the life of the mind without falling into idolatry of the mind.

CORNEL WEST

Our responsibility is to carry our generation one step forward.

MARY MCLEOD BETHUNE

Personal experience is important in any scholarly activity, but it cannot substitute for scientific research.

JAMES CONE

Repetition is the mother of knowledge.

S. B. FULLER, *Entrepreneur*

I had gone to a fine university and learned to read some of the most learned books in it. But I had not learned the great truth that God never leaves us.

JESSE OWENS

The mind is the standard of the man.

PAUL LAURENCE DUNBAR

There are times when what you don't play is as important as what you do play.

J.J. JOHNSON, *Trombonist*

It is better to travel alone than with a bad companion.

Senegalese proverb

If you speak, speak to him who understands.

Senegalese proverb

No matter how you feel. No matter how you think the professor feels about you. It's important to have a consistent presence in the classroom. If nothing else, the professor will know you care enough and are serious enough to be there.

NIKKI GIOVANNI
Poet, Professor of English

The passing of knowledge and experience from one generation to the next is as old as time.

MILDRED GREENE
Armchair Philosopher

Papa always taught us that with every dollar you earn, the first ten cents goes to the Lord, the second goes in the bank for hard times, and the rest is yours, but you better spend it wisely. Well, it's a good thing we listened because we're living on that hard-time money now, and not doing too badly.

SADIE DELANY
Having Our Say: The Delany Sisters' First 100 Years

I never had any pretensions ever about "learning" till I'd gotten run out of college and was in the Air Force. Then I started to appreciate the "learning" process. And I actually did, then, become attached to that activity. I mean, it was then I fell in love with learning. But only after I'd come out of school.

AMIRI BARAKA

Don't be afraid of your brothers and sisters in the ghetto who don't know. If you would come and bring your knowledge, your expertise and share it with the brother who does not know, he will put you on his shoulder and carry you around.

ELIJAH MUHAMMAD

For me, every month is February because of my research. But what Black History Month also means to me, is like a mountain that has been submerged in the ocean—the mountain representing knowledge—and then reemerges. What we need to do is to continue to study, and to celebrate, so that the mountain always remains in view.

WILLIAM SERAILE
Professor of Black Studies

He who gives you the diameter of your knowledge, prescribes the circumference of your activities.

LOUIS FARRAKHAN

I've always made it a practice to use my *head* before I use my body. I looked upon playing football like a businessman might: The game was my business; my body and my mind were my assets; and injuries were liabilities.

JIM BROWN

Black people don't have a chance in the world without an education.

KENNETH GREGORY, *College Student*

WELFARE REFORM

Do for Self!

ELIJAH MUHAMMAD

As I traveled the country to a series of welfare-reform hearings late last year, I met many African-Americans who believe that the welfare system is one of the worst things that ever happened to poor people in general and to African-Americans in particular. Many people still remembered times when we, as a group, would do any kind of honest work and were too proud to accept "handouts." They believe that welfare has robbed us of our dignity and sense of self-determination. They feel that this system, ostensibly devised to help uplift women and children, has actually made us poorer as a people.

AVIS LAVELLE, *M.S.W.*

. . . you can continue to trash welfare if you want, but you can't trash the fact that all of welfare is less than half of one percent of the federal budget . . .

JUNE JORDAN, *Poet*

Cultivating is better than begging.

Ugandan proverb

Poverty is fierce.

Ugandan proverb

363

No one goes to another continent to get a lazy group of people to pick cotton when cotton is king of the economy.

GWENDOLYN GOLDSBY GRANT
Advice Columnist

. . . [I]f you're poor and ignorant, with a child, you're a slave. Meaning that you're never going to get out of it. These women are in bondage to a kind of slavery that the 13th Amendment just didn't deal with. The old master provided food, clothing and health care to the slaves because he wanted them to get up and go to work in the morning. And so on welfare: you get food, clothing and shelter—you get survival, but you can't really do anything else. You can't control your life.

DR. JOYCELYN ELDERS

. . . a key element of welfare reform must be an attack on the twin problems of inadequate child-support enforcement and teenage pregnancy. Although tens of thousands of children are living in poverty, there is no nationally coordinated network for child-support enforcement. It's shameful that we do a better job of repossessing cars when the owners don't pay than we do of collecting child support when absentee fathers don't fulfill their financial obligations.

AVIS LaVELLE, *M.S.W.*

A man's bread and butter is only insured when he works for it.

MARCUS GARVEY

When I was young, I used to watch a lot of political debates about welfare. One thing I noticed is that they always had somebody talking about it who obviously was clueless about what welfare is and how it shapes the experiences of our people. I was on welfare. It's a system that's designed to keep fathers out of the house, to make women and children unproductive. Until the concept of welfare is changed, black people in the underclass will continue to be unproductive.

SISTER SOULJAH

Nothing is free. Like these little programs that government got, saying it's free. It costs you your everything.

CORA LEE JOHNSON

We must push our state legislators to make child-support enforcement a higher priority and urge them to support the formation of a nationally coordinated information system so that "deadbeat dads" can be tracked down and prosecuted. But in addition to getting fathers to accept responsibility for their babies, we must also redouble our efforts to challenge and motivate young people not to become parents before they are ready.

AVIS LAVELLE, *M.S.W.*

People say I sound like Newt Gingrich because I'm moralistic, for family values and am antiabortion. But I'm not Newt. I don't bash welfare mothers. I don't agree with the sink-or-swim philosophy. But I do believe that welfare has to be changed.

SISTER SOULJAH

See, I'm one of those bleeding-heart liberals who believes one day we will be judged by how we treat the least among us. It's not just survival of the fittest.

DAVID DINKINS

WHAT DID YOU SAY?

Honey, I surely do love getting the last word, having my say, giving my opinion.

ANNIE ELIZABETH DELANY
Having Our Say: The Delany Sisters' First 100 Years

Some people say I'm feisty. Some say I'm tough. Combative. Bitchy. In the community where I come from—the community of survival—those were considered good qualities.

MAXINE WATERS
U.S. Representative, California

Harvard has ruined more Negroes than bad whiskey.

ADAM CLAYTON POWELL JR.

Dinner and dancing for them is a down payment on a piece of ass. A piece of pussy comes with a drive to the shore. A gift is ransom for your body, my dear, not a token of affection.

NTOZAKE SHANGE
Playwright, Wild Women Don't Wear No Blues

Democracy is an approximate solution to insoluble problems.

CORNEL WEST

Seventy-three percent of all those arrested in this country are White. Eighty-five percent of all rural arrests are White. Fifty-two percent of all in jail are Black. They're making a jail industrial complex of our children.

JESSE JACKSON

I am not a role model . . . just because I dunk a basketball doesn't mean I should raise your kids.

CHARLES BARKLEY

We must stop seeing none other than stars as role models, then complaining that black children take only stars as role models. By focusing on glittering role models, we are left too often not with role models but with models playing roles.

NATHAN HARE AND JULIA HARE
The Miseducation of the Black Child

I'm told people look to me as a role model. I've worked very hard in my career and people appreciate the work I've done.

WILMA RUDOLPH

Until 1971 it was kinky and nappy and burry, like any other black man's. Then one night I got into bed with my lovely wife, Henrietta, when suddenly my head got to rumbling. It felt like a volcanic eruption. Ping! Ping! Ping! . . . All them curls were straightening out and straightening up. Each strand stood erect, pristine and beautiful, reaching for the heavens on its own individual stimulation. . . . Being a religious person like myself, I looked up the Scriptures and found God did it to me. I thought, whaddya know, I've been chosen by God! He made every shank a citadel.

DON KING

There is a tradition at the Apollo Theatre that has been built up over the years. It's called borrowing from the best. You see, the Apollo Theatre is uptown. But many performers from downtown would come uptown to sit in this theater and copy down what the uptown people were saying so they could take it downtown. So that many of the famous comics would come and sit right where you all are—well not really—mostly in the back, because they had paper and pencil and they would copy down what the uptown person was saying and then take it downtown. Many dancers, choreographers, came uptown to copy down what they saw uptown and created it downtown. But they hadn't! They saw it uptown and kept it quiet about what part of town they saw it around when they wrote it down.

BILL COSBY
"Motown at the Apollo, Twentieth Anniversary"

I cannot believe that you came here from the other side of the river to shatter my dreams.

SAM CHEKWAS
Ogbanje: Son of the Gods

Why is there always the implication that the white woman is just mesmerized, just helpless, if she's with a black man? Everybody knows the smart, hip, twentieth-century white woman is in complete control of herself and does exactly what she damn well wants to do and nothing else.

JIM BROWN

Out of the intensity of her phsyical oneness had come a mystical communication in which she had taken his dying into the warm bed of her body, not to die with him, not to die for her, but to fight for his life with the supernatural strength the resisting flesh stores for the hour before eternity.

DOROTHY WEST
The Wedding

We can always see possibilities—*active* with a promise of development, and there's the *inactive*, struggling with internal demands for transformation. And, finally, there's the *active negative*—racing toward its own negation.

AKINSHIJU C. OLA

The end is in the beginning and lies far ahead.

RALPH ELLISON

POWER

What is needed is a realization that power without love is reckless and abusive, and love without power is sentimental and anemic.

THE REVEREND MARTIN LUTHER KING JR.

If you are a powerful person, gain respect through knowledge and gentleness of speech and conduct.

Sacred wisdom of ancient Egypt

Sisters, I ain't clear what you be after—If women want any rights more than they got, why don't they just take them and not be talking about it?

SOJOURNER TRUTH

The role of education is to train the student how to be a responsible handler of power.

JOHN HENRIK CLARK

As a teacher, my main thrust in the classroom has always been to encourage and equip people to respect their rage and their power.

TONI CADE BAMBARA
Novelist, Professor

It is a liberal arts education that develops excitement about learning, an excitement that lasts a lifetime. That's empowerment!

JOHNETTA B. COLE

We want power, it can only come through organization, and organization comes through unity.

ALEXANDER CRUMMELL

It's nonexistent. There's no such thing as power in Hollywood—that's illusion.

WHOOPI GOLDBERG

When you become sentimental about power, you don't have it any more.

JOHN HENRIK CLARK

By giving up the illusory power that comes from lying and manipulation and opting instead for the personal power and dignity that comes from being honest, black women can begin to eliminate life-threatening pain from our lives.

BELL HOOKS
Sisters of the Yam: Black Women and Self-Recovery

I manage myself and I wouldn't have it any other way. My mistake was that I wasn't doing it from the beginning! All the material that has worked for me I found myself—nobody sent me or brought me anything—no producers discovered any tunes. All the bookings, and negotiating of fees I did myself. You can't do it all, but you've got to know what's going on in your business. That's why I'm managing myself; more people should do it. It's not bad stuff and it's fun.

ROBERTA FLACK

Power only means the ability to have control over your life. Power implies choice.

NIKKI GIOVANNI

Take charge. Ignorance is no longer a valid excuse. Empower yourself.

ANITA BAKER

There is a lot to be said about controlling your own destiny. You can do what you want to do without fearing that others won't agree.

ERICK SERMON, *Rap Artist*

Historically, black colleges have produced 50 percent of all black doctors, 30 percent of all Afro-American lawyers and the vast majority of the trained clergy.

DANIEL ALDRIDGE
Political Activist

I'd learned about the strength of the mind and seen that mental toughness, more than brawn, determines who survives and who buckles.

NATHAN MCCALL
Makes Me Wanna Holler: A Young Black Man in America

Negativity can kill you. You have to take control of your destiny and if your destiny is full of negativity, then the first thing you have to do is sweep up your house.

ROLANDA WATTS
Talk Show Host

The puzzling, often fumbling search for meaning embedded in the unfair or the painful can sometimes force us to tap into a mother lode of shimmering, unknown strength.

MIRIAM DeCOSTA-WILLIS
Wild Women Don't Wear No Blues

We have been named; we should now become "namers."

LERONE BENNETT

I'm the most democratic fascist you'll ever meet. I listen to everybody and then I make a decision.

GEORGE C. WOLFE, *Producer*

Most people don't even believe in success. They feel helpless even before they begin ... We have the power to make it in this society, and so we can't blame the system for everything. It is the fear of failure that gets into the way.

JOHN H. JOHNSON

True power comes through cooperation and silence.

Ashanti proverb

Faith in God is the greatest power ... but great, too, is faith in oneself.

MARY McLEOD BETHUNE
Her Own Words of Inspiration

There is great power in teaching young black girls about Abraham Lincoln but never about the distinguished nineteenth-century black activist, Ida B. Wells. There is great power in that act of miseducation because the silence about black women activists suggests that we always have been, are now, and must always be no more than the recipients of what is done to us.

JOHNETTA B. COLE

A little subtleness is better than a lot of force.

Congolese proverb

If Black women are really tired of carrying the load in the Black community, we are going to have to express to our men a willingness to share power.

AUDREY B. CHAPMAN
Black Men and Women: The Battle for Love and Power

The heart of the wise man lies quiet like limpid water.

African proverb

As young African men and women, we have the power to change the quality of our lives. We have to educate ourselves, but not in the traditional public-school way because the curriculum is not enough to fill the heart, soul and mind of a black child. We have to use the libraries and spend time in bookstores looking for alternative forms of information. We need to make resources out of the elders in our community.

SISTER SOULJAH

The vast majority of U.S. political office holders use the power of their positions to defend or advance the economic interests not of those who elected them but of those who helped finance their campaigns and of those with controlling interests in the economic structures of their constituencies.

DON ROJAS
Activist Journalist

You see, my grandmother was a woman who spoiled us outrageously, who dared to just let me "be." ... I don't see myself as being empowered because of a certain job or status. I see myself as being empowered because of my grandmother, and people like her. It has really been that kind of transmitting that has given us power. My power may have gotten manifested in a different kind of politics than that of my grandmother. But nonetheless, it was the same power ...

TONI CADE BAMBARA, *Author, Lecturer*

That ultimate power over life and death is so much at the heart of masculinity in this culture, and feminism has done nothing to change that. You prove the depths of your manhood by your willingness to go down in struggle—whether it's in a pathetic fight with a friend over a bag of potato chips or whether it's in going to another country and shooting other people in the name of patriotism.

BELL HOOKS

White men grow up with an implicit belief that they are born to wield power over others weaker than they. And if these men find they have no power, then they must find the weakest of all and wield what they can. Monsters are thus created.

RALPH WILEY
What Black People Should Do Now

Broadway does not want our blackness, wasn't designed or intended for it, definitely doesn't want any strange new forms inspired by that very blackness. She is a contented fat white cow. If you can slip and milk her for a minute—well, then, more black power to you, brother. But we're telling you—it's a weird price she's asking.

WOODIE KING AND RON MILNER

Power is never given; it's taken. And almost always with a fight.

TONY COX, *Writer*

So many truths seem to be rushing at me as the result of things felt and seen and lived through. Oh what I think I must tell this world! Oh the time that I crave, and the peace, and the power!

LORRAINE HANSBERRY, *Playwright*

I am not anti-American or un-American. I think there are plenty of good people in America, but there are also plenty of bad people in America—and the bad ones are the ones that seem to have all the power.

MALCOLM X

It's not about us. That power to captivate 20,000 people when we go on stage, or millions when a song is on the radio—no human has that kind of power. That's God talking through us.

NATHAN MORRIS, *Boyz II Men*

Just as lightning makes no sound until it strikes, the Negro Revolution generated quietly. But when it struck, the revealing flash of its power and the impact of its sincerity and fervor displayed a force of frightening intensity.

THE REVEREND MARTIN LUTHER KING JR.

ᴀNGER

I was furious. Even if everything he [Henry Louis (Skip) Gates Jr.] said was true, it was inexcusable not to mention what might have motivated blacks to feel this way, and to fail to talk about all the Jewish neoconservative racists who are undermining blacks in every way they can. Now that wouldn't excuse anti-Semitics, which is awful, but it would at least provide a context for this anger and make it less likely that Skip's piece is used by whites to justify cutting back spending on social programs.

DERRICK BELL

Two birds disputed about a kernel, when a third swooped down and carried it off.

Congolese parable

One camel does not make fun of the other camel's hump.

Guinean proverb

To be black in America is to live in a constant state of rage.

JAMES BALDWIN

The way America looks at the Black male hasn't changed since the day they sold us cut-rate and cutthroat ...

MEL TAPLEY
Arts and Entertainment Editor, Amsterdam News

Never before have you heard so many black male voices yelling at the world.

Rap star CHUCK D.

There is something religious in the anger and intensity of such men as Malcolm X, Medgar Evers, Don L. Lee [Haki Madhubuti], Senghor—almost as if they prepare for a coming Jihad, having realized at long last that ones blooming must be fed and inspired by action, by movement, by dedication to the principle that only those die well who have lived freely. And to live freely is to interject chaos into the universe, to disrupt the pretensions of order and serenity, promulgated by those who man the concentration camps.

ADDISON GAYLE JR.
Literary Critic

Uprisings are bound to be the order of the day, because our struggle here has been reduced by the white man, by his choice, to black versus white.

WINNIE MANDELA

I've spent an entire life making sure that I got into any place I wanted to get into. It was also a given that once I got into the room, I was supposed to open up the windows and doors and let in other people ... a channeled rage can become a fuel.

GEORGE C. WOLFE, *Producer*

A scared Negro is one thing. A mad Negro is something else.

DICK GREGORY

You don't owe the truth to your enemy.

UNITED AFRICAN MOVEMENT MEMBER

I'm very fierce. If I feel I'm right, if I feel I've been violated, then I am like a warrior from hell.

GEORGE C. WOLFE, *Producer*

As the wound inflames the finger, as thought inflames the mind.

Ethiopian proverb

White people will do anything and they always have. But then they started to say that we would do anything and now they've got us believing that.

LILY JEAN RUSSELL

Too much discussion means a quarrel.

Ivory Coast proverb

Because a man has injured your goat, do not go out and kill his bull.

Kenyan proverb

Why are middle-class blacks enraged and disillusioned? Because they have learned that playing by the rules does not shield them from racial prejudice, and that even with a "first-class" background, education and demeanor, they can still expect to sit in the second class coach.

CARRIE B. ROBINSON, *Writer*

[Racial harmony] will not come to pass as long as we insist on dividing people into different camps, swearing that differences don't count or that repeated blows to the soul shouldn't be taken seriously.

ELLIS COSE, *Author*

After winning the bronze medal . . . the most difficult thing was going back and getting angry inside about how people perceived black people where I lived. That's when you rebel.

WILMA RUDOLPH

I am boldly and unashamedly anti-Europe. I do not believe there are any European solutions for the problems Europeans set in motion.

JOHN HENRIK CLARK, *Historian*

If you hate someone, it only eats away at your being. Oftentimes they don't even know you hate them, or they don't care. You are the one who ends up suffering.

MEDGAR EVERS

But it was very difficult for me. I have painful memories of being called a "nigger"; of having stones thrown at me; of being chased by a gang of white boys; of riding the buses and having to sit or stand in that little section reserved for us with its barriers of chicken wire; of not being able to go to the pool; and of having to sit up in the buzzards roost in the movies. And I could go on and on.

Then, of course, when the threats started coming in, it made it very difficult for me to look kindly upon the white race, even though we had a few white people we considered friends.

When Medgar was killed, that suppressed feeling of hatred came alive and overtook me. It was a struggle to try to find some kind of balance that I could show to the public in terms of my feelings. I would have people tell me, "Oh my dear, you are so brave, you are so strong, you are so forgiving," and I would smile and thank them, but underneath I would be saying, "You just don't know. I hate your guts."

But I had to deal with my feelings of hatred because I had three children who were watching me very closely and listening to practically everything I had to say. I recall vividly spewing out some hateful things in the presence of my children, and the two oldest ones looked at me with a look that said "Mom, you aren't supposed to say those things; you aren't supposed to feel that way." And I remembered what Medgar told me, that I should not hate, and that if anything were to happen to him I should also rear his children not to hate.

MYRLIE EVERS-WILLIAMS
Teaching Tolerance, *the semi-annual publication of the Southern Poverty Law Center*

Don't talk to me about *Negro* violence. The greatest violence this country has ever known has been on behalf of the various interests of white people, demanding whatever they were convinced were their rights.

JIM BROWN

It did not satisfy me to narrate wrongs. I felt like denouncing them.

FREDERICK DOUGLASS

Don't be afraid to be as angry or as loving as you can, because when you feel nothing, it's just death.

LENA HORNE

White people, quit moving around the country like a bunch of damned gypsies. Wherever you are, we'll be there.

REDD FOXX

Why, when I most want to be seen, am I suddenly rendered invisible?

ELLIS COSE
The Rage of a Privileged Class

The average ghetto Negro is so pent up and fed up with white lies, hostility, hypocrisy and neglect that riots don't *need* planning.

JIM BROWN

I am a 100-percent advocate that if a man slaps you, you should slap him back.

JIM BROWN

It was intended that you should perish in the ghetto, perish by never being allowed to go behind the white man's definitions, by never being allowed to spell your proper name.

JAMES BALDWIN

FREEDOM

We may well exclaim how event after event has paved the way for freedom.

FRANCIS WATKINS HARPER
Abolitionist, Poet

We know that he is armed to the teeth. But the determination, the thirst for freedom in children's hearts, was such that they were prepared to face those machine guns with stones. That is what happens when you hunger for freedom, when you want to break those chains of oppression. Nothing else seems to matter.

WINNIE MANDELA
Part of My Soul Went with Him

Later, we heard that the bus of the Freedom Riders had been burned on Mother's Day in Anniston, Alabama, and that another bus had been attacked by people in Birmingham. CORE was discontinuing the Freedom Ride, people said. We knew we were subject to being killed. This did not matter to us. There was so much at stake, we could not allow the segregationists to stop us. We had to continue that Freedom Ride even if we were killed in the process.

LUCRETIA COLLINS
Civil Rights Activist

When you're a black child who believes she has no control over her life, you create your own definition of freedom.

PATRICE GAINES
Author, Journalist, Wild Women Don't Wear No Blues

Freedom without civility, freedom without the ability to live in peace, was not true freedom at all.

NELSON MANDELA

Malcolm's basic goal or objective never changed: He was totally committed to freedom for oppressed people.

DR. BETTY SHABAZZ
Malcolm X: The Man and His Times

A freedom seeking people cannot afford to be intellectually sloppy.

WILLIAM STRICKLAND
Professor, Author

Know that individual responsibility is the basis of freedom, and that the limitations imposed by fate (whether fair or unfair) are no excuse for passivity.

SHELBY STEELE

Freedom can only exist if it is bound to principles and anchored in economics.

RUBY DEE

Well, we persisted, and finally Papa told us of the day his people were freed. He remembered being in the kitchen and wearing a little apron, which little slave boys wore in those days. It had one button at the top, at the back of the neck, and the ends were loose. And when the news of the Surrender came, he said he ran about the house with that apron fluttering behind him, yelling, "Freedom! Freedom! I am free! I am Free!"

ANNIE ELIZABETH DELANY, *D.D.S.*
Having Our Say: The Delany Sisters' First 100 Years

I had grown up in a society where there were very clear lines. The civil rights movement gave me the power to challenge any line that limits me.

CORDELL REAGON
Civil Rights Activist

What some people forget with Martin Luther King and the movement of the '60s is that *we won*. We wanted an end to Jim Crow laws and we got it. Now once that happened, we bumped into something else, which was racism, and that's another fight. But we achieved our aim—and the world watched.

DICK GREGORY

The South is to be a great theater for the colored man's development and progress. There is brain-power here. If any doubt it, let him come into our schools, or even converse with some of our Freedmen either in their homes or by the way-side.

FRANCIS WATKINS HARPER, *Poet*

Freedom brings its responsibilities and it is my earnest hope that the hurdle we have just cleared will not give rise within us to any complacency for what we have achieved, or any false illusions about the hard work that lies ahead.

KWAME NKRUMAH

Nobody gives you freedom! If you think the end of apartheid means the end of white dominance, you are dreaming. That country [South Africa] was taken with blood. That is the only way white dominance will be removed.

JOHN HENRIK CLARK, *Historian*

The Emancipation Proclamation [which freed the slaves] was issued in 1863, ninety-odd years ago. I believe in gradualism. I also believe that ninety-odd years is pretty gradual.

THURGOOD MARSHALL

I don't want any other demands on my conscience. I don't want anything on my schedule—it makes me crazy. I want the freedom to do nothing. If I speak to a group, it's going to be for poor people, and *I'm* going to pay for my own flight.

JOHN CHANEY
Basketball Coach, Temple University

[The] University is talking about his refusal to ride the gravy train that comes with successful Division I coaching. Instead Coach Chaney keeps his focus on his commitment to remember where he was born, and to be there for those near to him.

MICHAEL HARDEN
about John Chaney,
his college basketball coach at Temple University

My deepest-seated fear, the thing that would go against every fiber in my body, is that I would ever leave the common people, that I would ever become a high-and-mighty jackass.

JOHN CHANEY

Whenever I went to the library and there was a book in the adult section I wanted to read, my parents would write a note that said "Let her take out whatever she wants." I always felt that I had freedom in my reading.

RITA DOVE, *Poet Laureate of the United States*

We are not these bodies, we are spirits, God's ideas. But you must strive to be the best of what God made you. You don't want to be white, what you really want is to be free, and freedom is a state of mind.

INDIA ANETTE PEYTON
grandmother of Melba Patillo Beals

I train people to be free of the stereotype that if you're black and female and poor, nobody expects anything of you.

BERTHA KNOX GILKEY

Freedom without organization is chaos. I want to put freedom into music the way I conceive it. It is free, but it's organized freedom.

DIZZY GILLESPIE

It may be that God himself has written upon both my heart and brain a commission to use time, talent and energy in the cause of freedom.

FRANCES ELLEN WATKINS HARPER
Abolitionist, Poet

... I gradually came to the point where I did not look at another person and see their color first. And when I reached that level it was one of the most liberating feelings that I have had. It's absolutely amazing to me. People are people, and that's that. We have good and bad and not so good in every ethnic group.

MYRLIE EVERS-WILLIAMS

THINK POSITIVE

Good things happen to positive people.

LES BROWN

... But because we get so much violence on the news, why make film, which has such potential as a positive vehicle, negative too?

HALLE BERRY, Actress

Women are blessed with a jewel of strength that glows all the time.

JUDITH JAMISON

Nobody can do everything, but everybody can do something, and if everybody does something, everything will get done.

GIL SCOTT HERON

Removing mountains requires digging into everything around them.

LINDA H. HOLLIES

God doesn't make mistakes. My daughter has added years to my life. She's made me more vibrant. Look at pregnancy as something positive that's happening to you and go on with

388

your blessings because that's exactly what a child is. A child is a blessing. A child is a gift.

MARY E. FLOWERS
Politician, about the birth of her
first child after age forty

If you really think about it, racism can give you the blues so bad you don't feel like continuing on. But that's not the answer. I think you have to stay positive, stay strong, but stay aware.

HALLE BERRY, *Actress*

Indeed, we must acknowledge that our lives are conceptualized not by the negative forces (slavery, colonialism, imperialism, racism, sexism, and other marginalizing historical forces) but by the detailed recording of the positive outcomes of our lives as individuals. These outcomes are testimony to the enduring truths about our ability to reshape our destiny, to find peace in war zones, to seek friendship among enemies, to find shelter from the wind and rain, to preserve our soulless climate—to survive against all odds.

GLENDA P. SIMMS

Take your eyes off what you didn't get and focus, with thanksgiving, on what you did get. Joy and peace are found in what you have that is positive.

MILDRED GREENE
Armchair Philosopher

Accentuate the positive; we can't build on negatives.

LILY JEAN RUSSELL
Social Worker

. . . as you put out positive energy it comes back to you and if you put out negative energy it'll eventually come back to you too.

EVERETTE HARP, *Saxophonist*

When you get negative thoughts, use that as inspiration to empower your positive self.

ROLANDA WATTS
Talk Show Host

I have a natural ability to analyze the fundamentals and ferret out facts and opportunities, and through labor and effort and creativity, to bring value to those opportunities that in the end will result in superior returns.

REGINALD LEWIS

. . . true beauty encompasses far more than the merely physical. It means not only the superficial attractiveness of your face and body, but the deeper, more fulfilling beauty of mind and spirit as well . . . But as women have moved forward pursuing fuller lives, seeking better opportunities for themselves in the world, achieving better jobs, more fulfilling careers and higher levels of education, many of us have also come to the realization that outer goals as these are not enough if the nurturing of our inner selves is neglected. For example, as important as any work is to me, it's not the source of my self-worth. And it is self-worth that's the true source of beauty both inward and out.

BEVERLY JOHNSON
True Beauty

Deal with yourself as an individual worthy of respect, and make everyone else deal with you the same way. College is a little like playing grown-up. Practice what you want to be. You have been telling your parents you are grown. Now is your chance to act like it.

NIKKI GIOVANNI
Poet, Professor of English

To be *whole*—politically, psychically, spiritually, culturally, intellectually, aesthetically, physically, and economically—is of profound significance. It is significant because there is a correlative to this. There is a responsibility to self and to history that is developed once you are "whole," once you are well, once you acknowledge your powers.

TONI CADE BAMBARA
Novelist, Lecturer

Never accept the negative thought, "I can't make it because I'm black." You can't concede defeat before you even start.

JAMES EARL JONES, *Actor*

I don't know about all this greatness stuff. I just want to keep on keeping on.

AL GREEN

My mother is my root, my foundation. She planted the seed that I have based my life on, and that is the belief that the ability to achieve starts in your mind.

MICHAEL JORDAN

Laughter releases stress. Comedy is like a medicine that helps you relieve tension . . . it can help people cope with problems.

ALTURO SHELTON

We must reinforce argument with results.

BOOKER T. WASHINGTON

I have totally eradicated the word "failure" from my vocabulary. "Setback," every now and then. "Failure," never.

DON KING

Sometimes the sun will come in, making a bright yellow day.

SARAH WRIGHT, *Novelist*

In these times of uncertainty, we are often prone to succumb to anxiety. But we can turn to the Word of God and find the power to overcome it—and get on with the business of trusting in the Lord and abiding in His peace.

TONYA BOLDEN, *Author*

There will be no more praise for predicting rain. It is time to build some arks.

A CONTEMPORARY BLACK MAN

Some people say they can't go to a grave. They'll cry. But a day comes when thinking about your loved one makes you smile. Now when I visit my mom's [grave], I'm smiling.

JOHNNIE COCHRAN JR., *Esquire*

I just want to be a change agent. I want to do my part in helping people to change their negative attitudes about us as a people. And hopefully, if we have any negative attitudes about ourselves, I want to help change those, too.

CAMILLE COSBY

Life is forever awakening the mind to the realities of *existence*!

PATRICIA SPRADLEY, *Ed.D.*

We have to work for peace. If we believe in peace, we have to work for peace.

GIL SCOTT HERON

People need to respect each other's concerns and differences. And frankly, there's far more in common than divides us.

DAVID DINKINS

I think that the mixture of the marvelous and the terrible is a basic condition of human life, and that the persistence of human ideals represents the marvelous pulling itself up out of the chaos of the universe.

RALPH ELLISON

I heard Elsa Lanchester say, "An actor must be indestructible." She was right. That the show must go on is one of life's really great philosophies.

DOROTHY DANDRIDGE

When the going gets tough and you feel like throwing your hands in the air, listen to that voice that tells you "Keep going. Hang in there." Guts and determination will pull you through.

ALICE COACHMAN
*the First African-American Woman
to win an Olympic gold medal*

Believe in Life!

W. E. B. DU BOIS

Africa: Her Patriots and Philosophers

We do not confuse exploitation or exploiters with the colour of men's skins; we do not want any exploitation in our countries, not even by black people.

FRANTZ FANON

... independence has been turned into a cage, with people looking at us from outside the bars, sometimes with charitable compassion, sometimes with glee and delight.

PATRICE LUMUMBA

To be a Westernized African in today's post-colonial Africa means ultimately to be marked/branded—in one way or another—by the historical experience of European colonialism. We should not try to "hide" from this all-pervasive element of our modern African historicity. Rather, our efforts to surmount it must begin by facing up to and confronting this enigmatic actuality.... for ultimately the antidote is always in the poison.

TSENAY SEREQUEBERHAN, *Philosopher*

Africa will not really attain its cultural [historic, political, and economic] maturity as long as it does not elevate itself resolutely to a profound thinking of its essential problems, that is to say, to philosophical thought.

MARCIEN TOWA, *Philosopher*

It was under the guise of introducing the "maturity" of the modern age that European colonialism imposed on African its present subordinate status. Thus, to be able to transcend this deplorable situation we contemporary Africans need to confront the question of our "maturity" at its most fundamental level— on the plane of philosophic reflection.

TSENAY SEREQUEBERHAN, *Philosopher*

The cultural [historic] memory is ceaselessly renewed retroactively by new discoveries. Our past, by continually modifying itself through our discoveries, invites us to new appropriations; these appropriations lead us toward a better grasp of our identity.

OKONDA OKOLO, *Philosopher*

When the white serpent has once bitten you, you will search in vain for a remedy against its bite.

BAHTA HAGOS
Eritrean Anticolonialist Leader, 1894

In Africa, the interest in hermeneutics also arises out of the reality of crisis: a generalized identity crisis due to the presence of a culture—a foreign and dominating tradition—and the necessity for a self-affirmation in the construction of an authentic culture and tradition.

OKONDA OKOLO, *Philosopher*

... colonialism can be considered as the paralysis or deviation or even the halting of the history of one people in favour of the acceleration of the historical development of other peoples.

AMILCAR CABRAL

Man aspires to know truth and the hidden things of nature, but this endeavour is difficult and can only be attained with great labour and patience. . . . Hence people hastily accept what they have heard from their fathers and shy from any [critical] examination.

ZAR'A YA'AQOB
Sixteenth-century Abyssinian Philosopher

For a long time, in the night, his voice was that of the voiceless phantoms of his ancestors, whom he had raised up. With them, he wept their death; but also, in long cadence, they sang his birth.

CHEIKH HAMIDOU KANE

. . . the effort of philosophy . . . is directly aimed at . . . overcoming the limits of human finitude.

TSENAY SEREQUEBERHAN, *Philosopher*

The African so propagandized strives to be those things most unlike himself and most alien of the culture that produced him.

EDWARD BLYDEN

He who lives with an ass, makes noises like an ass.

Ghanian proverb

We are always gaining experience by working in the present for the future. Not just in Africa, but everywhere. We have to mix. It's the best way to live.

SALIF KEITA, *Singer*

Ancestor Speak

But before the truth can be told of those days—and before it is time for us during this rainy season to feast upon the carcass of the boar—we must remember the first legends and myths, the secrets before the flood and regeneration, before our queen mothers gave us the privilege to play our songs on the balafons and talking drums.

HERB BOYD
African History for Beginners

Only the eagle announces his death.

Ugandan proverb

The one you heal is the one who kicks you.

Ugandan proverb

Every problem has a solution!

Saying

It is a poor squirrel that has only one hole.

Mother wit

A man with too much ambition cannot sleep in peace.

Ugandan proverb

397

He who is free of faults will never die.

Congolese proverb

A man who continually laments is not heeded.

Kenyan proverb

He who has done evil expects evil.

Guinean proverb

Do not leave your host's house, throwing mud in his well.

Zulu proverb

Do not tell the man who is carrying you that he stinks.

Sierra Leonean proverb

The bird forgets, but the trap doesn't.

West Indian folk saying

When the fool is told a proverb, its meaning has to be explained to him.

Ashanti proverb

A fool looks for dung where the cow never browsed.

Ethiopian proverb

A fool and water will go the way they are diverted.

Ethiopian proverb

When a fool is cursed, he thinks he is being praised.

Ethiopian proverb

The fool is thirsty in the midst of water.

Ethiopian proverb

A fool will pair an ox with an elephant.

Ethiopian proverb

When the master is absent, the frogs hop into the house.

African folk saying

He who is bitten by a snake fears a lizard.

African folk saying

The flood takes him in, and the ebb takes him out.

African proverb

She is like a road—pretty, but crooked.

African folk saying

Do not dispose of the monkey's tail before he is dead.

Congolese proverb

You do not teach the paths of the forest to an old gorilla.

Congolese proverb

A single bracelet does not jingle.

Congolese proverb

He is meaner than a junkyard dog.

African-American folk saying

The witness of a rat is another rat.

Ethiopian proverb

Cactus is bitter only to him who tastes of it.

Ethiopian proverb

One who recovers from sickness, forgets about God.

Ethiopian proverb

Termites live underground.

Ethiopian proverb

Her horns are not too heavy for the cow.

Ethiopian proverb

A cat may go to a monastery, but she still remains a cat!

Ethiopian proverb

I have a cow in the sky but cannot drink her milk.

Ethiopian proverb

When one sets a portion for oneself, usually it is not too small.

Ethiopian proverb

He who wants to barter, usually knows what is best for him.

Ethiopian proverb

She who does not yet know how to walk, cannot climb a ladder.

Ethiopian proverb

Saying that it's for her child, she gets herself a loaf of bread.

Ethiopian proverb

Even over cold pudding, the coward says: "It will burn my mouth."

Ethiopian proverb

A single stick may smoke, but it will not burn.

Ethiopian proverb

One is born, one dies; the land increases.

Ethiopian proverb

If there were no elephants in the jungle, the buffalo would be a great animal.

Ghanian proverb

A crab does not beget a bird.

Ghanian proverb

If you find no fish, you have to eat bread.

Ghanian proverb

A cow that has no tail should not try to chase away flies.

Guinean proverb

The toad likes water, but not when it's boiling.

Guinean proverb

He who talks incessantly, talks nonsense.

Ivory Coast proverb

A man who has once been tossed by a buffalo, when he sees a black ox, thinks it's another buffalo.

Kenyan proverb

He who does not know one thing knows another.

Kenyan proverb

Try this bracelet: if it fits you wear it, but if it hurts you, throw it away no matter how shiny.

Kenyan proverb

When you take a knife away from a child, give him a piece of wood instead.

Kenyan proverb

He who is unable to dance says that the yard is stony.

Kenyan proverb

If a dead tree falls, it carries with it a live one.

Kenyan proverb

There is no phrase without a double meaning.

Kenyan proverb

There is no cure that does not cost.

Kenyan proverb

Home affairs are not talked about on the public square.

Kenyan proverb

Good millet is known at the harvest.

Kenyan proverb

Do not measure the timbers for your house in the forest.

Kenyan proverb

Though the palm tree in the jungle is big, who knows how big its yield will be?

Liberian proverb

Don't kick a sleeping dog.

Madagascan proverb

An eel that was not caught is as big as your thigh.

Madagascan proverb

The dog's bark is not might, but fright.

Madagascan proverb

If you try to cleanse others—like soap, you will waste away in the process.

Madagascan proverb

Not all the flowers of a tree produce fruit.

Mauritanian proverb

When you are finished being sick, you know the remedy.

Haitian proverb

It's after the battle that you count the wounded.

Haitian proverb

The monkey caresses its child until it kills it.

Haitian proverb

The hawk missed you, but it didn't forget about you.

Haitian proverb

There is nothing that is hot that doesn't eventually become cold.

Haitian proverb

Rotten teeth are strong against ripe bananas.

Haitian proverb

When the river is rising, you don't put your foot in it.

Haitian proverb

In the midst of blind people, a one-eyed person is king.

Haitian proverb

When they want to kill a dog, they say it's crazy.

Haitian proverb

Your own house cat is the one who is eating your chickens.

Haitian proverb

Never leave the cat to guard the butter.

Haitian proverb

A loaded donkey does not stop.

Haitian proverb

In the place where they pluck the turkey's feathers, the chicken does not laugh.

Haitian proverb

It's nothing to lead the snake to school. Making it sit down is the hard part.

Haitian proverb

It's when the snake dies that you see its real length.

Haitian proverb

With Titid [Aristide] my heart is not pounding.

Haitian saying

To get a new bracelet is not sufficient reason to throw away the old one.

African proverb

He who wishes to barter, does not like his own property.

Nigerian proverb

Seeing is better than hearing.

Nigerian proverb

He who is sick will not refuse medicine.

Nigerian proverb

A wealthy man will always have followers.

Nigerian proverb

The dying man is not saved by medicine.

Nigerian proverb

Some birds avoid the water, ducks seek it.

Nigerian proverb

The house roof fights the rain, but he who is sheltered ignores it.

Nigerian proverb

Since he has no eyes, he says that eyes smell bad.

Nigerian proverb

He who is being carried does not realize how far the town is.

Nigerian proverb

The one-eyed man thanks God only when he sees a man who is totally blind.

Nigerian proverb

Someone else's legs do you no good in traveling.

Nigerian proverb

Fine words do not produce food.

Nigerian proverb

When the mouse laughs at the cat, there is a hole nearby.

Nigerian proverb

Before shooting, one must aim.

Nigerian proverb

He who has goods can sell them.

Nigerian proverb

When one is in trouble, one remembers God.

Nigerian proverb

A shepherd does not strike his sheep.

Nigerian proverb

A bird can drink much, but an elephant drinks more.

Nigerian proverb

Horns do not grow before the head.

Nigerian proverb

Time destroys all things.

Nigerian proverb

Earth is the queen of beds.

Nigerian proverb

Little is better than nothing.

Nigerian proverb

One little arrow does not kill a serpent.

African proverb

Do not be like the mosquito that bites the owner of the house.

Liberian proverb

If your mouth turns into a knife, it will cut off your lips.

Zimbabwean proverb

The monkey does not see his own hind parts; he sees his neighbors'.

Zimbabwean proverb

When the leopard is away, his cubs are eaten.

Rwandan proverb

If you are building a house and a nail breaks, do you stop building, or do you change the nail?

Burundian proverb

Nobody tells all he knows.

Senegalese proverb

A healthy ear can stand hearing sick words.

Senegalese proverb

If a little tree grows in the shade of a larger tree, it will die small.

Senegalese proverb

Count your blessings.

Sagacious axiom

ABOUT THE AUTHOR

ELZA DINWIDDIE-BOYD is the author of *Proud Heritage: 11,001 Names for Your African American Baby.* She teaches English Composition for the College of New Rochelle, School of New Resources at the New York Theological Seminary Campus. Boyd resides in New York City with her husband.

THE AFRICAN AMERICAN EXPERIENCE
from Avon Books

BULLWHIP DAYS   70884-1/ $14.00 US/ $19.00 CAN
edited by James Mellon
In their own voices, an oral history of the personal memories of the last survivors of American slavery.

CELIA: A SLAVE   71935-3/ $10.00 US/ $12.00 CAN
by Melton A. McLaurin
An account of a landmark courtroom battle that threatened to undermine the very foundation of the old South's most cherished institution.

PRIDE OF FAMILY   71934-7/ $10.00 US/ $12.00 CAN
by Carole Ione
The story of four generations of American women of color.

GROWING UP BLACK   76632-9/ $9.00 US/ $11.00 CAN
edited by Jay David
From slave days to the present–25 African-Americans reveal the trials and triumphs of their childhoods.

PUSHED BACK TO STRENGTH
by Gloria Wade-Gayles   72426-X/$10.00 US/$12.00 CAN

DOWN THE GLORY ROAD
by Herb Boyd   77523-9/$12.50 US/$15.00 CAN